Brazilian Foreign Policy in Changing Times

To my friend, Rebecca.
À minha amiga, Rebecca.

Gabi
30/11/2013
(11/30/2013)

Brazilian Foreign Policy in Changing Times

The Quest for Autonomy from Sarney to Lula

Tullo Vigevani and Gabriel Cepaluni
Translated by Leandro Moura
Foreword by Phillippe C. Schmitter

LEXINGTON BOOKS

A division of

ROWMAN & LITTLEFIELD PUBLISHERS, INC.
Lanham • Boulder • New York • Toronto • Plymouth, UK

Published by Lexington Books
A division of Rowman & Littlefield Publishers, Inc.
A wholly owned subsidiary of The Rowman & Littlefield Publishing Group, Inc.
4501 Forbes Boulevard, Suite 200, Lanham, Maryland 20706
http://www.lexingtonbooks.com

Estover Road
Plymouth PL6 7PY
United Kingdom

First paperback edition 2012

British Library Cataloguing in Publication Information Available

Library of Congress Cataloging-in-Publication Data

The hardback edition of this book was previously cataloged by the Library of Congress as follows:

Vigevani, Tullo.
Brazilian foreign policy in changing times : the quest for autonomy from Sarney to Lula / Tullo Vigevani and Gabriel Cepaluni; translated by Leandro Moura.
p. cm.
Includes bibliographical references and index.
1. Brazil—Foreign relations—United States. 2. United States—Foreign relations—Brazil. 3. Autonomy. I. Cepaluni, Gabriel. II. Title.
JZ1548.A57U6 2010
327.81073—dc22 2009033342

ISBN: 978-0-7391-2881-7 (cloth : alk. paper)
ISBN: 978-0-7391-2882-4 (pbk. : alk. paper)
ISBN: 978-0-7391-4348-3 (electronic)

Printed in the United States of America

∞™ The paper used in this publication meets the minimum requirements of American National Standard for Information Sciences—Permanence of Paper for Printed Library Materials, ANSI/NISO Z39.48-1992.

Contents

Acknowledgments

A book normally requires work over a long period. This one is no different. Some of the chapters of this book appeared in different versions and formats as academic articles. Many were discussed at important academic gatherings, such as those of the International Political Science Association (IPSA), International Studies Association (ISA), among others.

This book aims to reach a broad public: researchers and professors who study Latin America and people interested in international relations generally. Brazilian foreign policy from 1985 to the present is paradigmatic, as it displays a reasonable capacity to strengthen Brazil's role in the world, bolstering the country's development objectives. Brazil's higher profile on the international plane is not only the fruit of a wide-ranging domestic effort, but also of the exertions of the traditional Brazilian diplomatic school: the Foreign Affairs Ministry (Itamaraty). In its relationship with the United States, Brazilian foreign policy has related relatively well with different governments, be they more unilateralist, such as the Ronald Reagan and George W. Bush administrations, or more multilateralist, such as the Clinton administration and, probably, the Obama administration.

We thank our undergraduate, master's and PhD students, who have made us think about questions fundamental to Brazilian foreign policy. Several interlocutors have collaborated with criticism and suggestions over the course of our work, among whom: Moniz Bandeira, Andrew Bennett, Mauricio Font, Marco Aurélio Garcia, Giancarlo Gardini, Celso Lafer, Andrew Hurrell, Maria Regina Soares de Lima, Andres Malamud, Joseph Marques, Marcelo Medeiros, Reginaldo Moraes, Amâncio Jorge de Oliveira, Miriam Saraiva, Maria Hermínia Tavares de Almeida, Alcides Costa e Vaz, Sebastião

Velasco e Cruz. Among Brazilian diplomats, Paulo Roberto de Almeida, Carlos Henrique Cardim, Gelson Fonseca Jr., Antonio Patriota, Samuel Pinheiro Guimarães, Rubens Ricupero have been important interlocutors. Of course, none of these people should be held responsible for the contents of this book.

Some chapters of this book are deeply re-worked versions of earlier pieces. An earlier version of chapter 4, authored by Tullo Vigevani and Marcelo Fernandes de Oliveira and translated by Timothy Thompson, was published in 2007 ("Brazilian Foreign Policy in the Cardoso Era", *Latin American Perspectives,* vol. 34, n. 5). Chapter 5 originates in an article by this book's authors published in the *Third World Quarterly*, vol. 28, n. 7, 2007 ("Lula's Foreign Policy and the Quest for Autonomy Through Diversification"). Lastly, some arguments of Chapter 6 were based on the article "O Papel da Integração Regional para o Brasil: Universalismo, Soberania e Percepção das Elites", *Revista Brasileira de Política Internacional*, vol. 51, n.1, 2008, by Tullo Vigevani, Gustavo de Mauro Faverão, Haroldo Ramanzini Jr. and Rodrigo Alves Correia. We are grateful for these coauthors, and to the publishers of these papers, for permission to adapt these works for use in the present book.

With regard to the drafting and production of this book, Livia Yuri Enamoto provided fundamental support in the gathering of data, in the final revision of the chapters and in the design of tables and figures. Equally, we thank our translator Leandro Moura for his dedication, patience and suggestions in relation to the form and content of the book. Joseph Parry, our editor, has provided special encouragement to this publication since 2007, when we first met at the ISA Annual Conference in Chicago. Without his support, this book would not have been written. Marleida Borges, executive secretary of the Center for Studies on Contemporary Culture (Cedec), deserves all our gratitude for solving many of our administrative problems.

We also thank the universities and institutions for which we work and with which we have cooperated (National Institute for Studies on the United States—NISUS/INEU, Sao Paulo State University—Unesp, Campinas State University—Unicamp, Pontifical Catholic University of Sao Paulo—PUC-SP, University of Sao Paulo— USP, Georgetown University, and Cedec), as well as the funding agencies that have provided financial support to our research over the years (Brazilian Research Council—CNPq, The State of Sao Paulo Research Foundation-Fapesp, and Coordination for the Improvement of Higher Education Personnel-Capes).

Tullo Vigevani and Gabriel Cepaluni

Foreword

Philippe C. Schmitter
European University Institute

One of the most persistent deficiencies in the literature on foreign policy is its almost exclusive focus on the "core states" of Europe and North America—with an occasional sideward glance at China and India. Presumably, the reason for this is that other states do not really have foreign policies. Their capacity for independent reasoning and action in this domain is so limited by an international system dominated by the "central" actors that the effort to analyze their foreign policies is hardly worth while. If one understands what the core players are doing (and why), the actions of the peripheral ones should fall into line.

Here we have a book that breaks these bonds. Its central theme is "autonomy"—exactly what peripheral states are not supposed to have in their foreign policies. Admittedly, Brazil is a rather prominent member of the world's periphery—even a giant in its immediate neighbourhood of the Southern Cone of Latin America and, more recently, a distinguished and highly visible member of the BRIC Club. Tullo Vigevani and Gabriel Cepaluni follow Brazil's "quest for autonomy" from the mid-1980s when its regime became democratic to the present moment—through five consecutive presidencies—and they demonstrate that this quest has been an underlying strategic priority, but that its tactical expression has varied considerably. They delineate three ideal-typical tactics: gaining autonomy through *distancing* Brazil from dominant states and insisting on sovereignty; through *participating* with them in key institutional settings; and, finally, through *diversifying* its contacts with a wider range of states and settings. These are presented in sequential order, hinting at some evolutionary process of trial-and-error and selection of the fittest tactic, but the authors do not reify or even specify this notion. Nevertheless, their innovative conceptualization of Brazil's progress in gaining greater autonomy does suggest a "model" that might applicable to the foreign policies of other peripheral states with similar ambitions.

There are, however, several cross-cutting tensions in their account that seem (to me) to be more distinctively Brazilian. The first involves the obstacles and opportunities posed by external versus internal powers. Being on the periphery implies virtually by definition that the former is stronger than the latter. The dominance of core states (and most specifically that of the United States) should be a more important cause of continuity or change in foreign policy that the efforts of domestic interest groups—although by their account economic development focusing initially on the internal market and subsequently on regional integration did increase the role of national business corporations and associations, especially in pressuring for greater international (and regional) participation. Implicitly, they argue that democratization as such played a relatively secondary role in this policy transformation. The second tension is even more specifically Brazilian and that refers to the uniquely prominent role played historically by its Foreign Ministry, usually referred to as Itamaraty after the palace that used to house it in Rio de Janeiro. No other "third world peripheral" state has such a consistently well-trained and autonomous diplomatic service. Whatever the regime or government in power, Itamaraty had always guaranteed a high degree of continuity in its foreign policy. With the return of popularly elected presidents to executive office, especially ones who regarded themselves as empowered to conduct their own foreign relations, the locus of policy-making tended to shift back-and-forth. It is not clear from their account whether the evolution in tactics should be credited more to Itamaraty or to the last two presidents of Brazil: Fernando Henrique Cardoso and Luís Inácio ("Lula") da Silva.

In their conclusion, Vigevani and Cepaluni leave a very different Brazil than the one they found at the beginning. The country is now an important "semi-peripheral" player on the global scale and a potentially "dominant" player in South America. Paradoxically, it has been more successful at the former than the latter. MERCOSUR, the regional integration arrangement in which it is such a major participant, has languished at a very low level of institutional development and an even lower record of implementing its many promises—and much of this failure can be laid on Brazil's doorstep. Apparently, its dilemma is that the more the country gains autonomy on the world stage, the more reluctant it becomes to give up part of that autonomy within its immediate region.

Introduction

This book analyzes changes and continuities in Brazilian foreign policy from the mid-1980s to 2009. In order to examine this theme, the concept of autonomy is our chief analytical category. In this sense, Latin American intellectual production on international relations is fundamental to this work.

During the government of President José Sarney (1985–1990), the first civilian president after the military regime (1964–1984), the Brazilian democratic transition began. This generated pressures in favor of the reform of the country's institutions and culminated in the adoption of a new constitution in 1988. At that time, Brazil was going through a serious economic and social crisis. Inflation, low growth rates, and falling living standards were features of the patently difficult moments the country experienced. During the administration of President Ronald Reagan (1981–1989), the United States took on tough positions vis-à-vis traditional trading partners, as it faced strong economic competition from Japan and Germany and also from newly industrialized countries such as Brazil. Together with bilateral pressures on Brazil on the issues of information technology and patents, the United States was initiating efforts to incorporate "new issues," among them intellectual property, investments, and services into the remit of the General Agreement on Tariffs and Trade (GATT).

This combination of domestic and international pressures, added to the exhaustion of the import substitution economic model, encouraged a gradual alteration in Brazilian foreign policy. With the country's democratization, new actors, such as labor unions, business people, and public opinion, began to take more of an interest in and voice their opinions about foreign policy matters. On the domestic plane, the import substitution model, with its emphasis on the role of the State and the heterodox macroeconomic adjustments aimed at containing inflation and maintaining growth were insufficient to solve the country's economic and social problems. The 1987 foreign debt moratorium, the failed economic plans, and the successive falls of finance ministers were also signs of the model's exhaustion. The economic instability, blamed on the import substitution model by some, was harshly criticized by financial institutions such as the International Monetary Fund (IMF) and the World Bank.

International constraints made themselves felt. One of the most important international initiatives of this presidency was the attempt to coordinate its action with Argentina. This period represented an innovative moment in regional relations. Coordination with Argentina took on major significance, still within a perspective (at least initially) of development of the two countries' domestic markets. Historical tensions were overcome, thus opening up a period of partial integration that lasts to this day.

A discussion began on changes in economic orientation. The constraints made it difficult to maintain the import substitution model that had characterized the country since the 1930s, with the Getúlio Vargas presidency. For their part, supporters of the Brazilian economic model faced difficulties in arguing in favor of its continuity.

Despite the fact that the adoption of a democratic regime did not lead to sudden changes in foreign policy, President Sarney made important adjustments toward the end of his term. The government had to give some ground to the United States at a bilateral level—on the issues of information technology and patents—and a multilateral level, with the "new issues" entering the agenda of the GATT Uruguay Round. Actually, these pressures ended up being endorsed by developed countries in general. The Sarney administration also had to negotiate the payment of the foreign debt with more flexibility while putting into practice some of the policies advocated by the IMF and the World Bank. Therefore, President Sarney handed over to his successor a very different country. In 1988, Brazil not only had a new constitution, it had a new foreign policy taking shape, with aspects different from the ones that had prevailed during the military period. Brazil was seeking an insertion in the debate on some of the major international questions, believing this to be the way to strengthen national sovereignty. Hence the country gradually gave up on the idea of development guided by the protectionist practices that had characterized the corporate State, a feature of what we call in this book *autonomy through distance*.

During the 1989 presidential election campaign, Fernando Collor de Mello (president from 1990 to 1992), advocated drastic neoliberal reforms that, according to him, would modernize the country and make it stand out in the international setting. Initially, with Francisco Rezek as his foreign minister (January 1990–April 1992), Collor de Mello conducted a policy of rapprochement with the United States. However, the president did not win over US support to the extent that he had hoped. At the debt negotiations, for instance, the US position remained tough and intransigent. Accusations of corruption leveled at people linked with the government and an inability to deal with the economic crisis contributed to the political instability of the Collor de Mello years.

The 1992 ministerial reform put Celso Lafer at the helm of the Ministry of Foreign Relations. During his tenure, from April to October 1992, a new strategy for Brazilian foreign policy began to take shape. The ministry, which had lost importance in the formulation of foreign policy whilst attempting to minimize Collor de Mello's more extreme actions, regained a strategic role. Lafer sought to preserve the tradition of Brazilian diplomacy. At the same time he would make the necessary adjustments for the country to be able to adapt to the new opportunities and obstacles posed by the end of the Cold War and by the acceleration of the process referred to by many as globalization.

Lafer's reading of the world, along with that of the group that accompanied him, went along the lines of what was later termed *autonomy through participation*. Those who formulated this idea believed that for Brazil to enjoy more room to maneuver on the international setting, the country should not keep its distance from new international issues and regimes in order to safeguard its sovereignty. Rather, it should try to influence the international agenda with its values and its diplomatic tradition. An exemplary action of this new foreign policy conception was carried out at the United Nations Conference on Environment and Development (UNCED/Rio-92/Eco-92). At this conference, even if temporarily, the country was not seen as the destroyer of the Amazon, but as a player in defense of the environment. As shown by Hurrell (1991), there was a growing number of countries where public opinion, governments, businesspeople, social organizations, and intellectuals, among others, had been very critical of the deforestation of the Amazon region, which spurred a change in Brazil's environmental policies during the administration of President Sarney and, particularly, of President Collor de Mello.

According to Brazilian ambassador Gelson Fonseca Jr.:

> The attitude we adopted at Rio-92 exemplifies what I have called autonomy through the path of participation. At the meeting, we contributed, from the initial moments, to a broadening of the very scope of the conference, linking the development theme to the environmentalist theme and endorsing the concept of sustainable development. The balance in the resolutions and agreements adopted owes much to the Brazilian effort in ensuring consensus, in overcoming stalemates. The same positive attitude could be observed on the subject of human rights, when the Brazilian participation in the Vienna Conference was decisive for the meeting to end successfully (Fonseca Jr., 1998: 369).

The changes initiated by Lafer were partially continued following Collor de Mello's impeachment. The new president, Itamar Franco (1992–1994), formerly Collor de Mello's vice-president, toned down the liberal discourse, but the measures adopted by his predecessor in general were not reversed. It was inevitable that the country should seek greater international insertion. But high inflation rates, the foreign debt problem, and the country's negative image in the eyes of the hegemonic centers persisted. With regard to foreign policy, President Franco delegated its formulation and implementation to the Ministry of Foreign Relations, initially headed by Fernando Henrique Cardoso (October 1992–May 1993). During his brief period as minister, Cardoso set in motion a conceptual deepening of the idea of autonomy through participation initiated by Minister Lafer. According to Cardoso, Brazil would have to overcome the stage of authoritarian nationalism and of inward-looking development and strive to attain a competitive insertion in the world. Brazil should not rule out the possibility of partnerships in various corners of the planet, but the focus of its foreign policy was clear: establishing good relations with the United States and the central countries, and use the Mercosur as tool of international insertion.

With Celso Amorim's assumption of the ministry (May 1993–December 1994), while Cardoso went over to Finance, a foreign policy without labels was adopted so as not to generate specific expectations. However, certain aspects of the Independent Foreign Policy (PEI) tradition were taken up again. PEI was formulated by Affonso Arinos de Mello Franco, San Tiago Dantas, and Araújo Castro, foreign ministers of the last two civilian presidents before the April 1964 military coup, Jânio Quadros (1961) and João Goulart (1961–1964). In some cases, there was also reference to aspects of the "Responsible Pragmatism" developed by Minister Antonio Francisco Azeredo da Silveira, during the military government of President Ernesto Geisel (1974–1978). Amorim's foreign policy displayed some elements of what we call *autonomy through diversification*. This meant the country was seeking to enhance its strategic partnerships in order to have more bargaining power vis-à-vis the rich countries in multilateral forums and to broaden its spectrum of political, economic and technological interests, among others.

The Mercosur was thought of as a way of balancing the influence of the United States in the Southern Cone, but also as a way of preparing Brazil for a phase of enhanced competition in international trade in a context of reduced protectionism. At the UN, Brazil began to take more active positions, proposing a "Development Agenda" and advocating the democratization of the Security Council, which would allow the country to have a permanent seat. This new positioning was possible due to the country's history of peace,[1] to its new democratic credentials, and to the recent monetary stabilization brought on by the Real Plan in June 1994, which removed the foreign debt negotiation from the top of Brazil's international agenda. As had happened with Lafer and Cardoso, Amorim would have to wait a few years to be able to alter Brazilian foreign policy more intensely, since his stay at the Itamaraty[2] was not long enough to deepen the changes he had initiated.

In Cardoso's two presidential terms (1995–2002), first with Luiz Felipe Lampreia (January 1995–January 2001) and then with Lafer (January 2001–December 2002) at the ministry, Brazil was to establish a diplomacy guided by the logic of autonomy through participation. A foreign policy in line with democratic political values and economic liberalism took hold. An orientation that was unable to consolidate itself under Collor de Mello, and that was hesitant under Itamar Franco vis-à-vis economic openness, gained in strength. Hence, a foreign policy that almost until 1990 had been protectionist and reactive in some cases, which predominated during most of the Cold War—autonomy through distance—was substituted by a demanding international agenda aligned with liberal canons, whose influence seemed to be in expansion, and guided by the logic of autonomy through participation. Brazil should solve its domestic problems and have more control over its future if it wished to contribute actively to the formulation of international norms and regimes.

The aim of the Cardoso administration was not to adapt in passive fashion, but to redirect and remodel the international environment to the extent that the country's power and its limits permitted. It was necessary to take other States' interests and power relations into account, seeking forms of participation in the major negotiations and international questions by means of the formulation of international regimes more favorable to Brazilian interests. It was reiterated that the Mercosur was always thought of as a platform for international competition on the global plane. Greater convergence with global values and tendencies was also sought. This included, for instance, environmental protection, disarmament, trade liberalization, and greater participation in multilateral negotiations on the most varied themes. Lastly, political democracy and economic freedom were guiding principles of the logic of autonomy through participation.

With the end of the Bill Clinton administration (1993–2000), and especially after September 11, 2001, the multilateralist slant became weakened in the United States, and the trade issue lost strength vis-à-vis the conflicts that originated in the war on terror, with the emphasis shifting to the Middle East and fundamentalism. The interest taken by the United States in Latin America, which was not great as it was, diminished further. Consequently, toward the end of the Cardoso government, there were signs of change in Brazilian foreign policy. The policy, by tradition, advocates multilateralism, places economic development at the top of its agenda and security questions—if for no other reason, because the country has a history of very few conflicts—are not at the heart of its concerns. Cardoso began to slightly raise the tone of criticism to the foreign policy of President George W. Bush and to seek other partners more in tune with the country's agenda. During this period, growth rates in developing countries such as China, Russia, India, and South Africa were taking off. The Cardoso government was starting to outline a foreign policy oriented by the logic of reaffirming autonomy.

During the first term of President Luíz Inácio Lula da Silva (2003–2006), the partnership with China, Russia, India, and South Africa gained renewed emphasis. With India and South Africa, President Lula formalized a relationship meant to be strategic with the creation of the G-3 or IBSA (India, Brazil, and South Africa). With regard to Russia and China, Brazil has sought to increase commercial, technological, and military exchanges. The Lula administration has recognized China as a market economy, in spite of opposition from the most important business organization in the country, the São Paulo State Federation of Industry (FIESP). These relations, as will be seen, have taken on great relevance, with China becoming a major trading partner.

Toward the end of his administration, Cardoso established a dialogue—though not an institutionalized partnership—with the countries of the South. For its part, the Lula government has formed strategic alliances with developing countries with similar power capabilities and that enjoy leadership positions in their regions. During the Ministerial Meeting of the World Trade Organization (WTO), held in Cancun in September 2003 as part of the Doha Round, the Group of 20 (G-20) was created, with a leading role played by Brazil. The aim was to reduce domestic subsidies in rich countries and increase access to European and North American markets.[3]

Striving to deepen an international identity among developing countries with partly similar positions in the hierarchy of power and with similar social problems is part of the strategy of autonomy through diversification. This strategy is based on an attempt to influence the agenda of international regimes by means of coalitions of developing countries aimed at counterbalancing the agenda of developed nations. In this sense, Brazilian foreign policy has changed much if compared with the description made by Krasner of developing countries' strategy in the mid-1980s:

> (T)he desire to secure international regimes embodying authoritative rather than market allocation of resources has been an enduring aspect of Third World policy in the postwar period. It reflects the profound national weakness of most developing countries. This weakness stems from the inability to influence unilaterally or to adjust internally to the pressures of global markets. Larger

industrialized states are able to influence the international environment and can adjust internally (Krasner, 1985: 11).

Currently at the WTO, part of the developing countries, such as Brazil, adopt a more liberalizing sectoral agenda than the large industrialized countries, such as the USA and some European countries, on issues such as agricultural subsidy reduction. On the other hand, back during the Uruguay Round, developing countries gave up on trying to block the entry of "new issues," such as intellectual property, services, and investments, accepting their inclusion in the GATT/WTO. In the case of Brazil, the competitiveness of some of its products explains this liberalism. This was not adopted by the Lula government for other items on the agenda, such as financial issues, on which it allied with those who advocate greater State control.

Last, we argue that Brazil's plan to create a non-institutionalized Mercosur to preserve its autonomy and allow itself greater international insertion has combined with the logic of autonomy through diversification. This logic permitted Brazil to prioritize other partners. In relative terms, this took place to the detriment of its Southern Cone neighbors, making the integration process larger but lacking the depth expected of a customs union and of a common market. The recent emphasis in establishing partnerships with countries like China, Russia, India, and South Africa, among others, finds backing among interest groups, in business circles, and also within the government.

Having made the above remarks, the question remains: what are the main elements of continuity and change in Brazilian foreign policy since the mid-1980s?

We believe Brazil's key feature is the quest for international autonomy. In this book, autonomy means the country being able to pursue a foreign policy that is free from international constraints imposed by the more powerful countries. Clearly, autonomy is a concept with a certain gradation. A country can go from having extreme autonomy, allowing it to conduct its actions in unilateral fashion without depending on any other, to having an automatic alignment, a situation in which the foreign policy of *country A* is totally shackled to the actions and wishes of *country B*.[4] The idea of autonomy is a means of developing Brazil. At the same time, economic growth can also bring more room to maneuver at the international level. Therefore, on the general and abstract plane, the quest for autonomy and the quest for development are constant in Brazilian foreign policy at least since the mid-1980s. Its roots may be found in the past, even in the imperial period of the nineteenth century, and certainly at different points in the twentieth century. However, in this book, our central category of analysis is the idea of autonomy, while the notion of development plays a secondary role in our narrative.

With regard to the changes observed—our object here—, we believe autonomy may be sought, on the theoretical plane, in three different ways that are not mutually exclusive in reality, namely distance, participation, and diversification. In this book, we analyze the foreign policy of Brazil empirically from the mid-1980s to 2009. As will be seen, certain historical periods fit more neatly than others into each of the three notions mentioned earlier per style sheet.

During the Sarney years, the idea of autonomy through distance that had been meaningful in Brazil's foreign actions since the 1930s with President Getúlio Vargas, started to become exhausted as a strategic option. Toward the end of the Sarney government, the necessity of change was clear, but the way forward was not. With the Collor de Mello presidency, the country adopted a discourse whose pretension was alignment with the rich countries, particularly the United States. The failure of this strategy made it impossible to adopt a clear foreign policy course. The same can be said of the Itamar Franco administration, which had to deal with domestic crises and with the political instability present since the democratic transition began by Sarney. It was only under Cardoso that the country started adopting a foreign policy strategy oriented by the logic of autonomy through participation. Alternatives emerged for the country to strive for greater international autonomy with the changes in setting brought about by 9/11 and by the economic growth of the major countries of the South. With Lula's assumption of the presidency, South–South relations took on a new dynamic. The country has sought to broaden and institutionalize partnerships with non-traditional markets in Africa, Asia, and the Middle East. The search for these partnerships does not imply a return to the partial "third-worldism" of the 1960s and 1970s—though interrupted at the start of the period of military rule, during the Castelo Branco administration (1964–67). Rather, they are partnerships constructed taking into account the current liberal international order. They seek to increase Brazilian bargaining power in multilateral negotiations with developed countries, with a view to altering the hegemonic structure in existence since the end of the Second World War. In this book, we call this strategy autonomy through diversification.

ORGANIZATION OF THE BOOK

In chapter 1, we spell out the meaning of autonomy in the eyes of Latin American authors in the field of international relations. To this end, we establish a counterpoint to the mainstream position that privileges the debate from the point of view of sovereignty. From this perspective, the anarchy versus hierarchy contrast emerges as central. In this chapter we also describe three different ways of striving for autonomy. In chapter 2, we analyze the foreign policy of the Sarney government, and how domestic and international pressures forced it to promote changes in its foreign policy. In chapter 3, we show that the political instability of the Collor de Mello and Itamar Franco governments made it impossible for them to effect significant changes in foreign policy. Nevertheless, they influenced subsequent developments in Brazil's international action. In chapter 4, we argue that the Cardoso administration established a foreign policy guided by the logic of autonomy through participation. In chapter 5, we take the view that President Lula practices a foreign policy oriented by the strategy of autonomy through diversification. In chapter 6, we suggest that the great emphasis on the consolidation of partnerships with major developing countries like India, South Africa, China, and Russia may weaken the project of Mercosur institutionalization, in a context where the objectives of universalism and of being a global trader prevail. In the last chapter, we comment on Brazil–Venezuela relations, stressing the points of convergence and divergence between the proposals of presidents Lula and Hugo Chávez.

NOTES

1. The last and only war in which Brazil was the central actor was against Paraguay, from December 1864 to March 1870.
2. Name given to Brazil's Ministry of Foreign Relations because of the name of its first headquarters in Rio de Janeiro, the Itamaraty Palace. With the move to Brasília, the ministry's headquarters retained its name, which continues to be employed.
3. The G-20 is a group of developing countries established on 20 August 2003, in the final stages of the preparations for the Fifth Ministerial Conference of the WTO, held in Cancun, from 10 to 14 September, 2003. Its focus is on agriculture, the central issue of the Doha Development Agenda. Though known as the G-20, the number of members in the coalition has changed since its founding. In July 2008, the group had 23 members: 5 from Africa (Egypt, Nigeria, South Africa, Tanzania and Zimbabwe), 6 from Asia (China, India, Indonesia, Pakistan, Philippines and Thailand) and 12 from Latin America (Argentina, Bolivia, Brazil, Chile, Cuba, Ecuador, Guatemala, Mexico, Paraguay, Peru, Uruguay and Venezuela).
4. According to Carlos Escudé (1998), a peripheral State like Argentina should have a relationship of alignment with the United States in exchange for benefits that improve the social well-being of its citizens.

Chapter 1

Defining Autonomy

INTRODUCTION

In the works of Latin American academics, autonomy is a notion that refers to a foreign policy free from constraints imposed by powerful countries. Therefore, it is different from the understanding of most mainstream authors of classic international relations, who define it as the legal recognition of sovereign States considered as "equal units" in an anarchical international order.

According to Tickner (2003: 318), although international relations theories have referred explicitly or implicitly to the autonomy of the nation-State, the concept is normally associated with the domestic capabilities of the state. According to Krasner, domestic autonomy constituted a fundamental principle of Westphalian sovereignty, that is, "an institutional arrangement for organizing political life that is based on two principles: territoriality and the exclusion of external actors from domestic authority structures" (Krasner, 1999: 20).

In the Third World, autonomy is usually conceived of differently. Domestically, autonomy constitutes a basic symbol of the State, a primary means of ensuring distinct forms of autochthonous or non-dependent development. Beyond national borders, autonomy is considered fundamental for the practice of international relations in the Third World. Rather than being rooted in the legal notion of sovereignty, it is a political concept, a safeguard against the more harmful effects of the international system. "The concept of non-alignment, formulated in the 1950s, is just one example of the relationship between autonomy and internal/external freedom of action" (Tickner, 2003: 319). Consequently, from the privileged point of view of powerful countries, external autonomy is not a concern of great relevance.

Krasner (1999) argues that Westphalian sovereignty has always been a myth, for few States enjoy total domestic autonomy. He cites numerous examples when the sovereignty of western States, including the United States, was violated. Empirically this may be true, but from the Third World perspective, certain States are more sovereign than others (Neuman, 1998: 10). In this sense, the idea of autonomy becomes more pressing for those States with fewer power resources.

For this reason, Escudé (1998) argues that one must examine the origin of the myth of interstate anarchy in the discipline of international relations. In his eyes, the formal equality between States was legal fiction until the signing and ratification of the UN Charter. After that, it was not even fiction, as a Security Council with only five permanent members with veto power establishes the legal principle of the *inequality* between States in the security field. Furthermore, chapter 7 of the UN Charter *formally* grants the power of intervention to the Security Council. The same principle can be found in international regimes such as the Nuclear Non-Proliferation Treaty, in which it is *legally* established that some States have the right to possess weapons of mass destruction, whilst others do not. Questions regulated by these regimes are few in number, but extremely relevant in substance. "States are not formally equal; admittedly, informally they are even less equal" (Escudé, 1998: 62).

Hence, it is relatively clear that the myth of anarchy is part of the ideology of sovereignty. At the other end of the theoretical spectrum, in the socialist camp, Rosenberg (1994) also seeks to demystify the idea of legal equality, of equal sovereignty for all. According to Escudé, this fallacy is central to realist theories of international relations. "This logic ultimately stems from Hans J. Morgenthau and is clearly projected into the alleged anarchy that Waltz and other neorealists claim characterizes the structure of the interstate system" (Escudé, 1998: 63). It follows that the great powers and weak States are not "equal units" belonging to an anarchical order (Waltz, 1979). On the contrary, this difference between the great powers and weak States implies that the "structure" of the interstate system is predominantly hierarchical, not anarchical (Escudé, 1998: 65).

Russell and Tokatlian (2003: 1–2) have found three meanings for the term autonomy. Firstly, autonomy is a principle or right that has often been transgressed by the actions of state and non-state actors. The sovereignty of weak States is neglected in the name of other questions considered more important, such as democracy and human rights, for instance (Krasner, 1995/96).

Secondly, the concept is used as one of the objectives of the national interest, the other two being survival and economic well-being (Wendt, 1999: 138). According to Wendt, these interests, common to all States, are not only normative guides to action; they are causal forces that predispose States to act in a certain way (Wendt, 1999: 234).

Lastly, autonomy is seen as a condition that permits States to articulate themselves and attain political goals in an independent manner. According to this meaning, which is present in the Latin American view on the theme (including our own), autonomy is a property that States may or may not possess, falling within a continuum between two extreme ideal types: total dependence (or alignment) or full autonomy.

Therefore, the notion of autonomy is characterized by the capacity of the State to implement decisions based on its own objectives, without interference or restriction from without, by means of its ability to control processes or events beyond its borders. Autonomy is always a question of degree, depending on States' attributes of power (both hard and soft) and on the external conditions they face.

In this book, we advance the debate on autonomy using the historical example of Brazil from the 1980s to the present day. Our interpretation is that Brazilian foreign policy has been marked by a quest for autonomy, principally in relation to the United States. We ascertain that three ways of achieving this autonomy have existed: distance, participation and diversification. Over the last few decades, autonomy through distance has been characterized by autarchical economic development based on a strong nationalist sentiment, by a distancing from the major international issues and by a search for South–South alliances. Autonomy through participation relates to a greater international involvement and to an acceptance of liberal norms and of the main international regimes, in the hope of influencing and participating in the decision making of these institutions in the long term. Lastly, autonomy through diversification implies an approximation to the countries of the South in order to obtain greater insertion and more power in the framework of international regimes, betting on multilateral solutions and not on a unipolar world. Autonomy through diversification is characterized by the capacity to strive to diversify international partnerships, whilst not promoting ruptures with central countries. It aims to strengthen the country in a multipolar world with greater balance between States.

DEVELOPMENT OF THE CONCEPT OF AUTONOMY IN LATIN AMERICA

In Latin America, since the 1970s, the idea of autonomy has been thought of as a means to "liberate" the countries of the region from their external dependence.

Jaguaribe (1970: 91–93) describes the international system as a hierarchical order. Although countries that exert autonomy cannot guarantee the total inviolability of their national territories, they offer considerable obstacles to the actions of their enemies and enjoy enough room for maneuver to conduct their foreign policies. Dependent nations, in turn, though formally independent and sovereign, are strongly constrained by the great powers.

Autonomy is a function of the structural conditions that Jaguaribe (1979: 96–97) describes as "national viability" and "international permissibility." The first term refers to the existence of adequate human and social resources, to the capacity for international insertion and to the degree of sociocultural cohesion within national borders. The second concept relates to the capacity to neutralize external threats, and depends on economic and military resources and on alliances with other countries. Jaguaribe also identifies two fundamental factors for the existence of autonomy in the periphery: technological and entrepreneurial autonomy, and favorable relations with the center.

In his reflections on autonomy, Puig (1980, 1984), differently from realist authors like Morgenthau and Waltz, argues that the international system is not characterized by anarchy, but by an international hierarchy. According to Puig (1980: 149–155), the attainment of autonomy goes through four stages: the formal status of sovereign statehood; the material resources sufficient to formulate and put into practice a national project; the acceptance of the main power's policies in areas of strategic interest in exchange for the exercise of autonomy in sectors of equal importance for Latin American countries, like in the choice of their models of development, for example; and the breaking of dependence with the center and actions of non-obedience. For Puig, as much as for Jaguaribe, autonomy requires adequate degrees of "national viability," a considerable amount of domestic resources and an explicit commitment of the elites to a national project. The two authors also share the notion that autonomy requires the mobilization of power resources in the periphery. Regional alliances against the center, political and economic integration, and the improvement of negotiation techniques constitute the strategies to achieve this goal.

In an empirical analysis of Brazil–USA relations in the early 1980s, Moura, Kramer, and Wrobel (1985) use the term autonomy as a synonym for a Brazilian foreign policy that kept a certain distance from US interests. In their eyes, the process of political distancing between the two countries, from the 1970s, was well known. Hence, "the relatively long duration of this relationship makes one suppose that one is not dealing with momentary difficulties resulting from the specific policies of one government or another" (1985: 35). On the contrary, it suggests a long-term trend in the relations between the two countries. The defining elements of the discrepancy are, on the one hand, Brazil's wish to have a prominent role in the international setting as from the 1970s, and, on the other, US insistence in maintaining old-style "command" relations with Latin America. The backdrop to these changes was made up of the major transformations in the international system from the 1960s: the economic recovery of Western Europe and Japan; the growing role of the Third World in international forums, mainly in the GATT and UN; and the process of detente itself, which tended to loosen the ties of dependence within both the socialist bloc led by the Soviet Union (USSR) and the capitalist bloc led by the USA.

Advancing the understanding of the concept, Fonseca Jr. (1998) argues that Brazilian diplomacy during the Cold War period was characterized by autonomy through distance. By the 1980s, this same diplomacy would acquire new outlines due to the process of democratization in Brazil, the end of the Cold War, the deepening of the so-called globalization process and the arrival of "new issues" on the international agenda (environmental questions, human rights, reform of the international trade system, etc.). In sum, the very idea of autonomy was taking on new connotations.

For Fonseca Jr. (1998: 361), "the expressions of what autonomy is vary historically and spatially, vary according to interests and power positions." According to the author, the first expression of autonomy would be to maintain a certain distance from the actions and values of the Western Bloc. Next, it would mean a critical attitude in relation to the superpowers. On the other hand, autonomy in the contemporary world no longer means "distance" from polemical themes to safeguard the country from undesirable alignments. On the contrary, Fonseca Jr. argues that autonomy is translated by "participation," by a desire to influence the foreign agenda with values, by means of the Brazilian diplomatic tradition.

Along the same lines of reasoning, but with a more theoretical approach, Russell and Tokatlian (2003) argue that the acceleration of globalization over the last few decades has substantially changed the room that Latin American countries have for their action. This new global context demands that autonomy be defined differently. There would need to be a transition from *antagonistic autonomy* (similar to autonomy through distance) to *relational autonomy* (similar to autonomy through participation):

> This type of autonomy should be understood as a country's capacity and willingness, in conjunction with others, to make decisions of its own free will and to face situations and processes arising both within and beyond its borders. From this perspective, both the defense and the expansion of autonomy enjoyed by Latin American countries today can no longer depend on national or subregional policies of isolation, self-sufficiency, or opposition. Such policies are now either impossible or improbable, as well as undesirable (Russell and Tokatlian, 2003: 13).

Relational autonomy means growing interaction, negotiation and participation in the formulation of international norms and rules. Autonomy is no longer defined "by a country's power to isolate itself and control external processes and events, but instead by its power to participate in and effectively influence world affairs, particularly in all types of international organizations and regimes" (Russell and Tokatlian, 2003: 16).

For Russell and Tokatlian (2003: 19), relational autonomy must be achieved through commitments and negotiation with major participation from public opinion, strengthening the democratic aspect of this type of development of foreign policy. The partial abandonment of elements of sovereignty (a feature of antagonistic autonomy) is done with a view to developing institutions and norms for the promotion of the common good. We detect in this perspective the idea of a propositive insertion in the logic of the prevailing international regimes.

AUTONOMY THROUGH DIVERSIFICATION

In this section, we seek to refine and advance the debate on the concept of autonomy. Criticism common in Brazil of works about "autonomy" derives from them being authored by diplomats or from their ideas having entered the political vocabulary, as is the case of the notion of "autonomy through participation" formulated by Ambassador Gelson Fonseca Jr. Some believe that the debate about autonomy is contaminated by self-interested authors, whose analyses might serve to justify their own ideologies, political interests or even their bureaucratic logic.

However, a series of academic researchers have also reflected upon the question of autonomy in their studies, among whom we may cite Gerson Moura, Russell and Tokatlian. They influenced Anglo-Saxon production, chiefly in the 1980s and 1990s, as demonstrated by the works of Adler (1987), Evans (1995) and Hurrell (1986). On the other hand, we do not believe that engaging in a policy-relevant debate is demeritorious as long as one is careful not to appropriate these analyses uncritically, a precaution that should also be taken in the discussion of mainly "scientific" questions. Hence, differently from a certain body of political science work, we privilege political and historical aspects to the detriment of the scientific dimension of the discipline (when understood as that which makes great use of quantitative methods).

We define autonomy as the condition allowing States to formulate and implement foreign policies independently of constraints imposed by more powerful States. This term lies within a continuum whose extremities are total dependence (or alignment) and full autonomy. Obviously, between the two concepts at each extremity, there exists a gradation of foreign policies combining autonomy with dependence, although the autonomist trend is more marked in the Brazilian case.

In this book, we have found three ways in which a country can seek autonomy: distance, participation, and diversification. It would be possible to find other dimensions in the historical process, as well as foreseeing other developments. These three different ways of obtaining autonomy that we discuss get combined in reality and are more easily identified during certain historical periods than others (Weber, 1991). In this book, the change in means for achieving autonomy characterizes moments of transition,[1] although the quest for autonomy is a perennial concept in recent Brazilian foreign policy, with the possible exception of some policies of apparent alignment with the United States during the Collor de Mello presidency. Neither are these exceptions new in Brazilian history: some authors assess the period following the Second World War, until 1950, and the period following the 1964 military coup, until 1967, in similar light. In other words, a certain country can have a foreign policy that is more or less autonomist, but as autonomy is generally one of Brazil's goals, the changes in the country's external action are not characterized by ruptures with the past. Rather, they are more like adjustments and program changes, of more or less depth, for the country to come closer to its goals, such as external autonomy and economic development. Consequently, we define:

> (1) autonomy through distance—a policy of contesting the norms and principles of important international institutions (IMF, World Bank, GATT, etc.); a diplomacy that opposes the liberalizing agenda of the great powers, particularly the United States; the belief in autarchical development, guided by the expansion of the domestic market and by economic protectionism; resistance to international regimes interpreted as freezing world power, in favor of the status quo.
> (2) autonomy through participation—adherence to international regimes, including those of a liberal slant (such as the WTO), without losing the capacity to manage foreign policy. In this case, the objective would be to influence the very formulation of the principles and rules governing the international system. It is felt that the national objectives would be more effectively achieved along these paths.
> (3) autonomy through diversification—adherence of the country to international principles and norms by means of South–South alliances, including regional ones, and of agreements with non-traditional partners, such as China, Asia-Pacific, Africa, Eastern Europe, Middle East etc. The aim is to reduce asymmetries and increase the country's international bargaining capacity in its relations with more powerful countries, such as the USA and European Union (EU) countries. An important characteristic is the capacity to negotiate with more powerful countries without ruptures, with the perspective of breaking unilateralism and striving for multipolarity and greater equilibrium.

According to Velasco e Cruz (2007: 20), during the 1990s, Third World countries accepted tough measures to stabilize their economies by means of the "option for the market." At the time, the era of State intervention to strengthen and guide the economy in accordance with well-defined conceptions of the national interest seemed *passé*. The imperatives had changed: cutting spending, eliminating subsidies, opening up the economy, and creating a favorable environment for foreign investors, all in the hope of gaining access to capital and to global markets. Hence, if the autonomist strategy is a constant in Brazilian foreign policy, the different methods of seeking autonomy—distance, participation, and diversification—are ways for Brazil to adapt to international and domestic changes without effecting strong ruptures with the diplomatic tradition.

The approach we make to the three autonomies in this book, though based on the recent history of Brazilian foreign policy, may serve as inspiration for analyses of the foreign policies of other developing countries, even though they cannot be transplanted mechanically to totally different realities. Our analysis may also contribute to an understanding of the diplomatic action of Third World countries, in keeping with the Latin American academic tradition that has sought to develop in the region. Thus it may display a normative character.

In this book, we do not intend to construct a theory about autonomy, but merely an analysis grounded on historical observation. This analysis is neither a repository of truth nor in any way determinist. It is just a plausible interpretation of the world, with Brazil's experience as its vantage point. Our perspective is not valid for every time and space. It was constructed with the analyses of other authors as its starting point (Ayoob, 2002: 28) and intends to discuss Brazilian foreign policy—which remains little-known internationally. Hopefully, lessons will be learnt; hopefully, these may be useful to analyses of other experiences, that other researchers may come to develop.

FINAL REMARKS

In this chapter, we have spelled out the theoretical framework that is used in this book. We have defined autonomy basically as a country's capacity to practice a foreign policy free from external constraints placed upon it by powerful countries such as the United States, for example. The concept of autonomy may be seen as one extremity of a spectrum that goes from full autonomy to total dependence.

We believe there are three ways of obtaining autonomy: distance, participation, and diversification. Autonomy through distance is characterized by a country's isolation in relation to the hegemonic or dominant countries, with a view to preserving its sovereignty, and by a foreign policy marked by opposition to the agenda of developed countries and to a number of international regimes. Autonomy through participation refers to the acceptance of the values espoused by the main international powers and to participation in international institutions oriented by liberal principles. Lastly, autonomy through diversification refers to the participation in liberal institutions by means of South–South alliances in order to counterpose the agenda of certain developed countries, the United States in particular. The specificity of autonomy through diversification lies in avoiding a return to autarchical phenomena and ensuring that the counter-position does not become a rupture.

Distance, participation, and diversification are instruments that may be combined and may be more or less present within the same foreign policy. In other words, a certain historical period may display policies that are characteristic of autonomy through distance and also of autonomy through participation, mainly in moments of transition between the two categories. These instruments are analytic tools to simplify complex social phenomena. Normally, one of the three concepts gains more visibility than the others when we analyze Brazilian foreign policy from the historical point of view.

Each one of these concepts is embedded in the Brazilian diplomatic tradition. However, these strategies are not necessarily successful to the point of yielding clear results, for instance, in terms of increased trade, attracting direct investment to the country, having influence in international bodies, consolidating regional integration efforts or having political prestige and influence in questions of war and peace. Strategies or discourses do not always become political practice, which, in turn, does not necessarily bring concrete results. Furthermore, even when the strategies are actually implemented, they require some time to have a direct impact on the country's foreign policy. They must also be in line with the real power of a State, with its material and symbolic capabilities. Strategies, political plans and speeches normally precede concrete and quantifiable changes in foreign policy.

NOTE

1. In other words, these concepts would be in a gray zone, which explains the transition and the political change (Goertz, 2006).

Chapter 2

Pressure for Change

José Sarney's Foreign Policy

INTRODUCTION

An interesting issue which has not been thoroughly discussed by international relations specialists is the following: would a change of regime—for instance, when a military dictatorship gives way to civilian democracy—lead to an immediate change in foreign policy? In the case of Brazil, it has been argued that "the José Sarney administration foreign policy predominantly aims for continuity, when compared to the previous regime's" (Pereira, 2003: 91). Hence, the change of political regime in Brazil did not bring about any foreign policy ruptures.

We believe it was foreseeable that drastic changes in Brazilian foreign policy would not have taken place immediately after the end of the military regime. As the country's transition to democracy was gradual, significant changes in foreign policy also took place in a measured manner. On the other hand, the pressures for change were such that even though President Sarney tried to maintain his foreign policy within the logic of autonomy through distance, by the end of his term it was quite clear that the country was taking new foreign policy paths. By the late 1980s, liberal values were on the ascendancy and spreading from developed to peripheral countries.

In the first section we describe the domestic scenario during the Sarney administration. Thereafter, we analyze the changes that were taking place in the international system in that period. Lastly, we discuss four situations used to pressure Brazil into changing its foreign policy: (1) the Brazilian foreign debt moratorium; (2) the dispute with the United States over pharmaceutical patents; (3) the Brazil–USA conflict over information technology; and (4) the Brazilian position at the GATT Uruguay Round.

THE TRANSITION TO DEMOCRACY AND CHANGES IN THE FOREIGN SCENARIO

In the mid-1980s, Brazil was beginning its transition to democracy, bringing to an end over two decades of military governments that first took power through the 1964 military coup. The world watched the political changes in the Soviet Union, which led to the meltdown of its bureaucratic socialist system and to the end of the Cold War. Brazil was turning into a democracy, but it also faced a domestic economic crisis, originated in the exhaustion of a relatively autarchic economic model founded in the 1930s and based on import substitution, where the State played an important role.

Several policies from the military period were obsolete, though difficult to modify. According to Seixas Côrrea, international advisor to President Sarney from 1987 to 1990, it was not possible to make a drastic break with the past: "It became necessary to conduct changes of direction with an appropriate mix of boldness and balance" (Seixas Côrrea, 1996: 364).

After the demonstrations of popular discontent that were part of the *Diretas Já!* (Direct elections now!) campaign in 1984, most leading political and economic groups concluded that the government should search for a minimal consensus among Brazilian social actors to avoid institutional rupture. A few areas for convergence were created, which allowed for political and institutional advances: promotion of freedom of the press; adherence to formal rules for the protection of human rights; political and party pluralism, with direct elections at all levels; creation of a new Constitution (which was to be called "The Citizens' Constitution") promulgated in 1988; negotiation of the foreign debt; and political and economic integration with the Southern Cone countries.

The New Republic was supported by two great movements that helped consolidate its legitimacy. The first one, of a political nature, was materialized by the profound legislative reform, which became irreversible after the constitutional amendment that called for the Constituent Assembly, elected in November 1986. The democratic transition culminated with the new Constitution's promulgation on October 5, 1988. Presidential elections took place in 1989, and the new president took office in March 1990. The second movement consisted of the strenuous efforts made toward economic adjustment. The Cruzado Plan, an economic package launched in March 1986, was conceived to contain inflation, then at the highest rates ever experienced in the country. Its impact was significant, and President Sarney was invited to write an article in the journal *Foreign Affairs,* presenting the plan and its goals for Brazil's international insertion.

In his article, Sarney commented on the country's expectations upon his inauguration after 20 years of military dictatorship. These expectations were surrounded by concerns with the political and economic crisis, high inflation, the foreign debt, and an increase in social violence. His inauguration was preceded by the hospitalization and later death of President-elect Tancredo Neves, in April 1985, who should have been the first civilian president after the 1964 military coup. Sarney himself recognized the lack of confidence in him, having built a career in the National Renewal Alliance (ARENA), the official party of the military establishment that ruled Brazil from 1964 to 1985 (Sarney, 1986a: 105–106).

Sarney took office in a country that had doubts about his legitimacy and with the simultaneous explosion of three deep crises: political–institutional, economic, and social.

First, a legal–institutional apparatus built over 20 years of military governments remained in force. "Everything was in need of reform: the political party organization, the electoral system, the labor laws, laws governing freedom of opinion and information, even the constitution" (Sarney, 1986a: 107).

Second, the huge foreign debt had become a significant problem causing cuts in investments and loans. The inflation rate was the highest in history, there had been a recession for three years, unemployment rates were high, and there were shortages of food, as the sector had been neglected in favor of the export of high energy content products (Sarney, 1986a: 108).

Third, the chronic situation of poverty involving 30 million Brazilians was aggravated by the effects of the recession and the unequal distribution of income: 12% unemployment, a considerable fall of the real value of wages, increases in child mortality, hunger and malnutrition, millions of abandoned children, and an alarming crime rate (Sarney, 1986a: 108).

The main measure to deal with these three crises was to promote the country's economic growth, raising wages, and increasing the number of jobs offered. As such, President Sarney was opposed to those who espoused a monetarist policy with rigid controls, which would lead to domestic recession and, according to its advocates, make it possible for Brazil to meet its international financial obligations.

However, Sarney started to propose the replacement of the strategy based on autarchical economic growth, one of the hallmarks of autonomy through distance, by a market-oriented development policy, tending more to autonomy through participation. Some State agencies related to economic and foreign trade matters started conducting studies on the cost-benefit ratio of traditional economic policies, with less protectionist trends gaining ground. The international environment exerted its influence, but there were changes taking place among part of the Brazilian elite as well:

> In addition to the old concept of eschewing state control and of selling public sector assets, putting the Brazilian economy in private hands calls for a broad curtailment of the interventionist and regulating presence of the state in the economy. This is a new posture; economic development is now to be led by a well-structured private sector, free of the paternalism of the state. Thus is buried, together with its authoritarianism, the government's role as arbiter in the economy (Sarney, 1986a: 111).

On February 28, 1986, Sarney announced the Cruzado Plan (or Plan for Economic Stabilization) on national radio and television to deal with the high inflation rates afflicting the country. The plan, put in place by Finance Minister Dilson Funaro, consisted of a series of measures designed to reduce inflation. Among them was the complete elimination of indexing (situation where salaries were automatically adjusted when inflation increased) and a new national currency. In addition, a wide-ranging price freeze was put in place.

Lastly, in his article published in *Foreign Affairs,* President Sarney was harshly critical of the United States, which had been pressing Brazil on commercial issues and did not support the country in its democratic transition, showing the distance that separated the two countries' political proposals.

LATIN AMERICA

In the 1980s, Brazil was experiencing its "lost decade" in terms of economic growth (see Figure 2.1), having to administer its democratic transition in the midst of shortages and economic difficulties, unable to implement any consistent policy on one of the most significant problems of the time: the foreign debt (see Table 2.1 and Figure 2.2).

Along with these problems, the United States–Brazil information technology (IT) and pharmaceutical patents disputes and the start of the GATT Uruguay Round exerted pressure on the Sarney administration to change its foreign policies, particularly on economic issues. In spite of resistance, these changes started to take place toward the end of Sarney's term of office.

Sarney took office driven by Brazilian redemocratization, a process of political and institutional transformation. The issue of human rights was perhaps the first sign of a new direction in foreign policy. In the first months of civilian government, in 1985, Brazil joined the Pact of San Jose (American Convention on Human Rights), the United Nations human rights pacts, and

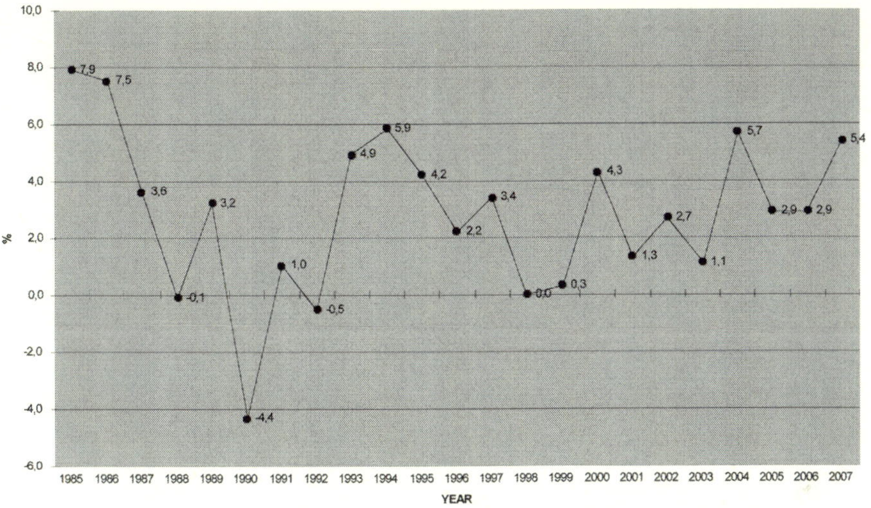

Figure 2.1. Brazilian Gross domestic product (GDP) – 1985/2006. ***Source:*** **IBGE.**

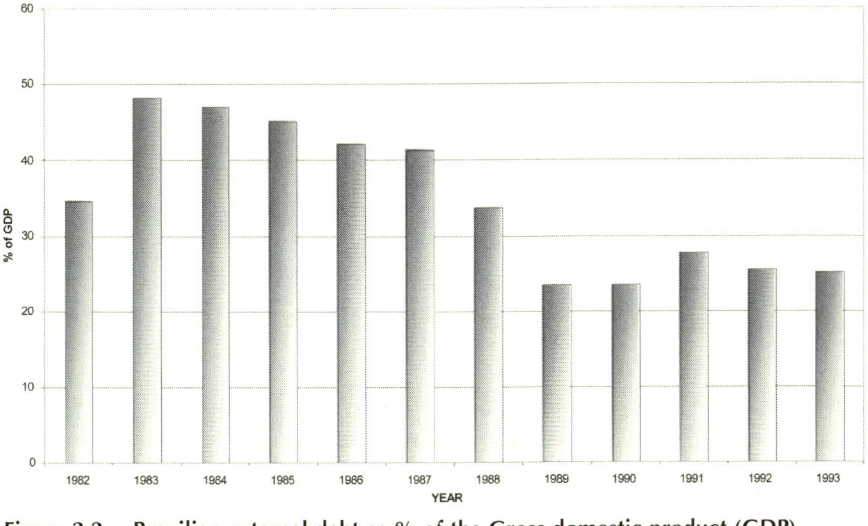

Figure 2.2. Brazilian external debt as % of the Gross domestic product (GDP) 1982/1993. ***Source:*** **World Book.**

the UN Convention Against Torture, thus rejoining the international system of human rights protection.

The recovery of the image of a democratic nation furnished the conceptual basis for Brazil to participate more actively in the international agenda. In this sense, the reestablishment of diplomatic relations with Cuba was one of the very first measures taken by the Sarney administration.

Table 2.1. Latin America External Debt—1982/1993

	1982		1983		1984		1985		1986		1987	
	US$ in millions	%	US$ in millions	%	US$ in millions	%	US$ in millions	%	US$ in millions	%	US$ in millions	%
Argentina	43634	79	45919	75.3	48858	65.8	50946	78.8	52450	66.9	58458	74.6
Bolivia	3328	101,4	4069	141,9	4317	167,6	4805	169,3	5575	151,4	5836	141,7
Brazil	92961	34,6	98341	48,3	105419	47,1	106121	45,2	113705	42,2	123837	41,4
Chile	17315	68,7	17928	87,6	19737	100,6	20384	126,1	21144	125,9	21489	110,1
Colombia	10306	16,8	11412	25,1	12039	28,6	14245	37,8	15362	37,9	17008	40,2
Equador	7705	64,2	7595	70,9	8305	82,6	8702	71	9334	83,9	10474	101,8
Mexico	86081	52	92974	63,8	94830	52,9	96867	52,4	100889	78,2	109469	73
Peru	10712	37,8	11343	52,4	12157	52,9	12884	73,1	14888	60,2	17491	64,9
Uruguay	2647	27,9	3292	60,8	3271	64,2	3919	85,7	3906	61,6	4299	53,5
Venezuela	32158	32,9	38303	38,8	36886	48,4	35334	41,9	34340	47,3	34569	61,3

	1988		1989		1990		1991		1992		1993	
Argentina	58741	62,4	65257	118	62234	58	65397	45,4	67770	40,6	74473	40,3
Bolivia	4902	115,2	4136	92,3	4278	96,6	4076	83,1	4220	79,5	4212	76,1
Brazil	115712	33,7	111373	23,6	116417	23,6	117350	27,7	121063	25,5	132749	25,1
Chile	19582	81,4	18032	61,4	19227	50,6	17947	34	19134	25,4	20637	26,4
Colombia	16994	36,6	16878	35,5	17231	34,2	17337	28,3	17197	20,9	17173	19,5
Equador	10746	111	11317	118,5	12109	114,9	12468	106	12280	94,9	14110	104,1
Mexico	99213	57,2	93838	44,5	106026	41,2	115362	34,9	113423	29,3	118028	28,7
Peru	18245	101,7	18583	64,8	20069	57,4	20719	37,8	20293	35,8	20328	32,4
Uruguay	3821	45,2	5246	62,1	5850	66,7	6149	60,6	6659	54,6	7259	57
Venezuela	34788	54,1	32377	68,9	33170	52,1	34122	44,8	37774	47,4	37464	47,9

Source: World Bank

In addition, Brazil agreed to participate in the Contadora Support Group, along with Argentina, Uruguay, and Peru. With the objective of cooperating with the efforts made by the four Contadora countries (Mexico, Colombia, Venezuela, and Panama) to ensure the pacification of Central America, the Support Group represented the involvement of four important South American diplomacies in search of solutions for the problems threatening peace and security in the region.

Brazilian redemocratization was decisive in changing the pattern of mutual distrust which had characterized diplomatic relations between the two most powerful countries in the region. Brazil–Argentina relations had been improving gradually since 1979, when the Tripartite Agreement was signed, including Paraguay, with the objective of using the River Parana to generate hydroelectric power. The November 1985 meeting of presidents Raul Alfonsín and José Sarney, where they signed the Iguaçu Declaration and later the Economic Integration and Cooperation Program (PICE), in July 1986, opened up a phase of far-reaching understanding, which strategically modified mutual relations. The 1988 Brazil–Argentina Common Market Treaty (precursor of the Asunción Treaty, of March 1991, which created Mercosur) was the result of a long process, now driven by the two presidents' personal commitment. Both vowed to cooperate right at the beginning of the process precisely in the field where mutual suspicion was strongest: the nuclear industry. This, in turn, generated beneficial consequences for relations between the two countries' armed forces, avoiding the rise of mistaken perceptions due to the mastery of the full nuclear fuel cycle, achieved by Argentina and the following year by Brazil. The two countries—beginning with President Sarney's visit to Argentina's secret nuclear installations in Pilcaneyeu—reciprocally disclosed their nuclear programs.

The four cases below illustrate the international pressures sustained by Brazil during the Sarney government. All these cases were top priorities of the foreign relations agenda at the time. Due to the international pressure, Brazil had to alter its foreign policy—drawing away from the strategy of autonomy through distance and gradually adjusting to the logic of autonomy through participation.

BRAZILIAN FOREIGN DEBT AND MORATORIUM

In 1985, the Brazilian Gross Domestic Product grew 7.9% (see Figure 2.1), and the trade surplus allowed the country to pay the interest on the foreign debt. However, the last Brazilian military government, commanded by President João Figueiredo, failed to meet the performance criteria agreed with the International Monetary Fund (IMF) between the end of 1984 and the beginning of 1985, postponing negotiations until the new civilian regime took office.

In the 1984 Cartagena Consensus, Latin American nations agreed they should persuade the governments of developed countries of the need to accept shared responsibility by creditors and debtors for the region's debt problems, with both seeking solutions and sharing sacrifices.

In September 1985, at the annual IMF/World Bank meeting, US Treasury Secretary James Baker proposed the first big plan to solve developing countries' foreign debt problem. The proposal suggested that creditor countries, multilateral credit agencies, and private banks provide new capital to debtor countries so that these might grow and restart debt payments. However, the objectives of the proposal contradicted with the means available for implementation, as it advocated "debt reduction through its increase" (Veiga, 1993: 53). Although the US government had obtained a formal agreement among the different players to enable the Baker Plan, it had not committed to actually investing significant funds, except in the form of small loans or by bringing forward its annual contribution to the IMF. Private banks, which supposedly would invest most of the funds, had no intention of loaning new money. Therefore, the form in which the Baker Plan was conceived only served to discourage Latin American countries, which in 1985 threatened to suspend interest payments. At the annual meeting of the IMF and World Bank in Seoul, where the Baker Plan was announced, James Baker suggested to Finance Minister Dilson Funaro that if Brazil made concessions on its IT policies, the United States would respond with some advantages in relation to the foreign debt (Veiga, 1993: 55–57).

Among other initiatives, Finance Minister Dilson Funaro disregarded any possibility of international negotiations where Brazil had to accept conditions imposed by the IMF. In January 1986, the negotiation on the foreign debt was frozen until November, when the legislators of the Constituent Assembly would be elected. But in June, an agreement was signed that restructured capital repayment of the 1985 US$6 billion debt. It also postponed to 1987 the payment of US$9 billion referent to 1986 (Lehman and McCoy, 1992: 613).

In 1985, the country had an annual inflation rate of 235.13% (see Table 3.1, next chapter). Consequently, Minister Funaro presented the Cruzado Plan on February 28, to combat so-called inertial inflation[1] without pushing the economy into recession. Initially, the plan had great results, but soon inflation started increasing again.

On November 21, 1986, the Cruzado Plan II was announced. It consisted of price increases in the public sector and selected price increases in the private sector, the closure of fifteen State-owned companies, an interest rate increase and a currency devaluation. Due to the general skepticism caused by the first plan, the population in general did not have highly positive expectations regarding the new plan.

In January 1987, the domestic crisis made Sarney negotiate a rescheduling of the foreign debt with the Paris Club[2] with no commitment to IMF programs or monitoring. Having refused to negotiate through 1986, the Paris Club agreed to reschedule more than US$4 billion in payments in January 1987, after the IMF sent a letter to creditor governments supporting the Brazilian economic policies established by the Cruzado Plan II, even though there was no formal agreement with the Fund.

On February 20, 1987, Brazil declared a temporary moratorium on the payment of interest on medium- and long-term debts to foreign creditors. The moratorium was decided as a response to the deterioration of the trade surplus, the depletion of the international reserves, and the need to postpone unpopular and recessive economic adjustments. On the domestic plane, influential figures on the left, such as the then leader of the Workers' Party (PT) Luíz Inácio Lula da Silva, the president of the Democratic Labor Party (PDT) Leonel Brizola, the CUT and CGT trade union congresses and even Party of the Brazilian Democratic Movement (PMDB—the largest party at the time), supported the moratorium, which favored President Sarney's decision (Lehman and McCoy, 1992: 617).

In April 1987, in the midst of a serious economic crisis and in response to the resulting political pressure, Bresser-Pereira from PMDB was named the new minister of finance. His objective was to reach a 6% annual growth rate and negotiate the foreign debt conventionally, with the participation of the IMF. But the question of involving the IMF was strongly opposed both by business leaders of the Federation of Industries of the State of São Paulo (FIESP) and labor leaders, as a strong recession was feared.

As a result of the lack of bargaining possibilities, Bresser-Pereira could not reach a new international agreement. In retaliation, banks imposed severe credit restrictions, negatively affecting the nation's balance of payments, which forced Brazil to reduce its foreign exchange reserves considerably.

Bresser-Pereira then suggested a "partial and negotiated conversion of present debt into new bonds, either with the same face value but fixed rates of interest below market rates, or with a discounted value and interest at market rates" (Bresser-Pereira, 1989: 6). However, the banks refused the proposal. In October 1987, Bresser-Pereira came up with another plan. He hoped to obtain US$10.4 billion in new credit to finance the interest on the debt. Once again, the banks showed no enthusiasm for the minister's plan. The counteroffer from the banks was the prepayment of US$500 million for them to restart negotiations. The banks got what they asked for, and later a further US$1 billion payment. The impasse between the banks and Brazil finally ended in November 1987, with the signing of short-term measures which would serve as an interim debt agreement.

However, the banks continued pressing Brazil to pay the interest on the debt and accept the IMF policies. The banks and Brazil agreed the IMF would provide "consultancy" services to Brazil, but Bresser Pereira repeatedly refused to link negotiations to the adoption of the institution's policies.

In private talks with Sarney, Bresser-Pereira stated that if there was no chance to reach a definitive agreement by January 1988, it would be more advisable to negotiate with the banks individually. However, in December 1987, with growing domestic opposition against Bresser-Pereira and inflation out of control, the minister stepped down, stating that the government was not "ready to seriously fight the public deficit by demanding effective sacrifices from workers and from business enterprises" (Bresser-Pereira, 1989: 7).

In February 1988, the new Minister of Finance Mailson da Nobrega managed to sign an agreement with the banks. The banks would loan US$5.8 billion to refinance old interest on the debt, restore short-term loans, and reschedule medium- and long-term debt to the tune of US$61 billion. Brazil committed to pay overdue interests and promote some domestic reforms.

In May 1988, an IMF mission arrived in Brazil to work on a new loan from the Fund and to conclude an agreement with private banks, which continued to demand the IMF's approval before signing an agreement. In early June, the IMF agreed to grant a loan worth US$1.5 billion. On June 23, 1988, the bank advisory committee signed an agreement on the debt, rescheduling US$62 billion and providing new loans worth US$5.2 billion. In July, a letter of intent was signed with the IMF, and the banks approved the deal in September.

The Constituent Assembly decided in late August 1988 that Congress should approve the foreign debt agreement. Noticing that there was domestic opposition to the agreement, Nóbrega rushed to sign it on September 22, before the new constitution was promulgated. He thus avoided submitting the agreement to formal congressional ratification (Lehman and McCoy, 1992: 634).

However, compliance with the international agreement was difficult because the government had failed to achieve economic austerity. The wage freeze implemented by Nóbrega in April and May 1988 was declared unconstitutional. Cuts in the federal budget were not approved by Congress in October 1988, and negotiations for an anti-inflation social pact, between labor unions and the private sector, collapsed in the same month.

On March 10, 1989, the government of President George Bush announced another plan for the foreign debt crisis, the Brady Plan. The most relevant aspect of the plan was the endorsement of the principle of debt relief if debtor countries adopted monetarist economic policies, therefore with recessive consequences (Veiga, 1993: 57–62).

In mid-1989, the creditor banks refused to disburse US$600 million until the government reached a new agreement with the IMF. In response, Brazil stopped making interest payments, a veiled moratorium. In July 1989, Brazil suspended interest payments of US$812 million to the Paris Club. Hence, as will be seen in the next chapter, the debt issue remained an important topic on the Brazilian agenda during the Collor de Mello administration.

THE DISPUTE OVER PHARMACEUTICAL PATENTS

On September 14, 1987, Gerald Mossinghoff, then chairman of the PMA (Pharmaceutical Manufacturers Association, now Pharmaceutical Research and Manufacturers of America—PhRMA), stated that Brazil had been chosen as a target of actions by the pharmaceutical sector and the USTR, due to its status as a developing country economic and diplomatic leader (Lyrio, 1994: 43). This statement confirms the belief of the USTR that changing the Brazilian position on intellectual property would make it easier to alter the same policy in other countries, using measures against Brazil as an example to other developing nations with patent laws seen as flexible. The latter were seen as inadequate for the universal standards that were sought through multilateral and bilateral negotiations led mainly by the United States (Lyrio, 1994; Tachinardi, 1993). Therefore, such pressure would be useful to convince Brazil and other countries of the need for a stricter international intellectual property regime (TRIPS) within the GATT (General Agreement on Tariffs and Trade).

The USTR, which had started adopting a tough stance with trading partners, was pressing Brazil to amend its Industrial Property Code (Law 5.772/71). In the 1980s, the USTR and the US Trade Act (1974) underwent several changes. As a result of actions carried out by US associations such as the PMA, the 1984 Trade and Tariff Act explicitly linked protection of intellectual property to trade. The 1984 amendment added three new features to US trade legislation. It gave the USTR the authority to initiate cases on its own. It explicitly determined the failure to protect intellectual property as liable of legal action under Section 301. Lastly, it included the protection of intellectual property as a new criterion to maintain and/or extend the benefits that certain countries are given according to the US Generalized System of Preferences (GSP) (Sell, 1995: 172).

In 1984, eight organizations, representing over 1,500 companies, gathered to form the International Intellectual Property Alliance (IIPA), which campaigned for tougher rules to protect the rights of patent-holders around the world. The association lobbied the US government to review the contents of the Trade Law in 1984 and 1988. The IIPA and the PMA lobbied in the United States to include respect for intellectual property as a prerequisite for developing countries to access the benefits of the GSP (Sell, 2002: 174–175).

At the GATT Uruguay Round, launched in 1986, US positions were among the most ambitious ever. With approximately 100 members at various stages of development and following very diverse political philosophies, it seemed unrealistic to think that wide-ranging trade agreements in the service, investment, and intellectual property sectors might be accomplished.

The USTR's goals were made clear in the 1988 Trade Act. Regarding intellectual property, the United States intended to create a new international regime under the GATT that was stricter than previous agreements. Thus, the US government's goal was to create an international intellectual property institution that would penalize member countries that did not follow the rules and standards in their agreements (United States, 2002b: 1102–1103).

As regards pharmaceutical patents, the USTR took on board the PMA's demands, pressing the Brazilian government to change its intellectual property laws. On June 11, 1987, the PMA presented a request to the USTR, complaining about the lack of protection for pharmaceutical patents in Brazil. In this document, the PMA stated that the USTR should apply Section 301, because Brazil's acts, practices, and policies were unreasonable and restricted United States trade. According to the complaint, the PMA member companies had suffered damages of "not less than $160 million in the period from 1979 to 1986 as a result of the Brazilian failure to afford patent protection to pharmaceutical inventions" (PMA, 1987: 168). According to the association, numerous countries did not protect pharmaceutical patents adequately. But Brazil was a unique case: it failed to protect patents both on pharmaceutical products and processes:

> In addition to Brazil, there are a number of other countries that refuse to provide effective patent protection for pharmaceutical products. These countries provide the convincing justification for the evident unfairness of the policy based on taking the property rights of others. Brazil is virtually unique among these countries because Brazilian law denies both product and process patent protection (PMA: 1987, p. 173).

In this petition, in addition to complaints against Brazil, the PMA supported the US initiative to create stricter intellectual property rules, arguing that many developing countries had agreed to negotiate "a new international code designed to ensure that intellectual property rights are protected" (PMA, 1987: 171).

In June 1988, the Sarney government expressed a willingness to adopt patents for pharmaceutical processes, postponing the adoption of patents for products. The measure did not please the United States, which also pressured for the approval of patents for products, because if the patents were restricted to processes, "national companies could arrive at the same product by means of reverse engineering" (Tachinardi, 1993: 110).

During the Sarney government, it was believed it was best to protract the negotiations, suggesting new measures only in unavoidable cases, as there was a perception that any change in legislation would result in losses for the country (Albuquerque, 2000). This strategy delayed some measures considered contrary to national interests in the sector of pharmaceutical patents, but resulted in trade sanctions against Brazil under Section 301. Such sanctions were implemented by President Reagan starting October 24, 1988, affecting the paper, chemical, and electronic sectors. This was one of the periods of toughest friction between Brazil and the United States during the 1980s (Presidential Documents, 1988).

The US measure was disproportionate to the losses in the pharmaceutical sector; the Brazilian pharmaceutical industry held no more than 15% to 20% of the domestic market (Tachinardi, 1993; Lyrio, 1994; Novaes de Almeida, 1994). In that light, the retaliation against Brazil had the objective to show other countries that the United States was prepared to confront major trading partners in order to create an intellectual property protection system with stricter international standards and regulations. However, many countries had reservations about the unilateral actions taken by the United States. Many developing nations such as India and Egypt opposed the unilateralism of the retaliation taken against Brazil under Section 301. Subsequently, the European Community also began to support the Brazilian cause. Both the European Community and Japan were in a comfortable position in relation to the conflict between Brazil and the United States. If the results were favorable to Brazil, it would be a blow to the USTR's unilateral actions; if the United States were favored, there would be better chances of creating stricter international rules on Intellectual Property Rights (Lyrio, 1994: 53).

In December 1988, with growing support from the international community, the Brazilian government requested a panel to examine the American sanctions. However, in order to open a GATT panel, a consensus of all members was required. Therefore, it was not possible to examine the Brazilian case, as the US position was to veto the Brazilian request. In February 1989, even when opinions mostly favored Brazil's request (50 countries), the United States, now under George H. W. Bush's government, stood alone in rejecting the opening of a panel.

With the prolonging of the dispute, the United States called for a broad discussion on Intellectual Property Rights, which at that time was virtually paralyzed due to the impasse in negotiations at the TRIPS group (Lyrio, 1994: 53).

Hence, the creation of an international institution for intellectual property (TRIPS) met the long-term aims of the pharmaceutical industry, but had as its main goal the recovery of US economic competitiveness. Hence, the United States pursued its own objectives, but it also required the explicit consent of other member countries. As for Brazil, US pressure pushed the country toward adopting more flexible intellectual property laws and beginning to change its position at the GATT Uruguay Round.

THE INFORMATION TECHNOLOGY (IT) DISPUTE

On September 7, 1985, Brazil's Independence Day, President Ronald Reagan devoted part of his weekly radio program to the South American country: "I am directing the US Trade Representative to start proceedings [. . .] against a Brazilian law that has restricted US exports of computers and related products and squeezed out some American computer firms operating there" (Reagan, 1985).

Initiated on the basis of Section 301 of the 1974 Trade Act, the case was presented as part of a strategy aimed at "stepping up [US] efforts to open markets abroad and create American jobs by increasing exports" (Reagan, 1985). Such a strategy was possible due to the Trade and Tariff Act approved by the US Congress in 1984. President Reagan's first complaint against Brazil was that it "restricted US exports of computers and related products" (Reagan, 1985). At the time the official announcement of the case was made, US exports had neither been eliminated, nor reduced. The problem was that they had grown at a slower pace than the Brazilian market.

Section 301 of the 1974 Trade Act requires the USTR to "take all feasible and appropriate action" if "an act, policy, or practice of a foreign country is unreasonable or discriminatory and burdens or restricts United States commerce [. . .]". These actions are not only reactions to commercial practices considered illegal, but also "unreasonable": "an act, policy, or practice is unreasonable if the act, policy, or practice, while not necessarily in violation of, or inconsistent with, the international legal rights of the United States, is otherwise unfair and inequitable" (United States, 2002a).

The companies more likely to suffer losses in Brazil were those which had already made heavy investments in the country, such as IBM and Burroughs. They were the most vulnerable to changes in US legislation, as they had already adjusted themselves to the restrictive Brazilian policies.

The fact that the United States did not take the case to the GATT even one year later suggests that the US government agreed with the view that Brazil would prevail if the two countries were to negotiate by the rules of the institution. According to Ralph Buck, then a State Department official and US consul in Brazil for economic affairs, "It's not possible to negotiate an issue like this (computers) within the GATT. [. . .] It is better to negotiate bilaterally."[3] The Brazilian Ambassador to the GATT, Rubens Ricupero, painted a good picture of the Brazilian viewpoint, showing that the succession of disputes and retaliations against Brazil "are nothing more than a clear message that the Brazilian government has to change its negotiating position at the GATT" (*Gazeta Mercantil,* 1988).

The September 1985 cases,[4] including the dispute over the computer market, consist of a combination of policies that could be distinctly regarded as typical of a declining hegemony. The countries chosen as Section 301 targets were not only regarded as violating the rules of free trade, but also as successful rivals, or potential rivals, suspects of adopting neomercantilist practices to improve their position in the hierarchy of nations, in relation to fair players such as the United States (Evans, 1989: 221).

According to Adler, there was a "'pragmatic anti-dependency' school of thought, prevalent among the Brazilians responsible for Brazil's computer policy" that sought to reduce the dependence of the country through technological autonomy, which would be reached by achieving "control of foreign technology and investment, development of the domestic capacity for innovation, and direct state intervention aimed at linking domestic industry with the scientific and technological infrastructure" (Adler, 1986: 675).

From the Brazilian point of view, as expressed by President Sarney, it seemed that the United States was trying "to freeze countries in their present state of scientific and technological development," which would ascribe to them the production "of simple manufactured goods involving little technical expertise" (Sarney, 1986b).

According to the provisions in Section 301, the USTR had a one-year period to make a recommendation to the president, who could act as he believed fit to remedy the situation. Almost every case analyzed on the basis of Section 301 was solved by means of negotiations before the fatal deadline, but the dispute over the computer markets became a different case due to the domestic situation in Brazil and because of its exemplary meaning. During the six months that followed the announcement of the case, Brazilian reaction was minimal. The Washington law firm that represented the Brazilian Computer Industry Association (Abicomp) started legal action at the USTR, but the Brazilian government did not respond.

Finally, a special meeting was held in Caracas, in February 1986, where the US delegation led by Trade Representative Mike Smith, met a Brazilian delegation headed by the Under Secretary of the Special Information Technology Department (SEI) José Ezil.

The Brazilian delegation was essentially willing to listen to American complaints, but was not authorized to negotiate anything at all. On both sides, agencies which regarded the dispute as a conflict between economic principles rather than a diplomatic issue to be negotiated were responsible for the case. According to then Economic Policy Secretary of the Ministry of Finance Luiz Gonzaga Belluzzo, "we could never set up an agenda. We always negotiated separately." Furthermore, "we could not discuss the market reserve, or intellectual property or anything else, or, say, retaliations on

Brazilian exports, without including the question of the Brazilian foreign debt, for example. [. . .] Sarney didn't want to resolve anything."[5]

In the United States, the USTR was the leading agency, together with the Department of Commerce. In Brazil, although officially under the jurisdiction of the Ministry of Foreign Relations, in practical terms the case was managed by the SEI, created in 1979 specifically to implement the computer industry market reserve policy. It had a strong interest in maintaining the policy.

In the beginning of April, 1986, US Secretary of State George Shultz started a direct dialogue with the Brazilian Ministry of Foreign Relations. In a letter he sent to Minister Abreu Sodré, Shultz stated that the United States was not interested in changing the Brazilian law (which seemed to be the main objective in Reagan's radio speech), but in a more flexible implementation (Evans, 1989: 227).

The Shultz/Sodré correspondence was followed by a visit of Under Secretary of State John Whitehead to Brazil at the end of May. This visit had a conciliatory tone and paved the way for a meeting of the two sides in Paris on July 2. Trade Representative Clayton Yeutter headed the US delegation and General Secretary of the Ministry of Foreign Relations Paulo de Tarso Flecha de Lima led the Brazilian delegation. The Paris meeting was the first of a series of confidential gatherings which turned a trade dispute into a State affair.

In the beginning of September 1986, President Sarney visited Washington as the victorious leader of a recently democratized Brazil, which made *The New York Times* publish an editorial under the heading "Admire Brazil, Then Negotiate."

Still more symptomatic was the controversy over software. For US transnational corporations operating in Brazil, the lack of adequate protection for software was the single most menacing element within the Brazilian situation. The fact that the intellectual property over their programs was being appropriated by Brazilian companies was a real nightmare for multinationals such as IBM, Digital Equipment Corporation (DEC), and Data General.

Eventually, those pushing the dispute were unable to generate an open rupture, despite both parties' continuous tension and frustration. Sarney managed to approve an acceptable proposal on software, which included the protection of copyrights, through the National Informatics Council (Conin). When the one-year period for deliberations expired, President Reagan announced that even though Brazilian policies harmed US commerce, he would only make a final decision by the end of 1986.

By mid-October, an IBM-Gerdau[6] joint venture had been officially approved by the Special Information Technology Department (SEI) as a "national company" qualified to sign Brazilian government contracts. In the beginning of November, the SEI started to implement "administrative reforms" to accelerate the processing of requests from companies. Companies' concerns included the creation of an ad hoc USA–Brazil group to review individual claims made by US companies.

At the start of December 1986, Sarney's new software bill was sent to Congress. By the end of 1986, Brazil looked more fragile in political terms and less menacing as a case of "affirmative industrialization." The shortages that followed the price freeze forced the country to import beef and other foodstuffs, making the trade surplus with the US fall by half. Thus, foreign exchange reserves dropped rapidly, and Brazil's ability to service the foreign debt became seriously questionable (see previous section).

On November 30, 1986, the White House announced it was giving up on the investigation of the computer market, except as far as software and investments were concerned, putting off legal action on those issues until July 1987. Before the end of the 6-month postponement, the Brazilian Congress passed a law protecting software, which in the US government's eyes "adequately [addressed] US concerns about software copyright protection."[7] When the deadline for decisions consequent on the investigation expired, President Reagan suspended the part of the case dealing with intellectual property and requested that the USTR carry on the issue of investments, albeit without stipulating a deadline.

In the initial stages of the case, companies with no investments in Brazil had been only marginally involved in the process. From 1987 onward, as the conflict extended and the government's commitment not to give in became clearer, new players joined the controversy (Evans, 1989: 231). In October 1987, the SEI turned down a request from six Brazilian companies to license Microsoft MS-DOS, on the basis that similar Brazilian software had already been developed. Microsoft's interest once more stirred up concerns on the software issue, which had now become the heart of the matter. Meanwhile, Apple, one of the few important multinational companies which had not entered the Brazilian market, became concerned about the possibility of the SEI approving a new MacIntosh clone, the MAC 512, as a legitimate Brazilian product.

By mid-November 1987, as a partial response in addressing the interests of these multinational companies that had joined the dispute, the US government decided to impose punitive tariffs on US$105 million worth of Brazilian exports to the United States.

The Conin discovered a formula to meet US interests without contradicting the SEI directly. The Conin determined that MS-DOS 3.3 (but not 3.1 and 3.2), had no similar Brazilian product and therefore could be licensed. Meanwhile, the SEI decided they could not authorize the MAC 512, unless the Brazilian manufacturer proved the independent development of more software systems (Evans, 1989: 232).

By the end of 1988, three years after President Reagan's statement of September 7, 1985, despite the fact that the United States did not manage to force the Brazilians authorities to rescind Information Technology Law, several concessions had been obtained. It was an example of possible future achievements, as determined in the 1984 Trade and Tariff Act. In an interview on June 19, 1987, President Sarney stated that which would be his administration's new guidelines: "the Brazilian computer industry market reserve policy has been excessive and has prevented the country from having a modern economy" (*Gazeta Mercantil,* 1987). He thus confirmed that new measures for this sector would be implemented. On October 6, 1989, the US government decided to close the investigation carried out against Brazil on the basis of Section 301 of the 1974 Trade Act.

BRAZIL AND THE GATT[8]

In the context of the launch of the Uruguay Round in 1986, and at least until the 1990s, the United States negotiated with Brazil under threat of retaliation against the Brazilian computer industry market reserve policy and the lack of protection for pharmaceutical patents (see sections 2 and 3 in this chapter).

The period between the attempts to launch the GATT Uruguay Round starting in 1982 and the first meetings held after the 1986 Punta del Este Ministerial Meeting is illustrative of the positioning of wealthy nations on the one hand, and of Brazil on the other. During the time spanning between the 1982 Ministerial Meeting and the 1988 Mid-Term Review, the developed countries proposed new issues and questioned the special and differential treatment, according to which poor countries would have special privileges due to their stage of development. During the same period, Brazil questioned the feasibility and legitimacy of the so-called new issues and made efforts to maintain the special and differential treatment.

From a few months before the 1988 Montreal Mid-Term Review up to the 1990 Brussels Ministerial Meeting, the positions held by the developed countries and by Brazil started to converge. Between Brussels and Marrakesh, in 1994, the main clash was between the European Union (EU) and the United Sates. The intensity of the disputes between the big powers and the peripheral countries had already diminished. In the case of Brazil, between 1987 and 1988, the country stopped questioning the new issues and tried to negotiate them by means of more specific proposals.

Brazil was strongly criticized at that time with regard to its development model. A statement by Reagan during Sarney's visit to Washington in 1986 clearly shows such pressures. According to the US president, "no nation can expect to continue exporting freely to others if its own domestic markets are closed to external competition" (*Gazeta Mercantil,* 1986). In the midst of the serious foreign debt crisis, a drop in the flow of exports would mean a loss of foreign currency to pay off the debt.

Within the scope of the Uruguay Round, pressures on Brazil on the eve of the 1988 Mid-Term Review were put on the record by the Brazilian ambassador to the GATT when he stated the following to the press:

> Brazilian delegate, Ambassador Rubens Ricupero, said heading as it was towards the mid-term review in December, that the negotiations had so far failed to meet third world expectations for "balanced results." Ricupero also expressed concern over violations of the standstill accord, and cited as a clear example of this the US announcement about its intention to impose unilateral restrictive measures on selected Brazilian exports, purportedly for alleged insufficient protection for patents in pharmaceutical industry in Brazil. The U.S. actions were not only a clear infringement of the standstill, but a measure for putting pressure on Brazil to change its stance in the negotiating group on TRIPS (*Suns On-line,* 1988).

The strong US pressures exerted on Brazil were even clearer in a paper sent by the Brazilian Government to the GATT Secretariat in August 1988 on the issue of patents. It emphasized the United States' disrespect for GATT norms and the fear for Brazilian exports:

> On July 2nd, 1988, the Government of United States of America announced its intention to impose trade restrictions on a number of Brazilian export items, because alleged damage to the US pharmaceutical industry resulting from Brazilian legislation on patents [. . .] This unilateral and discriminatory action constitutes a blatant disrespect of the provisions of the General Agreements. The declared intention of the US Government's action is to force a modification of long-standing Brazilian legislation. This legislation is in full agreement with the appropriate international conventions regarding intellectual property rights [. . .]. The implementation of the announced measures will cause a serious disruption in the bilateral trade. The mere announcement of this action is already causing serious damage to Brazilian export interests (GATT, 1988).

These statements seem to indicate that the Brazilian mission in Geneva reacted negatively to US threats with regard to Brazil's positioning. In fact, such positioning started leaning toward the acceptance of new agreements, particularly as regards intellectual property issues. In that context, Brazil could hardly avoid negotiating new agreements related to copyrights and services. US threats did affect the Brazilian position regarding new regimes taking shape. The country changed its foreign policy toward greater acceptance of international norms of a liberal nature in line with the logic of autonomy through participation. Finally, as of 1988, the country seemed to alter its strategy definitively. There was no room left for the defense of special and differential treatment without negotiating issues of services and intellectual property. Hence, it was necessary to soften obligations deriving from new agreements in order to safeguard the domestic capacity to legislate and prevent the advance of international harmonization of public policies according to rules over which the State would have no control whatsoever.

The Brazilian delegation in Geneva, aware of the need to negotiate in the face of external coercion, tried to attenuate new international obligations in a 1992 confidential document, as follows:

> . . . texts related to intellectual property, subsidies, safeguards, investment measures regarding trade and others, although acceptable in general, could have topical amendments (proposed by Brazil), so as to preserve in a more complete fashion our commercial interests and/or attenuate obligations we will have to assume because of agreements negotiated, which, in some cases, imply the revision of relevant domestic legislation.[9]

Diplomats Ricupero and Didonet (1995) came up with justifications that corroborate our argument with regard to the change in the Brazilian position at the Round. The bulletin clearly shows the dilemmas and anxiety the country underwent when pressed by the United States. In this sense, defending the old notion of autonomy through distance became increasingly complicated. Hence, the country had to be more participative and at the same time build up its capacity to bargain more effectively on the international plane.

> The unilateral character of the Brazilian trade liberalization has often been the object of criticism, for the country did not manage to negotiate anything in return. [. . .] It should be noted that the opening of trade barriers resulted from Brazil's own immediate interest, and not as a concession to foreign interests. [. . .] We must also not underestimate the pressure that began to be exerted on the country by industrialized partners when Brazil improved its balance of payments. [. . .] Brazil only escaped a serious dispute with the USA because of the decision adopted in March 1990 to remove non-tariff barriers. [. . .] Therefore, it was not true that Brazil could continue to implement its protectionist arsenal with impunity. On the contrary, if liberalization had not taken place, it is likely that trade conflicts would have significantly affected Brazilian trade performance (Ricupero and Didonet, 1995: 118).

Our understanding is that this change in strategy was the way the country found to maintain its autonomy in the conduct of its foreign policy while at the same time it enhanced its international participation. Top decision makers came to believe that greater adherence to prevailing international regimes resulted in greater capacity to influence decisions.

FINAL REMARKS

In this chapter we have ascertained that Brazil was strongly pressured by the US government and a number of companies. These pressures, together with changes in the international system resulting from the acceleration of globalization and the end of the Cold War, as well as the domestic democratic transition, caused deep alterations in the course of Brazilian foreign policy toward the end of the Sarney government. These changes made it impossible for Brazil to continue adopting a foreign policy guided by the concept of autonomy through distance, as had been practiced, with variations, since the Getúlio Vargas presidency in the 1930s.

Some changes were driven by domestic dynamics, which influenced Brazilian foreign policy. In accordance with the image of a more democratic country, topics such as human rights and the preservation of the environment started to play a relevant role in Brazilian foreign policy. The search for better relations with its Latin American neighbors was partly driven by the attenuation of the tension that existed among military governments, which had emphasized conflictive aspects of their foreign policies, when these were replaced by democratic regimes in the region. As we show in chapter 6, the quest for greater regional integration had the aim of increasing the capacity of bargaining and of insertion by countries that were to act in a coordinated manner on the international setting, as well as boosting trade among themselves. The most important result obtained during the Sarney administration was a much closer relationship with Argentina, which has become a new and long-lasting guiding principle.

Other changes in Brazilian foreign policy were driven by international pressure, particularly from the US. Thus, in this chapter we have attempted to show that the four cases analyzed (foreign debt negotiation, dispute over the IT industry, dispute over pharmaceutical patents and negotiations at the GATT Uruguay Round) are examples where Brazil had to alter its foreign and domestic policies due to international pressure at a time when the country was undergoing a serious economic crisis and a period of transition in its political regime. In this sense, both domestic and international pressures made it impossible for the country to remain distant and resistant; absence from negotiation fora where the leadership of the central countries was strong was not an option.

The four cases analyzed here provide evidence that by the end of Sarney's term of office the strategy oriented by the logic of autonomy through distance had started giving way to autonomy through participation.

In the first case, tough negotiations between Brazil on the one hand and the USA, private creditor banks and international financial institutions on the other, made Brazil gradually adopt less developmentalist and autarchic policies and lean toward more liberal ones. The adoption of such policies was a consequence not just of external pressure, but also of the need to overcome the import substitution economic model. As regards patents, US pressures made the Brazilian government ponder the alteration of the Brazilian intellectual property law, which was considered unfair by the American government. In the case of the computer industry, Brazil had to change its protectionist law and gradually open its market to the computer industry and to service sector companies from the USA and other countries. Lastly, such pressures plus the threat of removing Brazil from the US Generalized System of Preferences induced the country to accept the introduction of "new issues" such as intellectual property, copyrights, services, and investments onto the agenda of multilateral trade negotiations. Such non-spontaneous alterations in strategy led Brazil to stop trying to block the US agenda. It adopted a more flexible position in an effort to embrace the prevailing logic of the international debate, thus envisioning the possibility of influencing the agenda and decisions of the future World Trade Organization (WTO).

NOTES

1. Inertial inflation refers to the idea of inflationary memory, where the current index is the past index plus the future expectation. Inflation maintains itself at the same level without inflationary acceleration as a result of indexing mechanisms. These mechanisms can be formal and informal. An example of a formal mechanism might be specific and legal increase rules, such as rents, school tuition, etc.; informal: when actors increase prices because everyone else is doing it. In Brazil, at the time of high inflation (the 1970s and 1980s), contracts of various types had correction clauses which were automatically applicable. This generated an inflationary behavior in the population: the inflation rate was transferred to the next month even if there were no demand or price pressures.

2. The Paris Club is an informal group of developed creditor countries with the mission of negotiating with debtor countries in economic difficulties.

3. Buck, Ralph. Interview with Tullo Vigevani, May 23, 1991.

4. The computer market case was not the only one initiated in September 1985. Reagan announced an investigation against Korea, due to the restriction on American insurance companies, and another against Japan, for restrictions against American

tobacco. Investigations already underway were accelerated, against canned fruit subsidies in the European Community and against Japanese restrictions to leather product imports.

5. Belluzzo, Luiz Gonzaga. Interview with Tullo Vigevani, April 6, 1991.

6. Gerdau is a multinational company of Brazilian origin, which invests mainly in the steel sector.

7. Statement by Assistant to the President for Press Relations Fitzwater on Brazil–United States Computer Related Trade, June 30, 1987.

8. This section has benefited from research conducted by Feliciano Guimarães.

9. Del Du Brésil—Génève—*Rodada Uruguai: O Estado Atual das Negociações e a Postura Brasileira* (Uruguay Round: The Current State of Negotiations and the Brazilian Position), no 0041227332834. CPDOC / FGV. Ref. MMM METP 1991.06.14, doc. 26, p. 2.

Chapter 3

Turbulent Times

The Foreign Policies of Collor de Mello and Itamar Franco

INTRODUCTION

The government of Fernando Collor de Mello (March 1990–December 1992) was an important period in Brazil's recent history. It was not just the impeachment process that left an indelible impression on Brazilian political life. Collor de Mello initiated changes in the country's foreign policy that have endured, albeit revised and adapted under the governments of Itamar Franco, Cardoso, and Lula. The most important changes included the opening of the Brazilian market to world trade and the open defense of free trade on the international arena—part of the hallmarks of autonomy through participation.

Although Collor de Mello's foreign policy has been interpreted on many occasions as a mere "automatic alignment" with the United States (Batista, 1993), the idea that it abandoned the traditional autonomist paradigm of Brazilian diplomacy (Cruz Jr., Cavalcante and Pedone, 1993; Hirst and Pinheiro, 1995; Campos Mello, 2000) is by no means consensual.

According to the Collor de Mello government's Secretary of Science and Technology, Hélio Jaguaribe (1996: 31–32), the government had two distinct foreign policy phases. Initially, the government distanced itself from the foreign policy consolidated under the Geisel administration and sought to align itself with the views and values of developed countries. The ministerial reform of April 1992 and the appointment of Celso Lafer as Minister for Foreign Relations brought closer relations between Brazil and the countries of the Southern Cone that characterized the resurrection of the concepts laid down by San Tiago Dantas for an independent foreign policy.[1]

It is also not established that this shift can be solely attributed to Collor de Mello. According to Canani (2004: 41), "the Itamar Franco government has been characterized as a simple continuation, with some hesitancy, of the Collor de Mello government's policies. It is also characterized by the major difficulties posed by the instability of the President which persisted up to the creation of the Real Plan." However, "by concentrating on the figure of Itamar Franco, the political analyst loses sight of the fundamental direction of his government and overlooks the complexity of Brazilian politics as a whole in the mid-1990s."

Our thesis is that the Collor de Mello and Itamar Franco governments were unable to establish a clear and coherent foreign policy because they faced very significant political and economic instability and were both characterized by the brevity of their tenure and the high turnover of their foreign ministers. In the domestic arena, the pressures generated by the return to democracy, the collapse of the import substitution economic model and financial crises were the main causes of instability. In the international arena, the end of the Cold War, the acceleration of so-called economic globalization and the shifting stance of the United States toward its trading partners were the main drivers of change. Despite this instability, foreign ministers Celso Lafer (in the Collor de Mello administration) and Fernando Henrique Cardoso and Celso Amorim, both of whom served under President Itamar Franco, were in the future to occupy positions of influence on Brazil's political stage and use their previous experience to develop better defined visions of the path for Brazilian foreign policy (see forthcoming chapters).

This chapter is organized as follows: (1) we review the main points of Collor de Mello's foreign policy; (2) we examine the role of the Ministry of Foreign Relations (MRE) in the same period; (3) we analyze the conceptual reform of Brazilian Foreign Policy from 1992; (4) we describe the main motives leading to the president's impeachment; (5) we set out the domestic and foreign scenarios at the time when Franco took office; and (6) we discuss the extent to which Franco continued the foreign policy reform initiated by Collor de Mello.

COLLOR DE MELLO'S FOREIGN POLICY

"Modernization," "competitive insertion in the international economy," and the quest for a "place in the First World" meant that foreign policy assumed a central role in the reforms that Brazil desired. These were also the objectives established by Collor de Mello in his election campaign in 1989.

For the then Foreign Policy Secretary at the Ministry of Foreign Relations, Marcos Castrioto de Azambuja, "the growing and competitive insertion" of Brazil in the international economy is a "basic component in the process of Brazilian economic structural reform." These reforms would lead to the modernization of Brazilian industry, the "cleanup" of public finances, a reduced role for the State, a deregulated economy, stimuli to free enterprise, and an expansion of technological capacity-building (Azambuja, 1990: 1–2).

According to Hirst and Pinheiro (1995: 6), Collor de Mello's foreign policy had three main objectives: the modernization of Brazil's international agenda in accordance with new international themes and practices, like intellectual property, the environment, human rights, and sensitive technologies; building a positive dialogue with the United States; and the undoing of Brazil's third worldist profile. Relations with the Southern Cone were maintained, the highlight being the signing of the Treaty of Asunción in March 1991. It created Mercosur, with the participation of Paraguay, Uruguay, and Argentina. The characteristics of Mercosur were adapted by general and trade policies conveying the hallmarks of what was known as open regionalism.

As regards developing countries, the new orientation did not go so far as to involve anti-Third World rhetoric explicitly. Brazil did not withdraw from the G-77[2] or from the then recently created G-15,[3] nor did it officially abandon its position as an observer of the Non-Aligned Movement. On the contrary, at the first meeting of the G-15 on June 15, 1990, Minister of Foreign Relations Francisco Rezek suggested that a common position on the foreign debt question be formulated. At the time, this contrasted with Argentina's position, opposed to the idea of a "debtors' club." It proposed that the G-15 nations consider the environment issue and the seriousness of the global ecological crisis (Campos Mello, 2000: 84–85). At the same time, the diplomatic language of the Collor de Mello government made clear that with the exception of the Southern Cone neighbors, the new priorities were based on relations with developed countries. According to Rezek, "international relations are based on the principle of exchange and the truth is the majority of poor countries have little to offer us" (*Jornal do Brasil,* 1990).

This stance, in the words of Collor de Mello, did not merely "seek to find a place in the First World—a concept that has, after all, lost much of its relevance with the dilution of the Second World and the diversification of the Third." It aims "to state that we cannot remain outside these discussions, directly or indirectly. We must *participate* [emphasis added] so that matters that are in our interest form part of the wider agenda and are dealt with in a balanced way" (quoted in Azambuja, 1990: 18). According to Secretary Azambuja, expressing ideas that would later be identified as autonomy through participation:

> The greater opening of Brazil to the world also corresponds with greater concern for an international scenario where new opportunities and uncertainties coexist. [. . .] In an interdependent world that is going through unparalleled and deep transformations, no country is immune to the risks present in the international setting, nor can it shrink away from the ample opportunities for cooperation that it offers (Azambuja, 1990: 18–19).

In trade policy field, the liberalization program aimed to eliminate the majority of non-tariff barriers and prohibitions in the import license system. It also sought the reform of export incentives and the introduction of a reduced tariff program that aimed to reduce average tariffs from 32 percent (with a maximum tariff of 105 percent) to 14.2 percent (with maximum tariff of 35 percent) by October 1993 (Abreu, 1997). Liberalization also reduced bureaucracy on imports and exports and abolished State controls of the trade in wheat, coffee, and sugar. The list of imports and exports subject to prior approval by the government was dramatically reduced, and the non-tariff protection of electronic goods was also abolished.

At the same time, on the multilateral trade policy plane, in the final phase of the GATT Uruguay Round talks in 1990, a new Brazilian posture clearly manifested itself, though a reorientation of the Brazilian position had been noticeable since 1988.

In 1989, according to Abreu (2001), the position of the G-10[4] had already shown signs of a lack of cohesion, mainly because of "[. . .] polarization in textiles and TRIPS negotiations" (p. 94). The discussion on TRIPS centered on the appropriate body for negotiations: the GATT or the World Intellectual Property Organization. Developing countries, particularly Brazil and India, initially resisted the US proposal to include international intellectual property in the GATT talks, though "as Indian opposition diminished, the position of developed countries gradually prevailed [. . .]" (Abreu, 2001: 94).

Shukla (2002) argues that India and Brazil ended up accepting the widening of GATT, in line with the US conception, because the United States was using unilateral measures against its trading "adversaries." Firstly, in 1988, the US government placed sanctions on Brazil regarding pharmaceutical patents. Later, in May 1989, India also became the target of retaliation. Furthermore, the domestic political situation in both countries was a concern, diminishing their capacity to take a stronger stance on the international stage. As a result the India–Brazil coalition weakened, leading to a lack of coordination in mutual consultations that produced mistrust between the two countries. As such, the position of developing countries weakened while industrialized countries saw opportunities to gain advantage in negotiations (Shukla, 2002: 265).

New directions relating to sensitive technologies were more clearly expressed. The closure ceremony of the Serra do Cachimbo nuclear weapon test site days before President Collor de Mello participation in the UN General Assembly in September 1990 marked a unilateral renouncement of the right to conduct nuclear tests, even for peaceful purposes.

Other marks of the Collor de Mello government's foreign policy include: the signing of the agreement creating the Brazilian–Argentine Agency for Accounting and Control of Nuclear Materials (ABACC); the signing of the Quadripartite Agreement on nuclear safeguards between Brazil, Argentina, ABACC, and the International Atomic Energy Agency (IAEA); the proposal to revise the Treaty for the Prohibition of Nuclear Weapons in Latin America and the Caribbean (Treaty of Tlatelolco), a joint initiative by Brazil, Chile, and Argentina that opened the way for these countries to finally ratify the accord concluded in Mexico City on February 14, 1967; a piece of legislation related to the export of sensitive military technologies; and a commitment made to the United States to begin to consider the possibility of adherence to the Missile Technology Control Regime (MTCR) (Hirst and Pinheiro, 1995: 6–7).

However, less than one year into his term, Collor de Mello's freedom of action was curtailed by the domestic economic and political situation, as well as by the difficulties in dealing with inflation and accusations of corruption. This situation rendered unviable the rapid reforms sought by the government to improve Brazil's foreign policy.

Initial expectations that foreign debt negotiations would produce quick results were frustrated at the end of 1990. Weaknesses in the monetary stabilization plan also became evident. Growing difficulties in overcoming macroeconomic imbalances in the first foreign debt agreement of April 1991 sent less than satisfactory signals to financial institutions about Brazil's ability to meet its financial obligations. Under Collor de Mello, the negotiations on the foreign debt, which had become the largest in the developing world, were conducted by a tough and "autonomous" negotiating team (Veiga, 1993).

In April 1991, Brazil was put on a United States Trade Representative (USTR) watch list due to its legislation on intellectual property. Expressing his frustration, Minister Rezek declared that "we did not see in return the intensity and pace of a country that wishes to progress quickly," while the president added, upon his return from Washington in June 1991, "there is no support for anything" (*Jornal do Brasil,* 1991).

The second year of the Collor de Mello government saw a gradual toning down of the rhetoric of cooperation with rich countries. At the

UN General Assembly in September 1991, Collor de Mello mentioned the growing imbalance between the developed and developing worlds, the persistence of the foreign debt, the barriers to technology transfer, and the protectionism of industrialized nations (MRE, 1996). At the same time, against a backdrop of growing political difficulties at home, the President became less and less involved in international matters, allowing the Ministry of Foreign Relations to act with more autonomy. With the April 1992 ministerial reform and Celso Lafer's appointment as Minister for Foreign Relations, the second phase of the government's foreign policy got underway.

As with the strategy adopted in the foreign debt negotiations, Brazil's stance on the Gulf War was identified as one of the main reasons behind the reversal in positive relations with the United States under the Collor de Mello administration. As opposed to its neighbor Argentina, Brazil did not send troops to the Persian Gulf; however, it did support the United States at the UN Security Council. Here again, one must distinguish the objectives of the Collor de Mello government's foreign policy from the difficulties involved in its implementation. In the early 1980s, Brazil had substantial military and trade links with Iraq. It exported arms to Baghdad, and individual members of the Brazilian armed forces cooperated with the government of Saddam Hussein. Furthermore, domestic economic restrictions—with the challenge of reducing an inflation rate that reached over 1,150 percent in 1992 and exceeded 2,700 percent in 1993 (see Table 3.1), and of fighting the recession—impeded the Collor de Mello government from practicing a foreign policy of automatic alignment with the United States.

The Role of Minister of Foreign Relations in the Collor de Mello Administration

Ambassador Nogueira Batista, one of the main critics of the Collor de Mello administration, believed that the Ministry of Foreign Relations did not have an active role in the formulation of foreign policy in the period. However, within the room for maneuver it had in the implementation of the policy, it was able to minimize "the cost of certain stances taken by the President." On this, Batista cites two examples of "Itamaraty ingeniousness": the Quadripartite Agreement on Nuclear Safeguards between Brazil, Argentina, ABACC, and the IAEA and the so-called 4+1 Agreement between the four members of Mercosur and the United States (Batista, 1993: 122).

In the first case, the Minister formulated an "indirect adhesion" instrument to the Nuclear Non-Proliferation Treaty. In the second example, the Ministry would coordinate a joint response by the Mercosur members to the Initiative

Table 3.1. Brazilian Inflation—1985/1995

	JAN	FEB	MAR	APR	MAY	JUN	JUL	AUG	SET	OCT	NOV	DEC	TOTAL
1985	12,64	10,16	12,71	7,22	7,78	7,84	8,92	14,00	9,13	9,05	14,95	13,20	**235,13%**
1986	17,79	14,98	5,52	–0,58	0,32	0,53	0,63	1,33	1,09	1,39	2,46	7,56	**65,04%**
1987	12,04	14,11	15,00	20,08	27,58	25,87	9,33	4,50	8,02	11,15	14,46	15,89	**415,87%**
1988	19,14	17,65	18,16	20,33	19,51	20,83	21,54	22,89	25,76	27,58	27,97	28,89	**1.037,53%**
1989	36,56	11,80	4,23	5,17	12,76	26,76	37,88	36,48	38,92	39,70	44,27	49,39	**1.782,85%**
1990	71,90	71,68	81,32	11,33	9,07	9,02	12,98	12,93	11,72	14,16	17,45	16,46	**1.476,71%**
1991	19,93	21,11	7,25	8,74	6,52	9,86	12,83	15,49	16,19	25,85	25,76	22,14	**480,17%**
1992	26,84	24,79	20,70	18,54	22,45	21,42	21,69	25,54	27,37	24,94	24,22	23,70	**1.157,84%**
1993	28,73	26,51	27,81	28,22	32,27	30,72	31,96	33,53	36,99	35,14	36,96	36,22	**2.708,39%**
1994	42,19	42,41	44,83	42,46	40,95	46,58	5,47	3,34	1,55	2,55	2,47	0,57	**909,67%**
1995	1,36	1,15	1,81	2,30	0,40	2,62	2,24	1,29	–1,08	0,23	1,33	0,27	**14,77%**

Source: IGP/FGV

for the Americas proposed by President Bush. The intention was to bolster the strength of Mercosur, which could have been threatened by the bilateral negotiation of any of its members with the United States.

The continuation of Southern Cone integration became a means to avoid the excessive centrality of relations with the United States in Brazil's agenda. In the context of negotiations of the Free Trade Area of the Americas (FTAA), subregional integration aimed to draw attention away from policies that were solely focused on developed countries, especially the United States. It also introduced a certain South–South dimension.

The objective of guaranteeing to the Ministry of Foreign Relations the role of chief decision maker of Brazilian foreign policy reflected the bureaucratic survival needs of the institution. According to Ambassador Celso Amorim, in 1990 there was a perception that of some of the MRE's responsibilities, particularly on the issue of trade liberalization, were being transferred to the recently formed Ministry of the Economy, strengthened by the merger of the ministries of Finance, Planning, Industry and Commerce (Amorim, 1997: 3). The Ministry's wish to lead the integration of the Southern Cone was a reaction to the creation of the Ministry of Integration in 1991.

As such, the diplomatic corps quickly created, with Minister Rezek's authorization, the Department of Latin American Integration, later elevated to the category of Deputy General Secretary's Bureau of Integration, Economic, and Foreign Trade Affairs, so as not to lose influence to other government ministries or agencies.

Therefore, the Ministry of Foreign Relations intervened in the foreign policy of the Collor de Mello administration to introduce elements of autonomy in the central axis of Brazil's international agenda: its relations with the United States. This action was also motivated by perceptions relating to the bureaucratic survival of the Ministry in the politico-institutional context of the early Collor de Mello administration.

Rethinking Foreign Policy Guidelines

The April 1992 ministerial reform with the appointment of Celso Lafer as Minister of External Relations began a phase of Brazilian foreign policy marked by the closer relationship between the minister and the diplomatic corps.

In a later evaluation of his tenure, Lafer emphasized that "Itamaraty's authority" is necessary for an effective foreign policy. "For this reason, what each foreign minister must do in order to preserve the authority of the Itamaraty and hence be able to execute the foreign policy, is to add quality to the thread of a tradition" (Lafer, 1993a: 45). The April 1992 cabinet, according to its most prominent members, sought to preserve the State in the course of the ongoing storm. The central question was not the direction of each sector of government, but the very preservation of the administration in the face of the deluge of events that culminated in the president's impeachment in December 1992.

Many of Lafer's speeches at the time refer to the two conceptual directives in the renewal of Brazilian foreign policy: "creative adaptation" and "future vision." An example of this future vision would be Agenda 21, concluded at the UN Conference on Environment and Development (Earth Summit, Rio-92 or Eco-92), which intended to bring about cooperation and the reinstatement of the right to development onto the international agenda, as well as the defense of democratization of the United Nations Security Council. The Earth Summit was an especially important symbol of Brazil seeking greater international participation without losing autonomy (Fonseca Jr., 1998). The Summit meant a change in the previous paradigm, much criticized by the international community, of deforestation to promote economic development (Hurrell, 1991). It amounted to a critique of the national sovereignty discourse on an issue that was becoming increasingly international, but where power relations still manifested themselves. Examples of creative adaptation included the climate change and biodiversity conventions, as well as Brazil's adhesion to the Quadripartitie Agreement on Nuclear Safeguards, the Chemical Weapons Convention, and the Tlatelolco Treaty.

Within this foreign policy frame of reference, two ideas featured in official diplomatic language of the time: Brazil's self-designation as a global trader and the concept of Mercosur as a platform for competitive insertion on the international plane. The term global trader conveyed the idea that Brazil, as opposed to Mexico or Canada, had global interests and therefore should not align itself automatically with any particular country. The conception of the Mercosur as a platform for insertion on the international plane constitutes second structuring axis of the new framework formulated in 1992. This sought to make the new priority placed on Mercosur compatible with the motto of the Collor de Mello government about Brazil's competitive insertion into the world economy. This effort was meant to adapt the priority accorded to relations with central countries (i.e., the major economic partners), to elements of continuity focused on the pursuit of autonomy. As Minister Celso Lafer himself argues, the idea that Brazil is a global trader does not mean that the country should have the maximum diversification of trading partners. Rather, it coveys the idea that Brazil has interests in various parts of the globe:

> I worked with the notion of operational partnerships. It was in part the idea that Brazil was a country with general interests, a global trader in the economic field

> that needed to build international partnerships. I thought in terms of partnerships with the United States, the European Community and Japan. After that came Latin America, which is not a partnership but is our circumstance (Lafer, 1993a: 7).

It is useful to consider here a specific aspect surrounding perceptions of the period regarding relations with the European Community. Although the Inter-Institutional Cooperation Agreement between Mercosur and the European Community had been signed in May 1992, and negotiations were being concluded on the Brazil–European Community Framework Cooperation Agreement, signed in June 1992, the foreign minister made it clear that in terms of a "strategic partnership" with Europe "frankly, at this moment there are not significant resources or solutions flowing from there" (MRE, 1993a: 67).

As Campos Mello states (2000: 115), "Celso Lafer's tenure built a new frame of reference for Brazilian foreign policy [. . .]. From the opposite paradigm, guidelines were maintained ensuring adhesion to international norms and regimes," having been partially diminished the excessive centrality of the United States on the Brazilian foreign policy agenda, which proved inadequate already during the government of Collor de Mello, who tried to promote it but without success, as we have seen. Furthermore, on Celso Lafer's watch the Ministry regained its role in the conduct of Brazilian foreign policy, in spite of the country being in the midst of an acute crisis.

The Domestic Setting

Collor de Mello emerged on the domestic arena in 1989, before which time he was a little-known provincial politician. He stood in the first presidential race since 1960. The rapid rise of his popularity reflected the dissatisfaction of certain segments of the population with the established political forces in Brazil. The 1980s began with a recession followed by rapid economic growth (1985–86) and ended in hyperinflation. The government seemed unable to put Brazil back on its traditional path of rapid economic growth. Brazil's Gross National Product (GNP) recorded average annual growth rates of 9 percent between 1965 and 1980, falling to around 2.7 percent in the 1980s.

The return to democracy created expectations that were not met. In the negotiations on the transition from military to civilian rule, Brazil's elites remained influential and sought to avoid deep political and social changes. The combination of disenchantment and a persistent feeling of crisis was fertile ground for the emergence of a "savior" (O'Donnell, 1992: 12). Collor de Mello made the most of this opportunity: young and dynamic, he promised economic modernity, greater social justice and efficient and honest government.

Collor de Mello did not win with a mass political party. He was one of the founders of the National Reconstruction Party (PRN) in 1989 himself. It served as an election vehicle, having little political force or organizational strength. However, during the presidential campaign a growing number of conservative politicians and business leaders[5] began to support him against his leftist opponent, Luíz Inácio Lula da Silva of the Workers' Party (PT).

The adoption of a liberal program boosted Collor de Mello's political objectives. He intended to implement a plan to modernize the economy, open Brazil to the international market, and force domestic manufacturers to compete with foreign companies. The project created controversy between business leaders of differing opinions. More technologically advanced companies, capable of competing internationally, favored the reduction of trade barriers imposed by neoliberalism. However, sectors that had emerged and grown thanks to the protection of the State and to subsidies (so-called infant industries) feared that with the loss of protection, international competition might harm their business or lead them bankruptcy. Consequently, the liberal project divided opinion in the business sector (Weyland, 1993: 11; Weyland, 1999).

Using the modernization policy as his tool, Collor de Mello tried to weaken business associations and labor unions by attacking the corporatist structure that still characterized these groups (Schmitter, 1979). In particular, Collor de Mello tried to abolish the compulsory union contribution that companies and workers paid to organizations recognized by the State.

The President tried to use these same reforms to decrease the influence and capabilities of the State. While the imposition of a neoliberal policy strengthened presidential power, the return of some functions of the State to the market weakened the public sector. The privatization of companies weakened the State's capacity for action and also challenged consolidated positions. The political reform proposed by Collor de Mello angered high level bureaucrats and led to strong resentment in the public sector as a whole.

The participation of the military in policymaking was reduced in various areas. Collor de Mello exercised his power even in matters that had a direct impact on the armed forces, such as the relative reduction in military salaries. The President also dissolved the National Information Service (SNI), the State intelligence service dominated by the military and used to not only investigate and intimidate people with leftist leanings, but also to investigate acts of corruption in government (Weyland, 1993: 12; Conca, 1992: 160).

In spite of his efforts to concentrate power, Collor de Mello was unsuccessful in effectively controlling the actions of many of his political allies, several of whom—such as Health Minister Alceni Guerra and the Labor and Social Security Minister Antônio Magri—were accused of involvement in illicit activities. These scandals were so damaging that Collor de Mello had to reshuffle his cabinet at the beginning of 1992. More importantly, the President himself seemed to be involved in an extortion racket organized by the ex-treasurer of his election campaign, Paulo César Farias. In a country with as high a degree of State control as Brazil at the time, the government used the resources of the State as political currency to attract allies (Geddes and Ribeiro Neto, 1999). Given that the Executive had used its powers to adopt recessive economic measures, companies dependent on government contracts now had to compete more fiercely for a dwindling number of projects and were ready to pay a high price for them.

The failure of Collor de Mello's economic stabilization plan weakened his support among Brazil's elites, particularly the more conservative political elements and business leaders that had supported him initially. The economic policy ushered in a deep recession that had a negative impact on all social strata and failed to dent inflation, which stood at between 18.54 percent and 27.37 percent per month in 1992 (see Table 3.1).

Business leaders intensified their criticism of the government's economic policy. Many sectors were worried about lower trade barriers that affected the economy as a whole. These reductions increased international competition that came to be seen as a potential threat. Liberalization was not offset with development policies that favored production.

When the opponents of the government, many of whom had initially given their support, began to demand investigations into the accusations of corruption against the President, his allies were unable to block the Congressional inquiry that finally resulted in his impeachment. His political isolation was decisive for the investigation to go ahead and come to a conclusion.

THE FOREIGN POLICY OF THE ITAMAR FRANCO GOVERNMENT

The Itamar Franco government inherited a troubled domestic scenario and a foreign policy agenda overshadowed by pressure from the United States regarding the strengthening of liberal economic reforms and especially in relation to the approval of new legislation on intellectual property.

Additionally, the growing ideological and economic convergence between the US government and some Latin American countries, notably Mexico, Argentina, and Chile reinforced Brazil's image as a problem case. In contrast to other countries, Brazil stood out owing to the delay in the monetary stabilization process and economic reform, as well as its lack of interest in adhering to the concept that had started to take shape in the opening of negotiations for the creation of a Free Trade Area of the Americas (FTAA).

Due to the urgency of domestic problems, President Itamar Franco delegated the formulation of foreign policy almost entirely to the Ministry of Foreign Relations. His choice of São Paulo Senator Fernando Henrique Cardoso of the Brazilian Social Democratic Party to head the ministry was a key appointment of the Itamar Franco government and allowed for less presidential involvement in the conduct of foreign affairs. This situation prevailed even after Cardoso's tenure at Foreign Relations (October 1992 to May 1993) to take up the post of Minister of Finance.

President Itamar Franco initially intended to replace Cardoso by a political appointee (Amorim, 1997). However, after a three-month interim tenure, Ambassador Celso Amorim was finally nominated, which marked the return of a diplomat to head the Itamaraty. This had not been the case since the Figueiredo government (1979–1985), when Ambassador Saraiva Guerreiro was the minister. Under Amorim, the Ministry of Foreign Relations continued to enjoy reasonable autonomy in the formulation of Brazilian foreign policy.

In his brief period as Minister of Foreign Relations, Cardoso took up again and deepened the foreign policy framework set out by Celso Lafer. The minister recognized the United States as the main trading partner "but privileged integration with them will be unviable due to the dynamism and vitality of our exports to the American market where they often face many restrictions" (Cardoso, 1993: 8). In his brief stay at Foreign Relations, Cardoso already saw the need for a "new foreign policy," characterized during his presidency as the quest for autonomy through participation:

> Why a new foreign policy? Firstly, because Brazil has changed. In the political arena, we have made the transition from authoritarianism to democracy. In the economic arena, after a period of accelerated development, we entered a period of crisis that could lead to the stagnation of growth. On the ideological plane, we have gone beyond the stage of authoritarian nationalism and autochthonous development to seek a competitive insertion in the world. Secondly, because the world has changed. In the political arena, the end of the Cold War redrew the power structure. In the economic arena, globalization looks like becoming the dominant trend. In the ideological arena, democracy and the market economy are the general rules. [. . .] Liberalization measures will not, however, be free of charge. Concessions must have matching measures and be obtained through our traditional ability in negotiation. [. . .] In this sense, it will be necessary to add value to a solid base in our own region, if for no other reason, to increase our bargaining power. [. . .] The regional economic integration process cannot emphasize exclusive ties, as Mexico has done in relation to the

> United States. This option would lead to poverty. However, this stance does not mean abandoning the priority of our relations with the United States, our single most important trading partner, with which Brazil has sought to develop a positive agenda (Cardoso, 1994: 185–188).

On Cardoso's initiative, the Ministry of Foreign Relations began a process of internal reflection on the priorities of foreign policy. The conclusions reaffirmed that "it would be wise to choose policies that give us the largest number of options, for it will be these that will give us the greatest chances to gain political dividends" (MRE, 1993b: 132).

With Cardoso's replacement by Amorim, a foreign policy without labels was proposed, so as not to generate specific expectations. At the same time, there would be a "diplomacy focused on development and democracy." In particular, Amorim resurrected the "Three Ds" slogan used by Araújo Castro, Minister of Foreign Relations in the João Goulart government from 1963 to 1964, and Brazilian Ambassador in Washington and the United Nations in the 1970s. "Disarmament, Development, and Decolonization" had been the slogan of Brazil's international agenda at the early 1970s. Amorim proposed its updating to "Democracy, Development, and Disarmament" (Amorim, 1994: 21).

The point was affirming Brazil's commitment to human rights, which was linked with the democratization of international relations, particularly the reform of the UN Security Council. In September 1994, in his address at the opening of the UN General Assembly, Amorim deepened and made more explicit the Brazilian stance. The launch of the new currency, the *real,* in July 1994, improved the image of the government among Brazilian public opinion due to the resulting monetary stabilization. It also placed Brazil in a more favorable position vis-à-vis international financial institutions in the renegotiation of its foreign debt. It was with renewed confidence that Minister Amorim stated Brazil's intention to secure a seat on the UN Security Council, should it be reformed (Canani, 2004: 97).

It was with a view to Security Council enlargement that the foreign policy of Minister Amorim most clearly expressed its objectives for the promotion of Brazil in the international arena. It was a Brazilian proposal, for example, to add to the "Agenda for Peace" being debated at the UN, an "Agenda for Development," already suggested by Minister Celso Lafer at the General Assembly in September 1992. In relation to the crisis in Haiti, Brazil supported an economic embargo and a policy approved by the UN Security Council, and later by the Organization of American States (OAS), aligning itself with another 32 countries in opposing military intervention in the country and agreeing only to a peacekeeping force after the fall of Haiti's military government. Outside the confines of the United Nations, the Brazilian government also pushed for the reintegration of Cuba into the inter-American system, particularly the OAS, and condemned the US economic embargo of the island.

Lastly, there was greater interest in the diversification of relations that anticipated certain trends of the notion of autonomy through diversification, which were to be more clearly implemented under the Lula government. Despite taking into account the importance of relations with the United States, in the Itamar Franco government Mercosur is thought of as putting the brakes on "the United States offensive for a free trade area of the Americas," allowing the future possibility that "Latin America could be united under a larger project" (Amorim, 1997: 14). Under his watch, the Ouro Preto Protocol, foreseen in the Treaty of Asunción, was negotiated and signed in December 1994. It elevated Mercosur from a free trade area to a customs union. There was also increased interest in Africa, particularly members of the Community of Portuguese Language Countries, and Cuba. For Amorim: "It was not that the Collor government had at any time taken a hostile attitude towards Cuba or Africa, it is just that these were not priorities at the time" (Amorim, 1997: 14).

According to Amorim, there was the notion that we could not "completely go back in time," but moderate language and practices in relation to certain issues: "I was Minister of Foreign Relations for only a year and a half, which is not enough time to make major reformulations" (1997:12). In general, the balance between continuity and change involved an acceptance of a new agenda and an adherence to its norms and regimes, but also affirmation that this adherence did not mean the renunciation of autonomy—though the term "autonomy" was not to reemerge with emphasis in Brazilian diplomatic language during the Cardoso government (Campos Mello, 2000: 127). It was in this context that Brazil took part in the Marrakesh Conference, when the GATT Uruguay Round was concluded with the creation of the WTO.

FINAL REMARKS

There are two reasons for including an analysis of the foreign policies of Collor de Mello and Itamar Franco in the same chapter: (1) both governments had short duration; Collor de Mello did not finish his term due to his impeachment, with the Vice-President taking over; and (2) both are difficult to fit into one of the three central concepts of this book, yet they have aspects that come close to more than one of them. In Table 3.2, we summarize some similarities and differences between the Collor de Mello and Itamar Franco foreign policies.

Table 3.2. Differences and Simularities between the Collor de Mello and Itamar Franco Foreign Policy

Brazilian Foreign Policy Agenda	*Collor de Mello Administration*	*Itamar Franco Administration*
Relations with the United States	In the first year of his government, Collor de Mello sought closer ties with the United States. As the benefits of this strategy were not clear, some aspects of Brazilian foreign policy went back to having points of disagreement with the USA.	Sought to preserve good relations with the United States and at the same time tried to deepen relations with other countries. As such, the USA ceased to be the main focus of Brazilian foreign policy.
Degree of Importance Given to the Minister of Foreign Relations	Collor de Mello's foreign policy was centered on the figure of the President. The Minister lost influence during the period mainly under the tenure of Francisco Rezek. Later, it was to gain more prominence with the arrival of Celso Lafer at the MRE.	The formulation of foreign policy returned to the MRE, as President Itamar Franco delegated power to it, mainly due to Brazil's domestic problems. Celso Amorim's appointment to head the Ministry marked the return of autonomy to the institution.
South American Integration	Collor de Mello, together with the presidents of Argentina, Paraguay and Uruguay, signed the Treaty of Asunción in March 1991, creating Mercosur, in order to build a customs union and a common market. Collor de Mello and Carlos Menem believed that Mercosur could serve as a platform for their countries' international insertion.	Itamar Franco continued the process of regional integration but Mercosur came to be seen as a first tool of Latin American unity in opposition to the USA's proposals for integration of the Americas. At the end of his Presidency, the Ouro Preto Protocol was signed. It converted Mercosur from a free trade area into a customs union.
International Security	There was a series of initiatives to reduce possible tensions with the United States in this area. As such, Brazil renounced for good its military-industrial ambitions set out during the military dictatorship (1964–85).	The government maintained the commitments made by Collor de Mello. However, Brazil once again manifests its interest in having a permanent seat on the UN Security Council, particularly during the tenure of Celso Amorim.
International Trade	At the GATT, the country began to adopt a less defensive stance as to the demands of developed countries in relation to "new issues" (intellectual property, services and investments).	At the GATT, Brazil maintained its less defensive position, but the country began to demand freer trade in agricultural products and textiles.

In our view, contemporary Brazilian foreign policy has been marked by the quest for autonomy since the 1930s. One finds traces much earlier, at the start of the Republican period at the end of the nineteenth century. It became an explicit goal during the first Getúlio Vargas presidency and remains until the present day, with inflections (sometimes sharp ones). This quest, though relative and with strong oscillations at times—such as during the administration of Castello Branco (1964–1966), who sought to maintain a close relationship with the United States in many aspects—has been possible due to the fact that Brazil has a large population, a large territory, is relatively far from the great powers, has a reasonably industrialized economy and reasonably sized domestic market, among other factors.

The possibility of an autonomous foreign policy, though, is not an end in itself. Rather, it aims to increase Brazil's room for maneuver to pursue its "national interests." As the question of national security has not been regarded as a priority due to Brazil's historical non-involvement in armed conflict, economic development has almost always been seen as the country's main objective. Successive administrations have placed more or less emphasis on an autonomous foreign policy, whether through distance, participation or diversification strategies.

As we have stressed, the period under Collor de Mello and Itamar Franco is characterized as a transitional phase, in which the "paradigm" of Brazilian foreign policy was not entirely exhausted but another had not yet been put in its place. There appears to have been a transition from autonomy through distance to autonomy through participation, which was very marked at the beginning of the Collor de Mello government. Despite this government not having discarded the autonomist tradition of Brazilian foreign policy, the plurality of interpretations of the period indicates that the path it took was not clear. In one extremity, the president in his first year in office seemed to break with the tradition of autonomy in Brazilian foreign policy, in the belief that modernization meant closer ties with the United States and the central countries. As we have seen, this route did not bring about the desired results. For its part, the Ministry of Foreign Relations sought to minimize the changes brought about by Collor de Mello's government. In the second phase with the arrival of Lafer at the head of the Ministry, foreign policy went back to being implemented almost exclusively by the diplomatic corps, even if this was due to the domestic political crisis impeding the President from taking a greater role in international affairs. With the impeachment, Itamar Franco continued to delegate the formulation of foreign policy to the Ministry of Foreign Relations headed by Cardoso. Amorim as Minister sought to resurrect traditional issues of the foreign policy agenda, strongly reinstating the theme of autonomy and consolidating the concept of South America. The acceleration of the phenomenon known as globalization, the failure of import substitution industrialization, the economic crisis ruining the country and the democratization process all demanded solutions to address Brazil's development.

The clash of paradigms, autonomy through distance and autonomy through participation, according to Fonseca Jr's (1998) definition, was part of the creative process of two international insertion strategies that were to be refined in later administrations, albeit with partial success, to substitute the distance strategy. These were autonomy through participation, consolidated during the Cardoso administration, and autonomy thorough diversification, being implemented by the Lula administration. There seems to be an affirmation of the idea that autarchical solutions no longer meet the country's needs. Simultaneously, the concept of autonomy has become deeply rooted. The paradigms have to do with the different ways of tackling and resolving these obstacles faced by Brazil.

NOTES

1. The Group of 77 (G-77) was established on 15 June 1964 by seventy-seven developing countries signatories of the "Joint Declaration of the Seventy-Seven Countries" issued at the end of the first session of the United Nations Conference on Trade and Development (UNCTAD) in Geneva. [...] The Group of 77 is the largest intergovernmental organization of developing states in the United Nations, which provides the means for the countries of the South to articulate and promote their collective economic interests and enhance their joint negotiating capacity on all major international economic issues within the United Nations system, and promote South–South cooperation for development.

2. The Group of Fifteen (G-15) was established at a Summit Level Group of Developing Countries in September 1989, following the conclusion of the Ninth Non-Aligned Summit Meeting in Belgrade. [...] A long-term goal of the G-15 was to be recognized as a logical dialogue partner of the Group of 7 (G-7, now G-8) highly industrialized countries.

3. The G-10 was a group formed by developing countries in 1982 with the objetive of blocking the entrance of new themes (such as services and intelectual property) in the GATT negotiations. This group, which was led by Brazil, won considerable protection at Uruguay Round of GATT/OMC (Narlikar, 2003).

4. The notorious presidential debate between Lula and Collor de Mello broadcast by the Rede Globo TV Network was edited in subsequent news programs to cast PT candidate Luíz Inácio Lula da Silva in a negative light.

Chapter 4

Brazilian Foreign Policy in the Cardoso Era

The Quest for Autonomy through Participation

INTRODUCTION

This chapter examines the redefinition of the premises and practices of Brazilian foreign policy during Fernando Henrique Cardoso's two terms in office (1995–1998 and 1999–2002). Our principal claim is that the Cardoso administration sought to internalize, absorb, and consolidate the liberal changes that globalization brought to international society during the 1990s, in contrast with the failure of the Collor de Mello administration and the hesitancy of the Itamar Franco administration in this regard. At the same time, the Cardoso administration supported some State instruments in the economy, like Petrobras and the National Economic and Social Development Bank (BNDES). Accordingly, we demonstrate here that over the course of his eight years in office, Cardoso sought to replace a reactive foreign policy agenda dominated by a logic of autonomy through distance—which prevailed throughout the greater part of the Cold War era and handed down a model of development based on import substitution—with a proactive international agenda aligned in some issues with the canons of neoliberalism and guided by a logic of autonomy through participation.

This new perspective held that Brazil would begin to resolve its internal problems more effectively and assume greater control over its future if it actively contributed to elaborating the norms and guidelines of the global order (Fonseca Jr., 1998: 363–374). By actively seeking to organize and regulate international relations in a variety of contexts, Brazilian foreign policy would also help to establish an environment favorable to economic development, which had been the goal of Brazil's external action throughout most of the twentieth century. In this regard, the Cardoso years were characterized by a constant search for international regimes and norms, a search aimed at fostering an environment as institutionalized as possible.

During this period, the foreign policy standard formulated by Araújo Castro (Amado, 1982) underwent a transformation, albeit not a total one. This standard had strongly resisted the consolidation of institutions and regimes, which would have frozen the Cold War hierarchy of power. In a new international environment dominated by a single great power—an environment in which the relative power of the Brazilian State had diminished—an institutionalist perspective was seen as favorable to Brazilian interests because it promoted respect for the rules of the international game, rules that once established would have to be observed by all parties, including the most powerful. In the context of Mercosur and of South America in general, the outlook differed, however. Here, a more favorable power relation was seen as a way to promote Brazil's universal insertion as a global player.

From this initial discussion we can conclude that the Cardoso administration's foreign policy helped secure a place for Brazil among nations embracing hegemonic values considered universal.

FOREIGN POLICY PREMISES

This paradigm shift in Brazilian foreign policy was stimulated by the emergence, during globalization, of new configurations for the international economy. Beginning in 1990, the North–South and East–West axes of international relations, as configured at the end of the Second World War, seemed in the process of being replaced by new forms of structuring international society. This structuring emerged from an agenda based on the so-called new issues in politics, values and economics, issues involving the environment, human rights, minorities, indigenous peoples, and drug trafficking. These "soft issues," as interdependence theory suggests, had begun to take on greater importance in the international arena (Keohane and Nye, 1989). From the Brazilian perspective in Cardoso era, this meant that "the relative importance of each country [came] to be measured less by its military or strategic influence and more by its economic, commercial, scientific or cultural projection" (Abdenur, 1994: 3). Officials responsible for the formulation of trade policy, industrial policy and development policy came to understand, in coordination with important segments of the business sector, that the cost-benefit ratio for Brazil would be more advantageous in an open environment. They understood that a lack of competitiveness would risk greater disparity in relation to wealthy countries—and even in relation to countries that although underdeveloped, seemed prepared for sustained takeoff. Openness, then, would serve as an antidote to economic risk.

The evolution toward autonomy through participation proved incremental, however. It intensified at the end of Roberto Costa de Abreu Sodré's tenure at the Ministry of External Relations (MRE) during the Sarney administration and continued into Francisco Rezek's tenure during the Collor de Mello administration. During Celso Lafer's stint at the MRE in 1992, the effort to refine the theory behind the model was advanced by a policy of "universal foreign relations, without alignments or tradeoffs, with the intent of preserving the autonomy [through participation] of the country in its international action" (Campos Mello, 2000: 92). The 1993 annual report of the MRE pointed to this intent and observed that, in 1992, MRE efforts had focused on creating "an appropriate conceptual framework for advancing the strategic action of Brazil" (MRE, 1993a: 347). The Itamar Franco administration—which began with Cardoso himself as foreign minister, followed by Amorim—was responsible for mobilizing the foreign policy objectives that had been outlined.

The redefinition of foreign policy actively involved the Ministry of Finance, including during the tenure of Ciro Gomes,[1] and came at a time when adherence to prevailing international values entailed a preoccupation with economic stability. This preoccupation led to the consolidation of tariff reductions, initiated by the Collor de Mello administration but ostensibly based on studies carried out by the Foreign Trade Department (Cacex) of the Bank of Brazil in 1988 and 1989. And it took further shape in the decision to sign the Treaty of Marrakesh, which created the World Trade Organization (WTO); in discussions on the Common External Tariff (TEC) within Mercosur, which was finalized by the Ouro Preto Protocol of December 1994; and in participation in the Miami Summit of the same month, which launched negotiations on the creation of the Free Trade Area of the Americas (FTAA). Taken together, these actions were responsible for solidifying the new foreign policy perspective.

According to its framers, the concept of change with continuity, which predominated throughout Cardoso's presidency, meant that the renewal of traditional paradigms ought to embrace both creative adaptation and a vision for the future. From Cardoso's perspective, which was shared by both his foreign ministers, Luiz Felipe Lampreia (1995–2000) and Celso Lafer (2001–2002), a vision for the future was essential vis-à-vis an unfavorable environment, within which diplomacy ought to take long-term action while seeking to adapt to current transformations. The administration's objective was not to adapt passively but to redirect and reshape the environment within the limits of its power, adjusting to the interests of other States and forces, and seeking ways to participate in international issues through the formulation of regimes more favorable to Brazilian interests. By adhering to international regimes that "even if not ideal still [represented] an unequivocal improvement in the matter" (Lafer, 1993a: 46–47), Brazil would be guaranteed an international legal reference point in its search to satisfy its national interests. The pragmatic side of the revamped paradigm that persisted throughout Cardoso's time in office was represented by the reiteration of the "global trader" concept, the interpretation of Mercosur as a platform for competitive insertion on a global level, and the idea—paramount but not exclusionary—of the possibility of participation with other countries and regions (MRE, 1993a).

It should be pointed out, however, that neither the consolidation of these concepts nor their renewal was passed off as neutral. By embracing the global trader concept, Brazil displayed its global interests and so was able to adopt diverse agendas and positions, seeking out markets and trade relations without tying itself to a single partner. This explains why the country took a non-institutionalist approach to Mercosur, whilst taking an institutionalist approach to its multilateral agenda, particularly regarding global organizations such as the United Nations and the WTO (Pinheiro, 2000).

In general, a global trader opts for multilateral trade liberalization in order to maximize benefits. Throughout the 1990s and until the end of the Cardoso administration, the MRE maintained that "our objective should be a global solution" (MRE, 1993a), which meant, in diplomacy-speak, that opting for the FTAA or for a free-trade area with the European Union would aid the establishment and full functioning of an international regime of trade liberalization. During the Cardoso presidency, this was translated into a model of "two steps into the pool": agreeing to specific accords would be like stepping in at the shallow end before easing into deeper water.

Universalism had already been part of Brazilian foreign policy, but its renewal through the global trader concept pointed to the diversification of foreign relations and the addition of a regionalist angle. The Cardoso administration consolidated a policy that had been practiced during the Collor de Mello and Itamar Franco administrations and that had placed Mercosur at the forefront of the Brazilian agenda. Mercosur was seen not only as an unprecedented project in South America but as a form of open regionalism that did not exclude other partners. The concept of development that prevailed from 1985 to 1989 was abandoned, one that held sway throughout Brazil's trade negotiations with Argentina at a time when the role of an expanded domestic market was particularly significant. In spite of the importance that this bloc represented to Brazilian administrations (as Lafer put it, "Mercosur is our future, part of our milieu. The FTAA is not our future, it is an option" [2001b]), none was willing to elevate Mercosur's institutional status or to bear the costs of its consolidation. Mercosur was seen, rather, as an important platform from which member states could participate in wider international trends. In Argentina, for example, the administration of Carlos Saúl Menem maneuvered to keep its options open, a decision that was reinforced during Menem's second term, which began in 1995. In the end, this influenced choices made by the Cardoso administration as it came to grips with the challenges of advancing regional interdependence.

THE INTELLECTUAL LEGACY

The renewal of the foreign policy paradigm, which had been taking shape since 1992, received systematic development once it was incorporated into the program of the State. Beginning in 1995, it was set out in several presidential statements delivered abroad at Stanford University, Colegio de México, the French National Assembly, the India International Center and elsewhere. In his first inaugural address, Cardoso affirmed the need for changes that would ensure more active Brazilian participation in the world, and highlighted the goal of "influencing the design of the new order [. . .] and the necessity [. . .] of updating our discourse and our action abroad" (Cardoso, Presidência da República, 1996: 137). Lampreia confirmed this position, asserting that the government knew how "to enact the right policy alterations in response to current changes in the world, on the continent, and within the country itself" (1995: 11). He asserted that these alterations would indeed move forward but that they needed to occur in the course of promoting both the country and its complete adherence to international regimes, which would enable Brazilian foreign policy to converge with global trends and thus avoid isolation from the international "mainstream." For the Brazilian government, seeking convergence and avoiding isolation did not mean accepting a subordinate position, however; on the contrary, it was the path toward strengthening Brazil's relative position in international society.

From Cardoso's perspective, another important tenet of his administration was the correspondence between universally prevailing values and national identity: "The Brazil that enters the twenty-first century is a country whose primary objectives for internal transformation and development are in harmony with values universally disseminated on the international level" (Cardoso, 2000: 6). For Cardoso, conformity with international regimes would prove beneficial in the end: in the unavoidably globalized world of contemporary history, "The same system that inflicts a setback will work toward our favor in the long run" (Cardoso, 2000: 3) as long as the country is capable of transforming external opportunities into internal benefits (Lafer, 2001c).

More precisely, the foreign policy of the Cardoso administration followed, according to Lampreia,

> A line that I would call "critical convergence" in relation to the values, commitments, and practices now orienting international life [. . .]. "Convergence" because transformations in Brazil have brought us, of our own choosing, into the central current of world history in an era when political democracy and economic liberty are the fundamental reference points (Lampreia, 2001: 2).

The juxtaposition of the terms "critical" and "convergence" stems from the reality of contemporary international relations, within which "the observance of 'mainstream' values and commitments continues to suffer from serious distortions and inconsistencies fed and facilitated by the predominance of power asymmetries over the principle of juridical equality" (Lampreia, 2001: 3). This interpretation is relevant because it elucidates the administration's own understanding, making its adaptation to the mainstream, in principle, correct. Throughout both of Cardoso's terms in office, insistent criticism was leveled at these distortions, upon which both discourse and action made their impact felt. Criticism of power-based policies arose from a lexicon and a diplomacy geared toward understanding. The goal at all times was to avoid irremediable tensions, whether with the United States or with other countries. In the case of relations with Argentina, even when disagreements were at their most intense in January 1999 with the devaluation of the real, the policies of the Cardoso administration were guided by an attempt to find forms of understanding.

The constant goal of the administration was to work within the system toward resolving disagreements. Inconsistencies between discourse and practice among the most powerful and influential actors in international society arose in various scenarios—in relations between States, in global trade, in the functioning of international bodies, in issues of security, in environmental concerns—as realities that could only be overcome through mutual understanding. The activism exercised in a few instances, as with the WTO, for example, was aimed at strengthening Brazil's position.

From the administration's perspective, the desired outcome of autonomy through participation was a proactive agenda asserting that Brazil must increase its ability to control its future. Foreign policy was thus seen as contributing to a domestic agenda of growth, development and social problem solving. In this context, formulations of the meaning of this policy, which could be traced back to 1930, were reiterated. In contrast to other phases, following Fonseca Jr. (1998), policy goals would be better achieved through active participation in formulating the norms and guidelines of international conduct. Such participation would constitute "an engaged and affirmative contribution to peace and stability" (Lampreia, 1997: 5).

The Cardoso administration, after renewing and consolidating the paradigm of Brazilian foreign policy in the second half of the 1990s, conferred a new meaning on the concept of autonomy, that of "autonomy through participation, meaning an autonomy connected to the international situation rather than isolated from it" (Lampreia, 1999: 11). "In other words, maintaining mainstream behavior while attending to the specific needs of Brazil, as much in its material conditions as in its objectives and interests" (Lampreia, 1999: 89). Lampreia characterized this notion as refining a line of thought that set autonomy through distance—characteristic of Brazilian diplomacy during the Cold War—in opposition to the necessary pursuit of autonomy through participation. According to Fonseca Jr.,

> The heritage of positive participation, always supported by criteria of legitimacy, opens the door to a series of approaches that have given new shape to the work of Brazilian diplomacy. Autonomy today no longer means "distance" from controversial issues for the sake of protecting the country from undesirable alignments. On the contrary, autonomy now means "participation," a desire to influence an open agenda through values that uphold diplomatic tradition and demonstrate that we can discern the path of international order with our own eyes, from a new perspective, a perspective that corresponds to our national complexity (Fonseca Jr., 1998: 368).

In the end it was through organizing and regulating international relations in various arenas that Brazilian diplomacy sought to establish an atmosphere of international goodwill favorable to the principal objective of the country and its partners in Mercosur, namely, generating and guaranteeing lasting and sustainable development. This became increasingly necessary, since major transformations in the post-Cold War world, according to the Cardoso administration, yoked specific Brazilian interests to general interests inserted in the international order. Conversely, this same order would be able to contribute to the legitimation and fulfillment of specific national interests.

The tenures of Lampreia (1995–2000) and Lafer (2001–2002) at the MRE, although trenchant in some respects, were characterized by a search for constructive moderation expressed in the ability "to tone down the foreign policy agenda, or rather to reduce conflicts, crises, and difficulties to a diplomatically manageable level in order to keep them from being exploited or magnified by short-term interests" (Fonseca Jr., 1998: 356). Or, as Lafer put it, "Preferring to resolve differences through diplomacy and the rule of law, reducing the allure of power politics and aggression" (Lafer, 2001a: 47). In this view, which could be classified as an intermediate position between a Grotian paradigm (a balance between realism and idealism) and a Kantian one (pure idealism), the goal was to safeguard victories (perhaps trusting the capacity for persuasion and dialogue too much), although the administration remained aware of the relevance of power and force.

In terms of foreign policy analysis, then, a cooperative perspective prevailed throughout the Cardoso era. Repeated denunciation of asymmetries, insistence on criticizing policies that relied on power, efforts to undermine the use of unilateralism (particularly on the part of the United States under the G. W. Bush administration), criticism of the distorted use of principles—all of these should be understood as part of the struggle for a global order of cooperation. This legacy seems to have been a response to the possibility for change introduced at a particular historical moment, at a moment when the end of the Cold War implied a new set of opportunities.

In sum, the major foreign policy premise of the Cardoso administration was conformity with the global agenda embodied in the formula of autonomy through participation, mixed with aspirations to a strong Brazilian position. The administration hoped to diminish the negative impression of Brazil in the international community, especially in the financial arena, and to convince its partners that Brazil was prepared both to take on the obligations of the world economy and to take advantage of the benefits thereof. And at first glance this strategy could be deemed quite successful. It led to a number of achievements, as will be seen, including closer relations with the United States, the return of foreign direct investment as the country linked into the supply chains of important industrial sectors, advances in Mercosur, "victories" at the WTO and so on. These achievements notwithstanding, in the long run costs grew and benefits shrank, once there was a downturn in Mercosur and in foreign investment as a consequence of successive international crises and the constant flouting of multilateral institutions—institutions in which the administration had hoped to exercise its policy of autonomy through participation. This scenario was accentuated when George W. Bush came to power in the United States, and principally after September 11, 2001.

It is in this vein that we analyze the concrete ramifications of Cardoso's policy: its mobilization and how it influenced negotiations in which concrete interests were at stake.

THE PRACTICAL LEGACY

In terms of concrete formulations, the two central concerns of Brazilian foreign policy during the Cardoso years were maintaining strong pro-Mercosur rhetoric and building up relations with the rest of South America, the latter receiving particular emphasis during Cardoso's second term. From the administration's perspective, these concerns would permit a better exercise of universalism and bolster the directive of autonomy through participation. In terms of the major issues faced by Brazilian foreign policy, the administration believed that the negotiating ability of the country would be strengthened if Mercosur could be consolidated and if greater participation throughout South America could be achieved. The country's initiatives took place on innumerable fronts and demonstrated a multifaceted perspective, even though the importance of each issue remained profoundly distinct. Among them, greater or lesser emphasis was given to a free trade agreement with the European Union, to hemispheric participation and negotiations on the FTAA, to alliances within the WTO and to the expansion of bilateral relations with important partners such as China, Japan, India, Russia, and South Africa—not to mention other important issues, such as nuclear nonproliferation, disarmament, the spread of terrorism, the environment, human rights, the defense of democracy, the candidacy for a permanent seat on the UN Security Council, the campaign for a new international financial architecture, relations with Portugal and the other countries of the Community of Portuguese Language Countries (CPLP), and relations with Cuba.

The question of democracy and the principle of self-determination were also values defended during Cardoso's tenure. In this regard, we would point to the position taken by Brazil during the crises in Paraguay (in 1996, 1999 and 2001); to the inclusion of a "democracy clause" in Mercosur after the joint presidential declaration of 1996 and the Ushuaia Protocol of 1998; to the position taken on the institutional crisis in Venezuela at the end of 2002—also the end of Cardoso's second term—when the Brazilian position meant a certain continuity with the incoming Lula administration; and, lastly, to the position taken on the "election" of Fujimori to his third term in Peru, in 2000, a position that according to the Cardoso administration highlighted its defense of the principle of self-determination.

For the Cardoso administration, the gains derived from participation and partial adhesion to the international mainstream would need to be sustained by a highly specialized level of competency, one directed above all toward economic and trade negotiations. According to the administration, therefore, in order to achieve results favorable both to Brazil and to the parties concerned, adherence to international regimes and competence in making use of them would be fundamental. In the meantime, the adjustment of the State to the negotiating context and the ability of private actors to respond and adapt to new levels of activity proved insufficient. Brazilian positions were often defensive ones, and when offensive, they concentrated on competitive areas such as agriculture, which even at peaks of importance did not represent the totality of national interests.

PRESIDENTIAL DIPLOMACY AND REBUILDING THE NATIONAL IMAGE

In diplomatic action, the Cardoso administration frequently made use of the figure of the president, appropriating methods increasingly employed by other States. The Collor de Mello administration had "rehearsed" presidential diplomacy, but this proved fragile because of the challenges of consolidation faced by the administration. To a certain extent, presidential diplomacy, on the coattails of the relative success of the Real Plan, contributed to the reconstruction of Brazil's image, solidifying and legitimating it in the eyes of multilateral institutions and numerous governments, even among wealthy countries. According to Genoíno (1999: 7), the administration's foreign policy constantly sought "to rebuild external credibility on the basis of internal stability." And consolidating this interpretation, Danese (1999) states that from the beginning the Cardoso administration attempted to combine, on the one hand,

> greater national power, thanks to stabilization and the incentives presented by the country's economic dimensions, including its participation in Mercosur, and by its economic openness—and on the other hand, the personal disposition and vocation of the president as protagonist in a presidential diplomacy of the sort now enshrined by top world leaders (Danese, 1999: 7).

But the improvement in its image abroad addressed only one side of Brazil's standing in international public opinion, which is greatly influenced by existing perceptions in rich countries. Sensitive issues involving human rights, minorities, children, indigenous peoples, crime, the environment, and drug trafficking all became factors in the deterioration of Brazil's image, factors that could hardly be offset by governmental activism or even by the country's compliance with hegemonic standards imposed in the arena of macroeconomic stability. Clearly, the government cannot be held solely responsible for these problems, since they are widespread throughout many poor countries, particularly in Latin America; nevertheless, they contribute to weakening the country's international standing.

Among the favorable results deriving from the changes implemented during Cardoso's tenure, one may cite the trustworthiness that Brazil inspired abroad, which enabled it to attract foreign direct investment, an element in macroeconomic stability, as well as the support of multilateral organizations and the governments of developed nations during situations that threatened to cause financial and economic crisis, such as the exchange rate crisis of 1999.

Meanwhile, significant trends linked above all to the weakness of economic growth in Brazil throughout both terms—with the exception of the 4.4% rate obtained in 2000 (Intal, 2003: 7)—limited the possibility of using foreign policy to gain leverage in strategic objectives, both political and economic. Brazil's participation in certain important international debates, such as over the attempt to create a new international financial architecture that in the understanding of the administration would help to regulate financial flows of volatile capital, which contribute to setting off crises, reflected the difficulties that it faced in influencing an agenda still not desired by relevant actors with greater power. These actors did not seem interested in either controls or limitations in the Cardoso period. It seems, therefore, that the strategy of autonomy through participation may have achieved its aims when permitted to do so by the international mainstream or when the goals of Brazilian interest combined with acceptance from some developed countries. This is because the gains achieved by the Cardoso administration resulted from the predisposition, goodwill, and collaboration of external partners. Without these factors, results proved negative, as in the attempt to alter the international financial architecture that induces crises of volatility in emerging markets and all over the world. In spite of broad Brazilian participation, the final result was not exactly the administration's desired outcome.

In the Cardoso administration, the question of foreign relations within the domestic agenda seems to have gained much greater emphasis, probably in tune with tendencies abroad. International relations, for various reasons—some related to criticism of government policy—inspired greater attention and interest among society and the media. "Never before had business associations, unions, non-governmental organizations, the Congress, and public opinion been so engaged in the debate over Brazil's relations with the world" (Silva, 2002: 302).

Relations with the United States and Argentina were of constant concern to the administration, and it devoted intense efforts to improving these relations, albeit not always successfully. In nonofficial meetings of heads of state and government on the idea of a "Third Way," a more positive image of Brazil began to emerge—tied especially to the intellectual and political status of Fernando Henrique Cardoso and affirmed by leaders such as Bill Clinton and Tony Blair. At the same time, however, this does not seem to have been enough to alter the negative public opinion about Brazil among developed countries. In many instances, the international community's respect for President Cardoso and his success in making himself heard in diverse global fora, owing both to presidential diplomacy and to the strategy of autonomy through participation, did not translate into concrete advances for Brazil on different issues considered strategic.

RELATIONS WITH THE UNITED STATES

The effort to improve bilateral relations with the United States began in 1995, the year Cardoso took office, and achieved positive results by overcoming longstanding disagreements, some of which had originated during Brazil's military regime. In particular, Washington looked upon Brazil's policy of macroeconomic stabilization favorably. Additional factors that encouraged greater cooperation between the two countries included Brazil's acceptance of the Missile Technology Control Regime (MTCR), its promise to sign the Nuclear Non-Proliferation Treaty (NNPT), which it fulfilled in 1997, and its general commitment to the importance of constructive relations with the United States. In 1995, Cardoso made the importance of these relations explicit, stating that "the United States is our fundamental partner because of its central position [in the world order]" (Estado de S. Paulo, 1995).

An analysis of United States–Brazil relations allows for greater understanding of Brazil's foreign policy makeover. The search for improved bilateral relations emphasized the autonomy of Brazil's international action while affirming its role as both a global trader and player. Conflicts that occurred during Brazil's military regime and questions relating to the foreign debt (which weighed heavily on the administrations of João Baptista Figueiredo, José Sarney and Fernando Collor de Mello), not to mention intense political or trade disputes strictly speaking, seemed to vanish—or at least were downgraded to the level of run-of-the-mill foreign relations conflicts. In other words, the option for autonomy through participation was seen as fostering greater closeness between the two countries without requiring either trade-offs or automatic alignment. According to this perspective, Brazil would be able to maintain the possibility of dissent when its interests were threatened by US action. And in spite of holding global and regional power, the United States would find its capacity for action curtailed in the emergent multipolar arena of the 1990s, thus opening the possibility of a new Brazilian insertion (Lima, 1999). In the last two years of Cardoso's presidency, particularly after the attacks of September 11, 2001, the evolution of international relations that seems to have marked the beginning of the twenty-first century brought new questions to the fore and to a certain extent demanded greater energy (perhaps also greater risk-taking) in order to maintain strong bilateral relations.

Cardoso's policy sought out more opportune forms of insertion and took US dominance into consideration—hence the explicit recognition of the importance of good relations with the United States, necessary to guarantee Brazil's autonomy and ensure its viability in South America. For Cardoso, "We must maintain both good relations with the United States and the capacity to organize the South American space of Mercosur" (Estado de S. Paulo, 1996). This is the kind of perspective often assumed by pragmatic administrations, for whom existing realities are considered "inputs" rather than outcomes to be minimized or neutralized. In short, a policy of cooperation was made clearly explicit in relations between Brazil and the United States.

Good bilateral relations and a policy of autonomy through participation with the United States were considered necessary to enhancing Brazil's role on the international stage, a process beginning from its platform in South America. This perspective has not always prevailed in Brazil's diplomatic action, but it has been embraced in other historical periods, including during the tenure of the Barão do Rio Branco (Bueno, 2003) and Oswaldo Aranha (Vigevani, 1989). According to Cardoso, Brazil's priority was "the consolidation of Mercosur, which is not only the sphere of participation in the short term but the platform from which we will reinforce our linkage to other centers of the international economy" (Cardoso, 1993: 9). In a context of open regionalism, "The necessity of always keeping our options open" is a logical inference (Cardoso, 1993: 9). Closer relations with the United States came against a backdrop of "not [. . .] limiting ourselves to exclusive partnerships or reductionist criteria of international action. We must act on multiple levels, deal with multiple partnerships and be present in multiple arenas" (Cardoso, 1993: 9). Cardoso's rationale in 1993, when he was foreign minister under Itamar Franco, helped set the boundaries of action for both his terms in office.

The guideline of acting in various arenas was indeed implemented. Analysis of the approach taken during Cardoso's first term vis-à-vis the FTAA served to assess the weight of the external constraints that this position implied. Simply put, after the Miami Summit of December 1994, to which Cardoso had accompanied Itamar Franco, who was at the end of his term, the administration decided to put off the FTAA for as long as possible. This policy was finally reformulated after the second FTAA summit, in April of 1998 in Santiago, Chile. During negotiations between 1995 and 1998, defense of the autonomy principle was filtered through a logic of deferment. The same approach was taken in maintaining priority for Mercosur in spite of the bloc's increasing difficulties. According to Cardoso, South America should be considered "our historical-geographic space" (Cardoso, 1997: 4), and therefore, "For Brazil, Mercosur is our strategic pawn, but it is not enough: we need this broader participation" (Estado de S. Paulo, 2000).

This was not a question of playing the game on two boards, as it were. For the administration, different negotiations should be complementary, not opposed. Statesmanlike behavior, however, in the understanding of the administration, implied being able to project various scenarios. In the event that the FTAA failed to cohere and that difficulties in Mercosur persisted, the issue of a South American space would regain significance, as it did during the tenure of Celso Amorim at the MRE in the second half of Itamar Franco's presidency. Nor was it a question of diminishing the importance of relations with the United States, which would continue to be central, but of improving both Brazil's capacity to negotiate and its bargaining power in hemispheric negotiations. Beyond this, Brazil's "South American option" would prove useful in its aspirations to a permanent seat on the UN Security Council, since it would afford the country recognition as a regional power (Lima, 1996: 152).

During Cardoso's second term, Brazilian policy on the FTAA suffered the impact of constraints in a more direct way. After the Santiago summit, the MRE, with the president's backing, pointed to the risks of isolation, which were particularly unwelcome in a context in which the US market represented a fundamentally important factor, and not just for Brazil. In this case, cooperation and autonomy through participation in the end strengthened the move toward a more active insertion in the negotiation process. The desire to participate actively in debates about the specific regimes that would govern the FTAA led to an assertive approach, one that achieved a few minor successes by inserting items and concepts important to Brazil and Mercosur into the broader agenda, such as the "single undertaking" idea, for example. In the end, however, Brazil was not able to substantially modify the docket of negotiations, the basic legal framework of which left little room for issues not geared toward North American interests.

Other bilateral issues, such as pharmaceutical patents on generic drugs, were remitted to the WTO as an international body in which Brazil could articulate a broader defense of its positions. Pragmatism and the search for a cooperative approach, without abdicating national interests, would permit a reasonable balance in these relations and avoid more significant losses even if advances should fail to reach desired levels. Meanwhile, we should observe that the strategy of autonomy through participation postulated that the United States, in spite of its dominance, would maintain a more cooperative, multilateral approach to international politics. When it ceased to do so, as it did during the final two years of Cardoso's presidency, relations with Brazil grew rockier and the tone of criticism sharpened. The WTO placed new demands on the United States, and the Brazilian position in the FTAA grew more rigid, in line with both the strategy of President-elect Lula and the renewal of Brazil's leadership in South America through new proposals, such as the Initiative for the Integration of Regional Infrastructure in South America (IIRSA) vis-à-vis the challenges faced by Mercosur.

MERCOSUR AND SOUTH AMERICA

During the Cardoso administration, at least in rhetoric, a geographically concerned policy took shape and became a constant reference point for external action. This might seem to be a given, but we know that in the past, even during the Sarney administration, regional policy was not entirely central. The interpretation of Mercosur—which coincided with the interests of the Argentine government under Menem—as open regionalism made it possible for Brazil, without exclusivism or alignment, to simultaneously adhere to the norms and international regimes of its preference while guaranteeing the preservation of "a reserve of autonomy" (Pinheiro, 1998) that could be actualized in a context of regional maneuvering. The adherence to certain norms and regimes led in certain cases to the strengthening of "soft power," which had made a comeback thanks to the country's improved image. For Campos Mello (2000) the relation between universalism and regionalism can be established as follows:

> The universalism of the 1990s was originally expressed through regionalism: it is in this area that Brazil found the principal space in which to reaffirm its autonomy, in resistance to hemispheric participation—namely, through the process of the subregional participation of Mercosur and in new initiatives in South America (Campos Mello, 2000: 112).

The discussion of a free trade area between Mercosur and the European Union and the search for strategic partners, such as China and India, are issues that should be understood together with the regional dimension. In the opinion of Lampreia (1999:12), "Although, on the one hand, it means in effect some loss of autonomy, on the other hand, Mercosur increases our capacity to act in a more affirmative and participative way in the formulation of international regimes and norms essential to Brazil." Particularly during Cardoso's second term, there was a strong interest both in maintaining a minimal consensus among Mercosur members, in view of negotiations on the FTAA, and after the Brasília meeting of 2002, in seeking to build an integrated space in South America.

For the Cardoso administration, two initiatives pointed favorably to the political consolidation of Mercosur. The first was the joint adherence of Argentina and Brazil to the NNTP in the context of an agreement with the International Atomic Energy Agency (IAEA), which put an end to the phase in which the military use of nuclear energy had been both an unknown factor in bilateral relations and the focus of concern in relations with other countries of the bloc. The two governments promised to develop nuclear research only for peaceful and controlled ends. The second was the defense of democracy during episodes of institutional crisis in Paraguay in 1996, 1999, and 2001, and the inclusion of the democracy clause in Mercosur, finalized in the Ushuaia Protocol of 1998.

Brazil's insertion in the regional framework of international public goods (Valadão, 2005) would entail both regional stability (Silva, 2002: 316) and the strengthening of its own positions in the international community as immediate corollaries. In this vein, other actions should be considered, such as the contribution to the solution of border conflicts between Peru and Ecuador and the defense of democracy in Venezuela during its crisis at the end of 2002, when the Cardoso administration acted in a coordinated way with the incoming Lula administration.

According to Pinheiro (2000), the combination of a Grotian approach in the global arena with a universal and cooperative perspective in "harmony with values universally disseminated on an international level" (Cardoso, 2000: 6) should be compared to policies implemented regionally. In the latter, the power differential seems to have been used to avoid forms of supranationality and guarantee autonomy vis-à-vis partners outside the region. In this sense, there was an effort to maximize benefits, implying differentiated policies, not homogenous ones.

Throughout Cardoso's administration, South America retained its centrality in Brazilian policy, not only through the effort to consolidate Mercosur as a customs union, with a common market on the horizon, but through other actions as well. By all accounts, this is not a circumstantial trend, since this policy was inaugurated by Sarney and continued by Itamar Franco and Cardoso, whose administration acted in a relatively coordinated manner in relation to the region, even if in incomplete fashion. In this sense, not only government ministries and private businesses were mobilized but also certain strategic linchpins. The restructuring of the country's energy matrix, for example, was solidified: this after having been highly dependent on Persian Golf imports, above all from Saudi Arabia and Iraq, until the late 1980s. In the 1990s, imports shifted to Argentina and Venezuela instead. Large projects of material integration were also carried out, such as the interconnection of electricity networks and gas pipelines. But at the same time, regional institutions were not adequately strengthened. On the contrary, Mercosur, beginning in 1998 but particularly in 1999, entered a significant crisis, reinforcing the perspective that the bloc would not be able to overcome its status as an incomplete customs union.

Put differently, the readiness to accept the costs and obligations of the pursuit of international objectives did not gain significant ground during the Cardoso era, either among Brazilian society or within the State. The devaluation of the real in January 1999, supported by the great majority of Brazilians, had serious consequences in Mercosur and associate countries, including Bolivia. Although the causes of these crises had diverse origins, a Brazilian initiative seeking out forms of compensation would have benefited regional strategies.

And on the political level, the administration demonstrated a certain timidity, as was the case with Colombia. Brazil's non-participation in the group convened by the UN, the European Union, and some Latin American countries in order to foster negotiating conditions for an accord between the Colombian government, the Revolutionary Armed Forces of Colombia (FARC), and the National Liberation Army (ELN), limited Brazil's influence in the arena of the Colombian crisis.

In the administration's perception, the growth in Brazil's regional role increased the country's extra-regional bargaining power, but there were difficulties in proportionally increasing the national effort devoted to this objective. It was not only a question of governance but also of other internal tensions imposed by regional and social sectors fearful of being burdened with the costs of participation. Beyond this, Brazilian leadership met with other difficulties, both in pragmatic terms and in terms of principle. This would be a particularly sensitive issue in relation to Argentina. Thus what prevailed was the understanding that if Brazil came to dominate, this would be only natural, given the country's larger population and more powerful economy. Conversely, the refusal of forms of supranationality would serve to guarantee autonomy, if necessary, in relation to other countries of the region.

Even so, it was assumed that the strong return of the South American question in the second term, along with the choice to strengthen Mercosur, was necessary to sort out relations with the United States. Negotiations on the FTAA demonstrated that the United States was central to numerous countries not only commercially but strategically, financially, technologically, and culturally. The concern of the Cardoso administration in putting real instruments of action into effect—through the resources of the Andean Development Corporation (CAF), the National Economic and Social Development Bank (BNDES), and the Financial Fund for the Development of the La Plata River Basin (Fonplata)—suggested the need for more realistic platforms for regional policy. All the same, the idea that there could be common interests in keeping with a sense of identity and a similar vision of the region was never strengthened to the point of making the issue of participation into a bond uniting these interests, whether in Brazil or among its neighbors.

THE WTO, MERCOSUR, AND THE EUROPEAN UNION, AND THE FTAA

From the perspective of autonomy through participation, a policy of simultaneous action on three main levels of multilateral trade negotiation predominated during Cardoso's presidency: the WTO, Mercosur, and the European Union, and the FTAA, with a clear orientation toward "giving priority to multilateral negotiations over bilateral ones in the belief that they offered greater possibilities of success for a nation with Brazil's characteristics" (Silva, 2002: 325). Among the negotiations, those developed under the auspices of the WTO were considered "the forum par excellence and the best fit for our interests in formulating economic regulations at the international level" (Lafer, 2001a: 231).

In the administration's understanding, which had broad-based political and social backing, this preference was justified because the WTO

> occasions coalitions of variable geometry in keeping with the variety of issues it addresses; because of this, "automatic alignments" do not prevail in trade multilateralism. In the WTO, the United States is not the only factor in forming these coalitions. [Each country has a measure of influence] and each possesses the power of initiative through the force of joint action. In the end, the rule and practice of consensus in the decision-making process brings an element of democratization that permeates the life of the organization (Lafer, 1998: 14–15).

Because of this, one of Brazil's objectives was to inject the WTO with renewed vigor (Lafer, 2002). Making such possibilities viable is not automatic, however; they must be understood, analyzed, and channeled through the State and through Brazilian society for the benefit of Brazilian interests, a process that demands effort and adequate resources. Still, this policy, in various contexts, led to clearly satisfactory results.

The WTO was considered the best option for Brazilian economic interests because "it would protect against abuses and would offer adequate resources for the reasonably just resolution of conflicts that in some other form would be resolved by the survival of the fittest" (Silva, 2002: 325). The principal mechanism in this regard was the Dispute Settlement Body (DSB), to which both the administration and Brazilian businesses had recourse in trade disputes. By using these instruments, in addition to ad hoc groups, Brazil did achieve certain victories—on the issue of gasoline, for example, with a decision favorable to Brazil and unfavorable to the United States.

Perhaps the most well-known and important dispute, however, involved the Canadian company Bombardier and the Brazilian company Embraer. For Canada, the conflict centered on the subsidies provided for manufacturing Brazilian aircraft, subsidies that ran counter to the rules of the WTO as established by the Act of Marrakesh. For its part, Brazil accused Bombardier of using inappropriate methods in marketing its aircraft. After several years of litigation, both countries declared themselves satisfied with the arbitration. The resolution adopted by the WTO gave Brazil the right to retaliate in compensation for losses, while recommending restructuring the Export Financing

Program (PROEX) in order to adapt it to the rules of the WTO, in response to Canada's petition.

Another point of contention of great social and economic relevance, in which Brazil achieved a clearly favorable outcome, was the dispute between the Brazilian government and big pharmaceutical companies, especially North American ones. The government demanded the right to break the patents of HIV/AIDS drugs, arguing from standpoint of the national and international relevance of the issue and its demographic impact. Using the argument that the public good ought to prevail over profit, the country legitimized its demand and won sympathy from a majority of WTO members, as well as the UN, non-governmental organizations involved in issues of public health and human rights, and especially from the World Health Organization (WHO). On the occasion of the Doha ministerial conference of November 2001, which initiated a new round of trade negotiations, the United States accepted the accord—which it had previously opposed—and allowed for the possibility of patent-breaking in questions of public health in developing countries. The ministerial decision of the WTO also favored Brazil. According to Ministry of Health officials, the formulation and the execution of this winning strategy were clearly driven by State agencies involved in the question. Regardless of implicit political and electoral questions, given that it was expected that Health Minister José Serra would run for the presidency in 2002, these events demonstrated the importance of interagency connectedness in the formulation and implementation of particular aspects of Brazilian foreign policy.

A short time after September 11, 2001, the WTO initiated its new round of multilateral trade negotiations in Doha and returned to the unresolved issues of the Uruguay Round. Throughout the 1990s, Brazilian intervention had centered on defending the liberalization of the agricultural trade, and the administration viewed the dismantling of non-tariff barriers and subsidies as a condition for the success of the round.

Regarding economic relations with the European Union, our reference point from the Cardoso era is the Mercosur–European Union Framework Cooperation Agreement. The summit of European and Latin American heads of State and government in Rio de Janeiro in 1999 gave new contours to these negotiations. Once internal difficulties had been overcome, the European Union made new proposals in July 2001 with a view to advancing negotiations. But the detailed and wide-ranging offer made by the European Union on trade liberalization between the blocs was not well received by Mercosur member-States. This was not only owed to the political and economic crises they had experienced, but above all because the offer was unsatisfactory on a central point that rendered any progress impossible, namely, it lacked major concessions on agricultural products.

The European attempt in 2001 to accelerate negotiations on a free trade area can be explained in part by a concern with the potential expansion of US influence. The European Union worried that US policy, which involved a reordering of international economic relations via a large number of bilateral free-trade agreements, could weaken multilateralism and above all jeopardize the position of the European Union as the world's greatest trading power. It also saw the FTAA as having potential consequences, whether economic or political, for relations between Mercosur and itself. For Brazil, relations with the European Union constituted a strategic angle that could be employed as an alternative if negotiations with the United States fell through. Beyond this, the European position, in contrast to that of the United States, consistently privileged bloc-to-bloc negotiations, an approach that resonated well with Brazil's.

The perspective of autonomy through participation encountered various obstacles in negotiations with the European Union, though. In its European counterparts, the Cardoso administration had searched a set of partners whose worldview seemed similar to its own—but relations did not flourish as expected. Shared values of democracy, human rights, the environment, the Welfare State and multilateralism were not sufficient to reconcile State and social interests when those interests, on numerous occasions, proved contradictory.

Partnership with the European Union, with a view toward the harmonization of positions and actions in international fora, could mean an increase in power for Brazil. "A European Union–Mercosur 'axis of good' would have reasonable political standing within the international community, closing the 'Atlantic triangle' and serving as a constructive interface between the North American hegemon and the rest of the planet" (Valadão, 2005: 131). For Brazil, this could guarantee the possibility of multilateralism in international politics via the guiding influence of global rules and codes of conduct, which are important to establishing, implementing, and defending international public goods—and it could do so constructively, without breaking with the logic of autonomy through participation. According to Cardoso, this would contribute to the effective management of foreign affairs, since Brazil would not be able to undertake such a proposal on its own (Cardoso, 2001). But the lackluster results in this direction resulted from, on the one hand, the diversity of real interests and, on the other hand, the position of Europe in the post–Cold War international system. In the case of Europe, negative public opinion in relation to poor countries, including Brazil, weakened the possibility of implementing policies more favorable to Mercosur members. Some of the administration's difficulty in fostering closer ties to the European Union stemmed from the lack of reciprocity by EU members in opening their economies to Brazil and its Mercosur partners, as the latter had done in the 1990s, when their openness yielded large-scale investment, particularly from Spain and Portugal. For Cardoso, an additional shock of liberalization, without the offset of open markets in developed countries, would certainly decimate many economic sectors in the developing world, handing down a liability even more negative than the one already in existence (Cardoso, 2000).

This context helps one understand why the FTAA arose both as a threat and an opportunity (though to a lesser extent during Cardoso's second term), as an option but not a future—in contrast to Mercosur (Lafer, 2001b). For Cardoso, speaking in April, 2001, at the Third Summit of the Americas, in Quebec:

> The FTAA will be welcome if its creation is a step toward giving access to more dynamic markets; if in fact it is the path toward shared rules on anti-dumping; if it reduces non-tariff barriers; if it avoids protectionist distortion of good health regulations; if in protecting intellectual property it promotes, at the same time, the technological capacity of our people; and furthermore if it goes beyond the Uruguay Round and corrects the asymmetries that were crystallized there, above all in the area of agriculture. If not, it will prove irrelevant or, in the worst-case scenario, undesirable (Cardoso, 2001: 3).

This was not a question of uncritical adherence, or even of adherence, but of a desirable possibility of improving the relative position of the country. It was a question of the demands of a country seeking a relevant international presence capable of making an impact on the world order and, above all, of influencing the rules and decisions that would weigh on its own future in an asymmetrical and sometimes hostile environment. At the same time, structural elements tied to historical trends, such as the attenuation of the position of Brazil and South America in the world economy, weighed negatively on the negotiating capacity of the country. It is worth highlighting that the situation intensified in large part when the Cardoso administration realized that the inauguration of a more unilateral foreign policy in the United States had undermined the premises of autonomy through participation. There was, moreover, a clear lack of willingness to shape new strategies of international insertion. In this way, the administration saw its international activism diminished during its final two years in office.

RELATIONS WITH OTHER STRATEGIC PARTNERS

The Cardoso administration sought to establish robust or privileged relations with other States that, for various reasons, it considered strategic. Thus it exercised universalism concretely, seeking to defend what were considered

Brazilian interests. Among those countries to which it devoted particular attention, in differing dimensions and at varying levels of intensity, were China, India, Russia, Japan, Portugal, and the CPLP, Cuba and Mexico.

Relations with China were significantly enhanced, growing in importance throughout Cardoso's eight years. In 2002, for example, China became Brazil's number two trading partner. The significance of the growth in these relations is far-reaching, not only economically but also politically and strategically. From the Brazilian perspective, closer relations with China actualized the concepts of universalism, global player, and global trader. Brazil presented itself as a global interlocutor and sought to maximize its advantages in different areas, not only in trade but also in science and technology, with bilateral cooperation in the development of satellite technology gaining particular salience. With diplomatic relations consolidated, Cardoso visited China and twice received Chinese President Jiang Zemin in Brazil. During one of Zemin's visits, in the middle of the Sino-American crisis caused by a US airplane invading Chinese airspace, Washington requested Brazilian intervention to help mediate a solution.

Brazil also clearly manifested its support—one of the first countries to do so—for China's admittance to the WTO. And so negotiations developed in the direction of bringing bilateral preferences in line with the rules of the WTO, even if this entailed reciprocal concessions from China and Brazil. In Geneva, there were outlines of policy coordination at the WTO in the light of the relative parallelism of interests stemming from certain common characteristics, such as the existence in both countries of broad consumer markets and large inflows of foreign direct investment. The different insertions of the two countries in the international economy did not permit consistent coordination, however, though Brazilian exports to China doubled during Cardoso's tenure. Finally, the protocol on cooperation in space research, within the ambit of the Agreement on Scientific and Technological Cooperation of 1982, bore fruit with the launch of the first of four Sino-Brazilian satellites, Cebris, which generated knowledge and wealth for both countries. In addition, Brazilian companies held trade shows in China and vice-versa.

In the case of India, significant commonalities in international political and trade positions, expressed in multilateral fora, pointed to the potential for productive relations between the two countries. During Cardoso's eight years, however, these commonalities did not translate into concrete results, in spite of Brazil's manifest interest. Trade between the two hardly increased, clearly demonstrating the objective difficulties that exist in relations between developing countries, in which the parameters and non-complementarity of their economies limit the possibilities for cooperation, even when desired. When India performed its first nuclear tests, which coincided with the negotiation phase of the Comprehensive Test Ban Treaty (CTBT), Minister Lampreia issued a statement declaring Brazil's disapproval and Brazil, accordingly, repudiated its nuclear cooperation protocol with India. Coordination of policies in international trade negotiations also suffered periodic difficulties because of more rigid positions adopted by India.

In terms of relations with Russia, we would highlight a substantial increase in commercial exchanges during the 1990s, even if the total remained relatively small. On the Brazilian side, exports of farm commodities increased substantially, principally those tied to the food sector.

The economic stagnation of Japan had repercussions for its bilateral economic and political relations. The country, seen in the 1980s as an emerging great power, saw its importance in the international arena partially diminished in the 1990s, and this also had repercussions for its relations with Brazil. From an economic perspective, Japan remained an important market and industrial power, but it did not participate as an investor during the process of privatization implemented in Brazil during the 1990s. This absence notwithstanding, Japan cooperated with important Brazilian development projects. The macroeconomic balance and financial stability achieved during the Cardoso administration instilled greater confidence in Japanese businesses, which began to partner with Brazil in certain projects, especially environmental ones, such as the development of ecologically friendly fuel for the automobile sector, specifically in the area of sugarcane ethanol. There was also important cooperation on infrastructure and on social concerns, such as basic sanitation, not to mention the allocation of resources—in some cases in the form of grants—for hospitals, schools, and municipal projects, among others. Also of great importance in bilateral relations has been the temporary or permanent migration to Japan of Japanese-Brazilians, who have become the third largest contingent of Brazilians living abroad. As a consequence, cash remittances to Brazil have increased substantially.

Relations with Portugal were marked by investments made through the purchase of privatized Brazilian State companies; in terms of these investments, Portugal was surpassed only by Spain among European nations. During Cardoso's tenure, in spite of the definite "low profile" of Brazil's diplomatic presence in Lisbon, the role of Brazil among CPLP member-nations expanded. Relations with the Portuguese-speaking countries of Africa were recuperated, even though in the complex of African politics Brazil continued to occupy a second-tier position. Brazil's deployment of a peacekeeping mission to Angola, its largest overseas force since the Second World War, stirred Brazilian companies into taking a renewed interest in the country. In terms of political and symbolic impact, Brazil's decision to send a small contingent of peacekeeping forces to Timor Leste also proved important. During Cardoso's second term, the relative success of Brazilian efforts to control the spread of HIV/AIDS permitted the development of horizontal international cooperation in this area through the Brazilian Cooperation Agency (ABC), which has implemented measures to combat the disease and has trained public health personnel in African countries (Silva, 2002).

The end of apartheid in South Africa allowed for closer relations between the two countries, relations that were formalized in a framework agreement between South Africa and Mercosur. But although Brazil and Mercosur acknowledged the role played by South Africa both internationally and continentally, economic constraints and non-complementary systems made the deepening of relations within the ambit of this agreement problematic.

In Nigeria, Brazilian interests were directed particularly toward prospecting for and importing oil with the participation of Petrobras.

Relations with Cuba remained stable, and the Cardoso administration remained a constant critic of the US economic embargo, making clear its support for Cuba's reinsertion into the hemispheric community. Whenever possible, and without provoking greater tensions, the administration sought to motivate the Cuban government to respect democratic and human rights. Economic and commercial relations remained stagnated, though some agreements were implemented in the fields of medicine, agriculture, tourism, and academic and professional exchanges. There was also an agreement on reciprocal investment protection, although it was insufficient to move Brazilian companies to take greater interest in the island. Brazil also supported admitting Cuba to the Latin American Integration Association (ALADI).

Throughout the greater part of the Cardoso era, relations with Mexico suffered the impact of Mexico's adherence to the North American Free Trade Agreement (NAFTA). In certain negotiations, particularly those related to the FTAA, the positions of the two countries proved extremely divergent, since Mexico's implicit objective was to maintain its preferential access to the US market. On the other hand, during Cardoso's second term, Mexico's economic growth and its high foreign trade potential, combined with Mercosur's worsening crisis, led Brazilian companies, particularly multinationals in the automotive sector, to seek out the Mexican market. Hence, beginning in 2000, trade relations between the two countries began to display considerable development.

We should acknowledge that most of these initiatives regarding relations with strategic partners, principally partners with some similarity in their level of development, such as China, India, Russia, and South Africa, although important, only occurred once the limitations of the strategy of autonomy through participation came to light. Or rather, the choice of maintaining cordial relations with developed countries limited the possibility—which had begun to emerge—of taking advantage of potential complementarities among partners of intermediate standing on the international arena.

FINAL REMARKS

In analyzing the Cardoso era, a particularly relevant question arises as to the structural conditions that influenced the relative success of autonomy through participation. In hindsight, all the endeavors of the 1990s—and particularly the eight years of Cardoso's watch—were insufficient to stop a certain deterioration in the international position of both South America and Brazil, a deterioration expressed in low growth rates, the consequences of which were manifested in the role that the nations of the region played in the world economy. Nevertheless, the Cardoso administration should be credited, as we have sought to demonstrate, for its effort to contain this trend through its foreign policy. We have also seen that real and symbolic values prevailing in the public opinion of wealthy countries contributed to this deterioration and spread to other regions. One such example occurred in the administration's concern to avoid including issues related to civil rights, labor rights, and environmental protection in WTO negotiations in an attempt to counteract the influence of these issues in the trade sphere. Some of the successes of Brazilian diplomacy can be linked to a cooperative international environment marked by widespread interdependence, an environment in which the possibility of using multilateral fora became a reality.

One policy of the Clinton administration, which coincided with six years of Cardoso's presidency (from 1995 to 2000), was the construction of multilateral rules and institutions, even amid extremely tough negotiations in which the United States categorically refused to abdicate the unilateralism of its legislation. The difficulties of negotiations on the FTAA derived from these constraints, never abandoned by US negotiators. In other words, the multilateral heritage of Brazilian foreign policy was renewed during the Cardoso administration through the operationalization of the concept of autonomy through participation; through it, and in order to fulfill the concept's development objectives, the country moved closer to the central poles of international relations.

After January 2001, however, the Bush administration modified the conceptual framework of international relations, bringing new practical and theoretical difficulties to every country. The renewed emphasis on unilateralism, focused on questions of security and accentuated after September 11, placed new burdens on the concept of autonomy through participation. The concept was not invalidated in principle, but it certainly took on new characteristics, which involved the necessity of surprisingly higher levels of both negotiating capacity and international linkage and, eventually, of having to seek out new paths to bypass possible situations of rupture or lack of participation and cooperation. This worried the administration, which insisted on relations with China, India, and South Africa, which sought to stabilize its dialogue with the United States in the framework of negotiations on the FTAA and which worked at the same time to strengthen relations between Mercosur and the European Union.

During Lafer's tenure at the MRE, from 2001 to 2002, the practice of autonomy through participation, under the weight of circumstances, was attenuated by systemic changes. There emerged, without eclipsing the former strategy, an attempt at "housecleaning" through a turn to "a diplomacy of the concrete" (Lafer, 2002).

The removal of Ambassador José Maurício Bustani from the post of Director-General of the Organization for the Prohibition of Chemical Weapons (OPCW), under US pressure, revealed the administration's wish to maintain cooperative international relations, especially with the United States. These came at a moment when the possibility of such relations being the norm seemed to be deteriorating due to changes that had occurred in international society largely on account of US actions. The departure of Ambassador Samuel Pinheiro Guimarães from the International Relations Research Institute (IPRI) at the MRE, happened, in the administration's understanding, as an attempt to hierarchy maintenance.

Cardoso's two terms in office strengthened Brazil's presence in some of the great international debates, especially through the practice of "presidential diplomacy." The government faced various external constraints and internal deficiencies that worked against a more prominent international presence, as we have observed.

In seeking to achieve a balance and undertake a cost-benefit analysis, which is always difficult, we would submit that the gains of autonomy through participation, arising from adherence to the international mainstream, would have exceeded the costs of autonomy through distance if the country had been internally prepared to take advantage of the alteration. However, the weakening of the State ended up undermining this capacity. The vitality of some negotiations, as in the case of ad hoc groups addressing controversies at the WTO, led to favorable results. But adherence to international regimes and norms was not counterbalanced by the internal adaptation that would have enabled the country to reap the rewards of the said adherence. Equally, this adherence was not always interpreted in a way that favored domestic growth, whether in terms of development or of an industrial policy.

During the last phase of the Cardoso presidency there was an effort to address the question of human resource development. The MRE itself took specific actions in this regard. Adherence to the international mainstream, intense participation in negotiations and the profile that the administration sought to maintain all revealed the urgency of this kind of development. Attempts at solving the problem led to specific paths of action, such as modifying the entrance exam of the Rio Branco Institute (IRBr).[2] The institute also began to require that applicants be graduates and reorganized its course as a professional master's degree program. In addition, there were some institutional changes in the structure of the ministry. The consolidation of the MRE, at the beginning of Cardoso's first term, as the epicenter of international trade negotiations brought home the necessity of acquiring high levels of specialization and keeping them up to date. Lastly, there was greater cooperative interaction with other ministries and liaison with academics of relevant expertise, as well as with businesses, unions, and NGOs—even if not to the full extent necessary.

At the same time, the image of the Brazilian State improved internationally. The peaceful conduct of the country was consolidated, and Brazil came to be respected for its constructive positions. On the other hand, however, weakness in promoting development perpetuated a historical trend of shrinkage in Brazil's world-economic standing, undermining the country's bargaining power in relevant international negotiations. The negative image of poor countries manifested in the public opinion of rich ones, as well as the internal problems that affect poor countries specifically, also complicated the maximization of advantages. In Latin America, Brazil's effort to play a more relevant leading role was impaired in the end by its own internal constraints.

These limitations left the Cardoso administration, in its foreign policy, without great achievements to be celebrated, even if it did not suffer losses either. Concurrently, however, some of its initiatives allowed its opponent and successor, Lula, to tread a creative path through the international field. The basic diplomatic premise of the Lula administration involved replacing the concept of autonomy through participation with that of autonomy through diversification, which led Brazil to consolidate a more affirmative foreign policy around the defense of its interests. In response to US unilateralism, the Lula administration chose to recover multilateralism and to bring it into play as a principle ordering international politics, understanding it as a broad movement toward decentralizing and regulating power in international society. Hence Brazil's initiative in forming the G-3, in creating the G-20 for the WTO Doha Round, in reaching out to African and Arab countries and so on. Another significant change vis-à-vis the Cardoso administration is the Lula administration's apparent willingness to bear the costs of its leadership both in the world and specifically in Mercosur and South America.

NOTES

1. Gomes served as finance minister for three months, from September to December 1994, stepping down before the start of Cardoso's first term. He assumed the post at a particularly sensitive moment, two months after the implementation of the Real Plan and one month before national elections pitting Cardoso against Lula.

2. The IRBr, educational branch of the MRE, is the gateway to the diplomatic profession in Brazil.

Chapter 5

Lula's Foreign Policy and the Quest for Autonomy through Diversification

INTRODUCTION

Most of the Lula government's discourse has been focused on the need for change in relation to the Cardoso administration, as stated by the president himself during his inauguration: "Change: this is the key word; this was the great message from Brazilian society in the October elections" (Lula da Silva, 2003: 27–28).

Many initiatives of the Lula administration are situated in the framework of international trade negotiations and the search for deepening political coordination with emerging countries, namely India, South Africa, Russia and China. Most of these partnerships began taking shape toward the end of the Cardoso administration, but Lula gave a new emphasis to this aspect of Brazil's international agenda.

With India and South Africa, the Lula administration formalized a strategic relationship with the creation of IBSA (India, Brazil, and South Africa), otherwise known as the G-3. As for Russia and China, Brazil has sought to enhance exchanges in the trade, technology and military fields. Regarding China, Lula has recognized it as a market economy despite opposition from the São Paulo State Federation of Industry (FIESP). This fact contributed to criticism from sectors affected by so-called unfair competition that Brazilian foreign policy leaves aside important sectors of civil society. As we write, in the first half of 2009, China has become Brazil's number one trading partner.

According to data compiled by Prates (2005/2006), based on figures from the Ministry of Development, Industry and Foreign Trade, from 2002 to 2005, Chinese participation in Brazilian exports increased from 4.2 percent to 5.8 percent, while imports rose significantly (from around US$2.4 billion to over US$5.3 billion). However, China did not support Brazil joining the UN Security Council as a permanent member owing to China's relations with Japan. China and Brazil did not even become partners at the non-agricultural negotiations of the Doha Round. After months of negotiation, Brazil supported Russia's entry into the World Trade Organization (WTO), on the basis of "ensuring that that country does not diminish, under any conditions, its market's access to Brazilian meat for five years" (*Valor Econômico,* 2005).

While there was no significant rupture from the paradigms of Brazilian foreign policy—some of the guidelines being reinforcements of actions already on course during the Cardoso administration—there was a change in the emphasis given to certain options opened previously. Both the Cardoso and Lula administrations have used different foreign policy means, trying not to sway too far from the constantly pursued aim of developing the country economically, whilst maintaining a certain political autonomy (Lima, 2005: 11–12; Lafer, 2001b; PT, 2002: 6).

The extent of political autonomy has always been a matter for debate in foreign policy since Independence and during the Republic. The search for a friendly relationship with the United States and an autonomy strategy (the maintenance of a certain room for maneuver with the enhancement of economic interdependence) are marks that go back to Rio Branco (1902–1912) and Aranha (1938–1943) (Bueno, 2003; Vigevani, 1989; Vigevani, Oliveira and Cintra, 2004). The idea of defending sovereignty and national interests, in spite of possible conflicts with the USA, is clear in the Independent Foreign Policy tradition, formulated by Foreign Relations Minister San Thiago Dantas (1961–1963), under President Goulart, and reiterated by Azeredo da Silveira (1974–1978), during the Geisel administration (Cervo and Bueno, 2002; Vigevani, 1974).

In this chapter, we pose the following question: has there been political change in Brazilian foreign policy since the swearing-in of President Lula?

In order to discuss the topic, we present three notions of autonomy to explain the changes that contemporary Brazilian foreign policy has been through. Secondly, we examine the empirical contents of the Brazilian international agenda, focusing on some of the foreign policy topics most debated during the Cardoso and Lula administrations. Lastly, we specify the differences between the international agendas of the two presidents.

THE THREE AUTONOMIES: DISTANCE, PARTICIPATION AND DIVERSIFICATION

The Brazilian political and economic context of the 1980s was marked by the crisis of the national development model, built in President Vargas' period starting in the 1930s, based on the existence of an entrepreneurial and protectionist State and an economic policy of import substitution.

This model was facing difficulties by the 1970s and was unable to provide satisfactory responses to the strong economic instability of the time. The foreign debt and the oil shocks, whose consequences lasted up until the mid 1990s, worsened the situation. In this context of political instability, a growing number of sectors, both from the elite, middle class and labor unions, started to call for the country's democratic reform and the end of the military regime. During the transition to democracy, which lasted throughout the Sarney administration, it was evident how critical the situation of the state apparatus was. This had an effect on Brazil's foreign policy, especially on the economic relations it had with the rest of the world (flow of investments, finance and trade).

From the late 1980s to the early 1990s, liberal ideas gained strength on the international and domestic agendas. In Brazil, this was due to a number of reasons: the evident crisis of the previous model, the role of some international agencies (i.e., the IMF and World Bank) and the conviction, both on the part of the elite and public opinion, that such ideas brought potential benefits. This influenced the adoption of economic reforms to face the challenges of so-called globalization and coincided with the difficulties faced by the political and social opponents of the new development model to formulate alternatives to it.

The domestic and international changes taking place with the end of the Cold War meant it would be difficult for Brazil to keep the same orientation as in the past, in a situation where the State was weakened. The country began to seek new approaches to dialogue with the world, which involved strategies formulated in the ministries of finance and foreign relations. The 1990s enhanced the visibility of the Ministry of Foreign Relations, owing to the emphasis placed on regional integration processes, the opening of the market and multilateral negotiations (Vigevani and Mariano, 2005: 14).

As from 1989, with the cooling off of East–West tensions, the country adopted a defensive posture in its foreign policy, still hoping to maintain its autonomy. The search for autonomy during the period of the Independent Foreign Policy (1961–1964) and some military governments—mainly from 1967, President Geisel's Responsible Pragmatism (1974–1979) in particular—was undertaken by distancing the country from the international power centers (Amado, 1982). These foreign policies, which were labeled by the Ministry of External Relations itself, despite having been implemented by very different regimes in domestic terms, are considered similar projects in some aspects, albeit not in all (Seixas Corrêa, 1995; Fonseca Jr., 1998). Under President Vargas, Brazilian foreign policy was able to have a relatively isolationist position during World War II, when the alliance with USA was considered necessary to strengthen national interests (Moura, 1980). In the 1960s and 1970s, with the increasing importance of Third World issues such as the Cuban revolution (1959), the Non-Aligned Movement (starting in 1961), the oil crises (1973 and 1979) and the Vietnam War (from 1959 to 1975), Brazil positioned itself as a capitalist country, but defending the importance of the South's demands. At the same time, during certain periods, like the Castello Branco administration (1964–1966), the political and anti-communist alliance with United States was espoused wholeheartedly.

However, in the post–Cold War period, a tendency for autonomy through participation was emphasized by foreign policymakers, believing it advanced Brazil's interests. As discussed earlier, according to Fonseca Jr. (1998: 368), "Autonomy [. . .] does not mean 'distance' from controversial international issues in order to protect the country against undesirable alignments [. . .] Autonomy means participation, means the wish to influence the open agenda with values that express traditional [Brazilian] diplomacy." In other words, while the parameters of foreign policy meant protectionist polices had made sense in the past, the new international configuration would require one to incorporate issues like human and social rights, environmental protection, democratic transition, social rights, liberal economic reform, free trade, competition, technology flows, investment, financial flows and the acceleration of South American integration. This agenda was implemented from 1990 to 2002, with varying intensity.

In the 1990s, issues that make up a country's soft power seemed to gain weight, contrasting with the visibly diminished importance given to international security, fundamental during the Cold War. The Brazilian Ministry of Foreign Relations created departmental divisions and adapted the subdepartments to fit these new themes. There prevailed the idea that Brazil would obtain more benefits within an international system where free trade predominated. The increase in competitiveness in a world with lower tariff barriers would make it possible for the country to integrate into the global market better. "Participation comes from the simple fact that, given the dimensions of the country, there are very few things that do not affect us" (Fonseca Jr., 1998: 367).

During the 1990s, various domestic measures were adopted in consonance with this vision of international insertion: currency liberalization, decreased subsidies for industry, new legislation for intellectual property, greater liberalization for imports, relative investment liberalization, privatization of State companies and renegotiation of the foreign debt. Several measures were taken over the course of the 1990s, but the privatization program did not include every State company, while instruments of macro-economic management and of support to development policies, such as the National Economic and Social Development Bank (BNDES), remained in State hands.

This evolution toward autonomy through participation was slow, having been enhanced at the end of Abreu Sodré's period at the Ministry of Foreign Relations (1986–1990), during the Sarney administration, and continued by Minister Francisco Rezek (1990–1991), under President Collor de Mello. However, there was a theoretical refinement of the new paradigm adopted by Brazilian foreign policy during Celso Lafer's brief stay at the helm of the Ministry of Foreign Relations in 1992, during the Collor de Mello administration (Campos Mello, 2000).

President Itamar Franco (1992–1994) put into operation the goals set out by the ministry, with Cardoso (1993) and Celso Amorim (1994) in charge of the portfolio. The search for a redefinition of objectives to be actively pursued involved the Ministry of Finance, when Cardoso, Rubens Ricupero and Ciro Gomes held the office of minister, while an adherence to international economic values meant focusing on domestic stability.

The decision to sign the Final Act of Marrakesh, which created the World Trade Organization (WTO) in 1994, and the discussion of a common external tariff in Mercosur, which was consolidated in the Ouro Preto Protocol of December 1994, thus initiating negotiations for the creation of the Free Trade Area of the Americas (FTAA), consolidated the autonomy through participation strategy (Vigevani, Oliveira and Cintra, 2004: 34).

The idea of change with continuity defended by Lafer (2001b: 8), which prevailed during the Cardoso administration, meant that a foreign policy renewal should be characterized by creative adaptation toward new international challenges. This being so, foreign policy changes do not need to be radical redirections of a country's objectives; usually they are just adjustments or changes in political program. What one saw in the Cardoso administration was the consolidation and sophistication of a policy initially formulated and practiced by the Collor de Mello and Itamar Franco governments. There was the abandonment of the idea of intrinsic development, which prevailed until 1988/1989, when the government's main objective was increasing both the domestic market and consumption, strengthening and extending the State, drawing in foreign investment and using import substitution policies. Part of the success of Brazilian diplomacy in the Cardoso administration was linked to a partially cooperative international environment, where a democratization of international institutions was believed to have taken place mainly in the field of trade. The economic growth of most countries in the 1990s, especially of the United States under Clinton, seemed to back up this perception.

As we said in chapter 4, the Clinton administration, which coincided with six years (1995–2000) of the Cardoso administration, sought to strengthen international rules and institutions amid tough negotiations. Issues such as security and strategic planning were important, but had less visibility in this period. The George W. Bush government began to modify the concept of international relations in 2001, bringing new difficulties to the Cardoso administration. This does not mean that autonomy through participation lost its validity for his government; it was adorned with new traits.

At the end of his term, Cardoso was worried about the difficulties resulting from the growth of American unilateralism. This led to an enhancement of relations with China, India and South Africa and a search for greater balance in the dialogue with the United States on the Free Trade Area of the Americas (FTAA). Despite not having reached agreement, the Cardoso administration attempted to use the Mercosur–European Union negotiations to take on greater maneuverability (Vigevani, Oliveira and Cintra, 2004: 57). This tendency and actual redirection would be taken further and defended more emphatically in the Lula administration, indicating a gradual change from autonomy through participation to the strategy we define as being the search for autonomy through diversification.

A summarized definition goes as follows: (1) autonomy through distance—policy of not automatically accepting prevailing international regimes; belief in partial autarchy; development focused on the domestic market. Consequently, a diplomacy that goes against certain aspects of the agenda of the great powers, putting forward as its main goal the idea of preserving the nation-State's sovereignty; (2) autonomy through participation—the adherence to international regimes, especially more liberal ones, but without the loss of foreign policy management. The objective would be to influence the formulation of principles and rules that govern the international system; (3) autonomy through diversification—an adherence to international norms and principles by means of South–South alliances, including regional alliances, and through agreements with non-traditional partners (China, Asia-Pacific, Africa, Eastern Europe, Middle East, etc.), trying to reduce asymmetries in foreign relations with powerful countries; at the same time, the maintenance of regular and good relations with developed countries, cooperating with them in international organizations and reducing their power.

With the beginning of the Lula administration, expectations arose as to the possible redirection of foreign policy. According to Cardozo and Miyamoto (2006: 3), some of Geisel's Responsible Pragmatism (1974–1978) guidelines, such as affirming autonomy in relation to the superpowers and enhancing ties with countries of the South, whether bilaterally or through international institutions, were undertaken again by Lula's foreign policy.

Geisel's foreign policy was marked by the effort to bring Brazil closer to the countries of the South, since closer relations with Third World countries would allow for diversification of interests and, consequently, less dependence on rich countries. On the other hand, he enhanced relations with some developed countries, like West Germany. The intensification of South–South relations would objectively put the North–South dialogue on new terms, inasmuch as the coordinated action between developing countries could decrease international power asymmetries (Cardozo and Miyamoto, 2006: 11). However, Responsible Pragmatism did not mean complete alignment with the southern agenda; Brazil was never a member of the Non-Aligned Movement, for instance. In fact, this was a policy associated with the context of the period: major increases in oil prices, high dependence on Middle East imports, particularly from Iraq and Saudi Arabia, human rights policy of the Carter administration, development of Brazilian nuclear power with West German support and the protectionist development project.

In the Lula administration, the international system does not differ considerably from the context of the Cardoso administration, mainly after September 11. On the domestic plane, the abandonment of the import substitution model seemed consolidated due to a certain consensus in society on the need for an internationally competitive economy.

The apparent changes in the Lula administration had some guidelines: (1) to contribute to the search for greater equilibrium and attenuate unilateralism; (2) to strengthen bilateral and multilateral relations in order to increase the country's weight in political and economic negotiations on an international level; (3) to deepen relations so as to benefit from possibly greater economic, financial, technological and cultural exchanges; (4) to avoid agreements that could jeopardize development in the long term. These guidelines, throughout the first period of the government (2003–2006), broadening in the second period, implied precise emphases: (1) intensification of relations with emerging countries such as India, China, Russia and South Africa; (2) an important role at the Doha Round of the World Trade Organization, as in other international negotiations; (3) maintenance of friendly political relations and the further development of economic relations with rich countries, including the United States; (4) forming and strengthening relations with African countries; (5) campaigning for the reform of the United Nations Security Council, including a permanent seat for Brazil; (6) defense of social objectives, allowing for greater balance between the State and civil society; (7) strong participation in international organizations and multilateral fora that discuss international governance.

THE SIGNIFICANCE OF SOUTH–SOUTH COOPERATION

According to General Secretary Pinheiro Guimarães of the Ministry of Foreign Relations in the Lula administration, "Brazil [. . .] has to react to the political initiatives of the great powers, especially [. . .] the United States. Brazil has to articulate political, economic and technological alliances with peripheral states of the international system to defend and protect its interests" (Guimarães, 2006).

Throughout most of the Cold War, Brazilian foreign policy defended themes on the North–South agenda, as opposed to the East–West conflict. Even at moments of greater political identification with the USA and western diplomacy under the Dutra and Castello Branco administrations, the issues of national development and division of countries into poor and rich still manifested itself. The support for the G-77, that sought a fairer international economic order, the sympathy for proposals of countries unwilling to align either to the USSR or the United States and closer ties with Middle Eastern and African nations, set forth a third-world-like foreign policy, more visible during the Responsible Pragmatism period (1974–1978). The Cardoso administration (1995–2002), which kept up good relations with developing countries, explicitly recognizing the asymmetries and the lack of fairness between nations, sought to move away from this position, emphasizing the cooperative aspects of the international system.

> The foreign policy that I pursued in my brief passage through the Ministry of Foreign Relations (October 1992 to May 1993) was that of autonomy through participation, within a changing international reality, in contrast to autonomy through distance from the world order of the time. [. . .] The Ministry of Foreign Relations, generally run by diplomats during those years of technocratic tendency, drew up a policy of defense of our interests that toyed with Third Worldism. [. . .] The military regime's foreign policy followed the guidelines of such a style of government, but had to review its central objectives after the fall of the Berlin Wall in 1989 and the accelerated economic process linked to globalization from 1980 to 1990 (Cardoso, 2006: 604–606).

At first, one might believe that Lula's foreign policy is an attempt to return to a Third World mentality. In Brazil, this interpretation is strong among the opposition parties, particularly the Brazilian Social Democracy Party (PSDB) and the Liberal Front Party (PFL, renamed "Democrats" in 2007), and resonates in the mainstream media and in business and intellectual sectors. However, whilst the will to place South–South cooperation back on the agenda does exist, it had to be reinterpreted within a scenario that brought with it two fundamental changes: the country's adherence to the universality of democratic principles and the acceleration of the globalization process, which made it impossible for the nation to maintain a foreign policy that had a low level of interdependence in relation to other countries (Lima, 2005: 33; Lima and Hirst, 2006: 25). This explains why the stances taken by the Ministry of Foreign Relations are not necessarily elements to weaken the ties with richer countries.

Even if the Lula administration could escape the constraints created and deepened by previous administrations, a mere return to the past would be impossible. The program of the Workers' Party (PT) initially suggested a distancing from the developed capitalist countries. But a nostalgic sentiment toward autonomy through distance within the government had to fall into line with certain realities that had changed very little in relation to the Cardoso administration.

The Lula administration "innovated" when it named Marco Aurélio Garcia, a PT intellectual who was its secretary for international relations from 1996 to 2002, to take over as special adviser to the president on foreign affairs. The only other occasion on record when a non-diplomat had the post dates back to president Kubitschek (1956–1960), when poet Augusto Frederico Schmidt held it. There have been rumors of conflicts between the adviser and the minister of Foreign Relations on occasion, which leads one to suppose there are disputes between the two as to who heads the country's foreign policy-making. A certain division of space dispelled some doubts: Garcia is meanly responsible for "ideological" topics of Brazilian foreign policy, particularly when there is the need for dialogue with South American leftist leaders like Hugo Chavez. On the other hand, Amorim takes care of the more "technical" aspects of the Brazilian international agenda like WTO and FTAA negotiations (Garcia, 2004).

The Lula administration has an assertive stance in the defense of national sovereignty and interests, seeking privileged alliances in the South. It must be made clear that South–South cooperation occurred in the Cardoso administration in the questioning of HIV/AIDS drug patents, with the leadership of Minister of Health José Serra, when Brazil joined South Africa, India and various NGOs (e.g., Oxfam and *Médecins sans Frontières*—MSF) in demanding the lowering of international prices on such drugs. However, this coalition was institutionalized only in the Lula administration on June 6, 2003, with the Declaration of Brasília, an agreement on issues ranging from trade to international security, resulting in the creation of IBSA or the G-3, with India and South Africa. With regard to intellectual property rights, Lula authorized Brazil for the first time to break the patent of an HIV/AIDS drug made by Merck & Co. and import a generic version from India instead (Amaral, 2007).

As for the WTO, both governments considered it important to take part in multilateral trade negotiations. The Cardoso administration devoted itself to dialogue, not to an institutionalized coordination of southern countries. Lula has formed alliances, such as the much talked-about G-20 and IBSA. The final outcome of these coalitions is still uncertain, but they were recognized in the Doha, Cancun and Hong Kong meetings.

After the IBSA agreement, some diplomats who had held relevant positions in previous governments criticized the lack of scope and undefined strategy of the alliance. The issues covered by the G-3 included not only foreign trade and international security, but also technological cooperation and incentives for tourism, among others (Almeida, 2004: 167; Souto Maior, 2004: 56).

The concern of the Lula administration in strengthening its own negotiating role in South–South coalitions became evident before the ministerial meeting in Cancun in September 2003, occasion of the formation of the G-20, a group of countries interested in the end of domestic subsidies for exports of agricultural goods and greater access to North American and European markets (Amorim, 2004). As with other southern alliances, the Lula administration believes that this coalition's interests go beyond the expansion of individual economic benefits and that it should have a common identity. Pinheiro Guimarães, ambassador at the time and currently serving as General Secretary of the Ministry of Foreign Relations, expressed the idea clearly:

> Despite the differences between Brazil and other large peripheral states, inasmuch as they share common characteristics and interests and are far away from one another, they do not have direct competitive interests and are therefore able to construct common political projects (Guimarães, 1999: 141).

As proof that real common interests exist, an assumption of Brazil's action in the Lula administration, the G-20 has been able to reach its objectives and has constituted itself as a negotiating power, even though its continuity is subject to the always asymmetrical logic of interests and power relations. The discussions between G-20 countries at the July 2008 WTO ministerial meeting held in Geneva confirm this conclusion, on continuity in the long term. According to Amorim,

> the so-called "failure of Cancun," was the first step towards the success of Geneva, almost a year later [2004], [. . .] in comparison with previous rounds, when the United States and the European Union set, between themselves, the bounds of the agreement that was then offered as "possible consensus" to the other countries. [. . .] Our priority is to successfully conclude the WTO negotiations. There, we will actually be able to eliminate the billion-dollar export subsidies and significantly reduce the domestic support for agricultural production of the developed countries (Amorim, 2005: 4–5).

REGIONAL ROLE, UNITED STATES AND DIVERSIFICATION OF PARTNERS

The Cardoso administration was characterized by multilateralism, attributing emphasis to international law. Recognizing the reality of strong power asymmetries in the international system, direct negotiation with central countries was prioritized without the need for systematic southern alliances (Lafer, 2001c). The WTO panels against the United States and the European Union regarding cotton and sugar demonstrate the meaning of the use of legal mechanisms. Whilst recognizing the strategic importance of Mercosur and of relations with Argentina, the administration at the same time pursued the constitution of a regional bloc in South America, particularly after the South America Conference of Heads of State and Government in 2000. There prevailed the conviction that activism would not solve the problem of scarcity of bargaining power. As for values, subject to the idea of autonomy through participation, Cardoso defended human rights principles and sustainable development, sought to preserve peace and democracy and advocated universal principles (Cardoso, 2006: 602).

Lula's foreign policy, maintaining multilateralism, defends national sovereignty more emphatically than the previous government. This characteristic, in agreement with the notion of autonomy through diversification, gained relevance and was interpreted at certain moments as a sentiment of regional leadership. Even if Lula's ideas, and those of his top-level staff, are merely rhetorical statements, they still have an impact on Brazil's relations with other countries. Governments and social groups do not only react considering the State's power resources, but also according to the potential for utilization of such resources. Therefore, political ideas and the perceptions of actors affect the behavior of States, as has been argued by authors of differing theoretical perspectives (Keohane and Goldstein, 1993; Wendt, 1999; Rosati, 1995).

The possible leadership role for Brazil was seen as an outcome of the country's economic prominence by the policy formulators of the Cardoso administration. Such leadership would be limited to a regional status due to the lack of resources (financial, military, political and professional) available for the State's action further afield. In contrast, the Lula administration believes a specific and important influence can be achieved by more active and dynamic diplomatic action, as well as by the country's importance in the region (Amorim, 2003: 77). At the same time, there is specific attention paid to actions supported by real measures. For this reason, this administration disagrees with international actions grounded more in ideological discourse than anything else.

The leadership role is difficult, given that its maintenance generates expectations and demands that cannot be easily met. This being so, leadership can bring about animosity. Even if this does not happen, there is always a price to pay (Burges, 2005; Mattli, 1999). The nationalization of Bolivian gas in 2006 by President Evo Morales, ultimately affecting the continuity of the concession of the Brazilian State company (Petrobras), demonstrates the difficulties of leadership. The same could be said about the difficulties in dealing with drug trade problems between Brazil and Colombia, a situation that demonstrates Brazil's incapacity to help Colombia deal with drug traffickers. The leadership role demands greater capacity from the state to mobilize resources. Brazil's wish to make both foreign policy and regional integration central pillars of its own national project is an issue to be examined.

Lula's foreign policy, seeking to increase its international and regional status, has taken on a preeminent role in Haiti, since 2004. In this case, the country has accepted the command of a United Nations Special Mission to establish peace in Haiti by sending a contingent of approximately 1,200 soldiers. Even in this situation, we cannot identify an action that implies goal changes in relation to the country's traditional foreign policy, but possibly one from the autonomy through distance period. The sending of troops to Haiti is part of Brazil's tradition, taking into account the country's peacekeeping role back in 1956, under President Kubitschek, when it sent forces to Sinai, having followed through in Angola and other countries, such as Yugoslavia and East Timor, with a small number of troops. The presence in Haiti, approved in 2003 under the Lula administration, is linked to the tradition of Brazilian diplomacy to cooperate in policies that seek to promote international (Sinai) or national (Angola) peace initiatives. This is also linked to the strong interest in obtaining a permanent seat on the UN Security Council. This is the reason why the government, as part of a more general international strategy, has accepted the mission and demonstrated a willingness to bear part of the peacekeeping costs.

The Haitian case perfectly exemplifies the meaning of autonomy through diversification. Diversification not only means the search for broadening the range of relations with non-traditional partner-States. It also implies the capacity for intervention in areas that are not of immediate interest and refer to internationally recognized public goods. Brazil chose to take on this responsibility, supported by other countries of the region, such as Chile and Argentina, because its objective strengthens the country's international status.

The Cardoso administration opted for a more moderate position, in which external actions would be collaborative and initiated through international institutions, thus avoiding a role that would result in responsibility and risk. Cardoso explains: "Aside from making the Brazilian position in the region clear, and this without arrogance, I am convinced that leadership is exercised, not proclaimed" (Cardoso, 2006: 621). As for a permanent seat on the UN Security Council, Cardoso prioritized other issues on the agenda, such as "inclusion in the G-7 as a better alternative" (Cardoso, 2006: 610).

The intensification of the domestic debate on foreign policy has been evident throughout the Lula administration. In the context of the country's modest growth since the early 1980s, international trade has developed significantly, reaching US$107.6 billion in 2002 and US$228.9 billion in 2006 (Secex, 2007). This partly explains why international economic issues gained relevance in the domestic debate. This was of interest to public opinion, the elite, entrepreneurs, unions, parties and Congress. On the other hand, innovations met with resistance, weakening what seemed to be a reasonable domestic consensus for a foreign policy that, according to some critics, should be of the State and not of governments. According to the opposition, especially the PSDB and the Democrats, the strong politicization was due to the lack of effort in favor of relations with traditional economic and political partners, particularly the United States and the European Union. In fact, the Lula administration chose to increase the list of relations with other countries, including African nations, specifically Portuguese-speaking ones, and not only on economic bases, but also redeeming the so-called human, social and cultural debt.

Relations with the United States throughout the Cardoso period were defined as essential and cooperative: despite good political relations, there were sectoral disagreements, especially in the trade area, where differences over intellectual property rights, agriculture and disputes in several areas won the spotlight. US cotton subsidies were questioned by Brazil, and this ended up serving as a catalyst and as experience in the use of WTO panels and conflict-resolution mechanisms. This environment made it difficult for any further negotiations on the FTAA, despite the conclusion reached in the final phase of the Cardoso government that such an agreement would be interesting. Opposition parties critical of Lula's trade policy say it lacks pragmatism. They insist that its disconnection from its time and its overly ideological nature negatively impact trade. In order to expand, it would have to go through the FTAA, a path desired by significant segments of the private sector (Giannetti and Marconini, 2006; Jank, 2006). However, a survey conducted with members of the Executive, Congress and the Judiciary, and also of social movements, NGOs and special interest groups, concluded that most of those interviewed (61 percent) believed that the Brazilian government should demand from the United States a lowering of its non-tariff barriers and subsidies before reaching any sort of agreement, while 16 percent believed that the agreement was not in the country's best interest. Only 8 percent of respondents supported it (Souza, 2002: 60).

During the 2002 Brazilian election campaign, US neoconservative sectors feared that Brazil would excessively oppose the interests of the United States. In the economic camp, rumors were such that the country's risk factor rose to 2,000 points. This had a strong impact on the election campaign itself and conditioned part of the government's economic measures as from 2003. It was believed in US business circles that the foreign debt would not be honored and that a "populist," State-driven program would be implemented.

However, the day after Lula's October 2002 election victory George W. Bush telephoned the future president of Brazil inviting him to go to the United States before his inauguration. The visit was positive and contributed to diminish the conflict that was in neither of the countries' interests. Bush's visit to Brazil in November 2005 consolidated the dialogue. Some even talk about the mutual empathy that appears to exist between the two presidents. Lula's negative image in the United States mainstream in 2002—as during the presidential campaigns of 1989, 1994 and 1998—gradually dissipated over the course of his first term and definitively ended during the 2006 election campaign. In its final phase, Lula's 2006 candidacy did not elicit strong opposition in the United States, though this did not mean that US elites were sympathetic toward him. At the same time, the American Federation of Labor–Congress of Industrial Organizations (AFL-CIO) and leftist groups supported him.

In March 2007, at the beginning of his second presidential term, Lula met George W. Bush again, first in Brazil, then in Camp David. Two topics of the meetings gained the media spotlight: a possible agreement on ethanol and the US attempt to block the actions of President Chavez of Venezuela. The Lula administration has always supported democratic and constitutional solutions for every conflict, be it political, economic or social. This principle is considered valid for all countries, including South American ones. On the question of Venezuela, the Brazilian government has shown little desire to confront Chavez. It has supported the maintenance of democratic rules and has always intended to strengthen economic relations between the two countries.

As for ethanol, the USA certainly needs to decrease its "addiction to oil," and Brazil wants more access to the US market, but it is not clear what the results of this partnership will be, since it is in its very beginning. According to Amorim, the approximation between Lula and Bush "is not a 'course correction' in Brazilian foreign policy. [. . .] Precisely for having an autonomous and sovereign foreign policy [. . .], Brazil is respected by developed and developing countries" (Amorim, 2007). With President Barack Obama, in office since January 2009, there surely is more political common ground, in international security and environment issues, for instance, but difficulties could grow over trade.

The relations of the Cardoso administration with the United States, like its positions on then-current international themes, can be placed within the autonomy through participation perspective, understood as the active attempt at influencing agendas. Certain social sectors, especially business and political ones, and high-level officials, constituted the political support base for this. They find relations with central countries to be more beneficial, potentially opening up opportunities for markets that are not found in other countries. In the perception of the Lula administration, the aim is to "maintain good political, economic and commercial relations with the great powers and at the same time *prioritize* [emphasis added] the ties with the South" (Lula da Silva, 2007). Objectively, the change in countries' weight in trade terms, China's rapid growth and the crisis in the USA since September 2008 suggest that this perception is up-to-date with structural changes that seem to be happening in the international economy.

The attitude of relative autonomy, in some cases of disagreement with the United States, and the silent proclamation of regional leadership are signs that fit into the autonomy through diversification notion. The changes brought about in the international environment because of American unilateralism, consolidated by the September 11 attack, served to strengthen the foreign policy espoused by the PT leaders who reached power in Brazil in 2003 (Alden and Vieira, 2005).

Lula's policy has risks and in part demonstrates the new geography of world power and of the world economy. Using Brazilian foreign trade figures, important though unable to explain the complexity of the scenario, we see that imports from the traditional markets (United States, European Union, Japan, Canada, Mexico and Mercosur) decreased from 79.3 percent to 67.2 percent of the total, between 2002 and 2005. As for non-traditional markets (China, Asia-Pacific, Africa, Eastern Europe, Middle East, etc.), their share increased from 19.7 percent to 31 percent over the same period (Prates, 2005/2006: 138). This reflects a specific worldview and represents risks, through the lack of attention to traditional international interlocutors, but is not colliding with the new tendencies of the twenty first century's international scenario. One of these tendencies is Asia's growing importance. The other is the delay in negotiations for the establishment of free trade areas (with the European Union and the FTAA) because the Lula administration seems to believe there is a possibility of keeping close relationships with core countries without conceding too much in order to establish asymmetrical free trade agreements. There are possible obstacles to this strategy, for instance, the difficulty in strengthening Mercosur and the partnership with

Argentina. Similarly, the lack of a strong and consistent development project for Brazil and Mercosur, which would demand a well-equipped State to put into practice, could place obstacles in the way of the country (and the region) fully benefiting from the changes taking place in the world in terms of the new geography of political and economic power.

CONCLUDING REMARKS: THE CARDOSO AND LULA FOREIGN POLICIES

In comparison with Cardoso's, Lula's foreign policy has elements of change with continuity as expressed by Lafer (2001b: 108). The Lula administration did not drift away from the historic principle on which Brazilian diplomacy is based, that of being an instrument of economic development and the consequent preservation of and increase in the country's autonomy. There are ideological and strategy changes to deal with problems brought about by the condition of underdevelopment, yet they are not essentially different from the problems faced by President Cardoso (see Table 5.1).

Analyzing the two governments' positions clearly indicates that Lula seeks strategic partners in the South in order to have more bargaining power in international negotiations. Moreover, this is owed to changing relationships in the world. There are structural limitations if the project is to be taken further. The objective of partial coordination of actions by different countries to act in concerted fashion on the international arena seems hard to achieve, as shown, for instance, by the difficulties existing between Mercosur and the Union of South American Nations (UNASUR) in terms of coordination. The economic costs, the small number of diplomats and the relatively low capacity—including in business and academic terms—for producing policies and enabling complex negotiations can impair the government's project. Political ability is necessary to interact with audiences as diverse as, for instance, the participants of the Davos World Economic Forum, the G-8 meeting in Gleneagles and of the Porto Alegre World Social Forum. But it is far from clear whether the demand for a fairer international order, which is present in most of the Lula's speeches, will come through. More importantly, Brazil's role in this "future new world" is not self-evident.

Results may well surface if the autonomy through diversification strategy is used successfully in the long term, consolidating historic Brazilian development goals and a less asymmetrical distribution of world power.

According to Lima (1990; 2005), the ideas of dependency and of autonomy are inherent to the international relations of middle powers. Being on an intermediate level of power, these countries' patterns of behavior vary. Sometimes

Table 5.1. Differences and similarities between the Cardoso and Lula foreign policies

Brazilian Foreign Policy Agenda	*Cardoso Administration*	*Lula Administration*
1. FTAA	Despite not considering it a priority for Brazil, the government did demonstrate a favorable posture. The strategy was to delay negotiations and only sign the agreement if it were favorable to the country.	Began negotiating in more demanding fashion, with the argument that negotiations would only move forward if Brazilian demands were met.
2. Fighting World Hunger	Not present on the Brazilian agenda during the Cardoso administration.	Gained the spotlight in Lula's international statements, especially in the beginning of his term, but did continue. Attempted to formally introduce it onto the international agenda, with dubious results.
3. UN Security Council	Wanted a permanent seat on the UN Security Council, but not enough effort was put into this objective by Brazilian diplomacy. Cardoso got to the point of declaring that he would prefer deepening regional integration and having a seat on the G-7.	Minister Celso Amorim firmly expressed the country's wish to obtain a permanent seat on the Security Council. The efforts put into this objective have been considerable. Brazil's mission to Haiti is an attempt to prove to the international community that the country is ready to be a permanent Council member.
4. South–South Cooperation	The Cardoso administration prioritized relations with developed countries, mainly the European Union and the United States. The approximation to large southern countries sought material benefits, principally in the field of trade. At the end of his second term, the government focused on improving relations with China, India, Russia and South Africa. In the case of	The approximation with the countries of the South has been given much emphasis in the Lula administration. Attention is paid to a more lasting relationship with developing countries. This was brought about by the worldview and ideological roots of the PT, partly in consonance with a tendency already in existence among some of the diplomatic corps. A partnership between Brazil,

(Continued)

Table 5.1. (*Continued*)

Brazilian Foreign Policy Agenda	*Cardoso Administration*	*Lula Administration*
	the pharmaceutical patent dispute with the United States, Brazil became closer to India and South Africa, but did not institutionalize this partnership.	India and South Africa was institutionalized, covering themes such as security, trade and technological exchanges. The results are still uncertain. The G-20, a group of developing countries seeking the liberalization of the agricultural trade and open markets for manufactured goods in developed countries, has gained visibility during the Lula administration. Such a coalition has a purpose: the reduction of economic and power asymmetries.
5. United States	The Cardoso administration based itself on the logic of active participation in international regimes, in which the US retained a key role. The Brazilian president developed personal relations with President Clinton. At the end of his term, already in the George W. Bush administration, especially after September 11, President Cardoso began criticizing US unilateralism. In this new phase, new commercial partnerships were sought with large developing nations to counterbalance the commercial power of the United States.	Recognizing the United States as the world's richest and most powerful nation, the Lula government's foreign policy has opted to deepen relations with big developing countries and with the European Union in an attempt to reduce the power asymmetry in relation to the US powerhouse. It has also sought to increase the country's bargaining power by diversifying its strategic options, such as strengthening Mercosur and Mercosur–European Union negotiations. With the European Union, results have not been good. In this context, the Lula administration has avoided confrontations with the United States.

Table 5.1. (*Continued*)

Brazilian Foreign Policy Agenda	*Cardoso Administration*	*Lula Administration*
6. Latin American Integration	South American regional integration has been on the Brazilian agenda since the country's return to democracy in 1985. In the Cardoso administration, Mercosur and regional integration were seen as an instrument Brazil could use to fight for more economic and political space in the world. There were difficulties with the Menem administration, but the idea of integration was consolidated.	The Lula administration remains interested in Mercosur and is strongly focused on the Union of South American Nations (UNASUR) project. Political relations with the Kirchner administrations have been good. Trade matters always lead to conflicts and negotiations. There is a rhetorical emphasis on the role of the region, especially demonstrated by the development of the Initiative for the Integration of Regional Infrastructure in South America (IIRSA). Integration is at the top of the country's agenda. In the Lula administration, emphasis has been put on maintaining a balance in relations with other countries, to capitalize on the apparent convergence in relation to integration and to avoid worsening potentially conflictive situations.
7. Brazilian Leadership	The Cardoso administration believed that leadership is not proclaimed, but exercised. In this sense, the issue of Brazilian leadership did not receive much attention.	The Lula administration has put the theme up for political debate, though not ostensibly. The wish to obtain a distinguished role among developing countries was introduced. On the other hand, certain South American countries, like Bolivia and Paraguay, are demanding much more from Brazil.

they are similar to those of weak countries. Sometimes they reflect standards of stronger nations. The variability of Brazilian conduct does not imply that it acts in an irrational fashion or that it does not pursue its interests, but suggests that "power is to be measured according to specific issues," hence questioning the notion of a single general power structure irrespective of thematic area (Lima, 1990: 11). Based on this and on the analysis of Lula's foreign policy, we can also say that the search for more balanced relations with rich countries does not result in ruptures with them.

Therefore, we emphasize the fact that the notion of autonomy through diversification, while not hegemonic among all social sectors that take an interest in foreign policy, is central in the eyes of key policymakers, especially Lula, Amorim, Pinheiro Guimarães and Garcia. Their approach is largely supported by Brazil's intellectuals and mass social movements, as well as part of the business community, all imbued with a worldview opposed to unilateralism.

Chapter 6

The Dilemmas of Regional Integration for Brazil

Autonomy and Diversification of Partners

INTRODUCTION

Brazil's position in the regional integration process must be understood in the light of structural and historical factors in the country's foreign policy. The constraints placed upon this process include not only economic issues and diverging views among the main Mercosur countries. There also seems to be some tension between the structural requirements for regional integration and the attitudes and positions of major social actors (elites and interest groups) and government players, such as the Presidency of the Republic and various ministries—not just the Ministry of Foreign Relations.

We may consider that two very important concepts used in foreign policy-making, namely diversification of partners and autonomy, both deeply rooted in civil society and the State, come together in the construction of a view of regional insertion that hinders the deepening of Mercosur.

Objective reasons explain the difficulties faced by Mercosur throughout its twenty-year existence. One of these reasons is, for example, the challenge of integrating developing countries with significant asymmetries among them, low interdependence and a tradition of macroeconomic instability. The argument presented by the Alfonsín, Sarney, Collor de Mello, Menen, Itamar Franco, and Cardoso administrations was that the low level of institutionalization and the intergovernmental character of the regional integration process—driven and controlled by the executive branches of the member countries—would ensure rapid progress, bypassing heavy bureaucracies. Brazil advocated the view that Mercosur should be based on relations between national governments. This position was not very different from that of Argentina and stemmed from the conception of the role that Mercosur was supposed to play in the country's international relations as a whole.

For some foreign policy-makers, the notion of diversifying partnerships has to do with the country's specific geographic, ethnic and cultural features. According to Lafer (2004), this idea reflects the multiple interests of the State and society, the historical and political affinities; it symbolizes the interest in diversifying international relations as much as possible and in creating plural, broad, extended channels of dialogue with the rest of the world.

The hypothesis of this chapter is that, from 1991 to 2009, Mercosur structure has suited the interests of part of the Brazilian elites. This model has been sufficient to bolster the country's international actions in the World Trade Organization (WTO) and its relations with the European Union (EU) and the United States, freeing the country from the constraints imposed by a customs union or a common market. From this perspective, a more robust institutional setting would limit the action of all States-parties, especially Brazil despite the power asymmetry in the latter's favor. This integration model is therefore consistent with an enlargement of the trade bloc, by making it possible to include new members such as Venezuela. The advantages of not having an institutional framework self-enforce Mercosur's intergovernmental nature and the low engagement between national policies of member countries.

In the mid-1980s, when Brazilian policy set out to strengthen its ties with Argentina, the idea of diversifying partnerships was not discarded, but rather gained new meaning. There was an attempt to intertwine national interests with the regional interest of the Southern Cone. In the case of Brazil, the prevailing idea was that the national interest would be better served by a regional integration process. The same was true in Argentina. Initially, this process incorporated not only the interests of the States, but of the business elites as well. Later on, labor unions and other groups, such as intellectuals, were to take part in the debate on regional integration.

While the notions of national and regional interest were aligned with one another by means of Mercosur, the concept of autonomy took on an essential role (Guimarães, 2006). Therefore, we may observe that "the definitions of autonomy vary through time and space; they vary according to interests and positions of power" (Fonseca, Jr., 1998: 361). From the 1930s to the second half of the 1980s, the idea of autonomy meant Brazil making its own choices individually, without constraints imposed by the great powers. Even though this notion was not possible, it was presented as an objective by various nationalist groups, as discussed in chapter 1. This outlook on autonomy was shared by the military, intellectuals, business groups, bureaucrats, unionists, schools of thought, such as the Military Club (during part of the 1950s), the Higher Institute of Brazilian Studies (ISEB), the formulators of the Independent Foreign Policy (PEI) and of Responsible Pragmatism, among others. In the 1990s and 2000s, an updated and modernized version of these ideas pervaded the Workers' Party (PT) of President Lula da Silva and other political forces in Brazil. Mercosur was not, and is not, seen as a factor limiting the country's autonomy. On the contrary, finding common ground with countries in the region was supposed to increase Brazil's ability to act internationally. Therefore, our objective is to discuss how these two concepts (autonomy and diversification of partnerships) were processed. From our perspective, there was a movement toward establishing, or reestablishing, the meaning of the notion of autonomy. The foreign policy outlined by this movement has reduced the significance of Mercosur, especially the importance of relations with Argentina. This helps explain the crisis of this regional trade bloc and the difficulties it has faced in affirming itself.

In analyzing Mercosur, we pay special attention to the role of Brazil and, to a lesser extent, to that of Argentina. The great importance of these two countries to the integration process is due to their economic significance, which is much greater than that of the two other member countries, Uruguay and Paraguay. Therefore, Brazil will be highlighted not only because this is the main purpose of this book, but also because it is the main economic power in the region.

First, we provide the economic and cognitive reasons for Mercosur's poor institutional development throughout its twenty years of existence. Second, we address the position of the Brazilian elites that have advocated a Mercosur with a low level of integration.

THE MEANING OF MERCOSUR: REASONS FOR ITS NON-INSTITUTIONALIZATION

In the 1980s, as discussed in chapter 2, the country's economic development model was reexamined, including relations with the rest of the world. Among the factors contributing to this reexamination were the exhaustion of the import substitution industrialization model, the foreign debt crisis (Figure 2.2 and Table 2.1), high inflation (Table 3.1), economic stagnation; particularly in the early 1990's (Figure 2.1), and reduced foreign investments (Figure 6.1), which began to recover during the Cardoso administration as of 1995.

With the global ascendancy of neoliberal values, various studies on international economic relations were conducted in the two last years of the

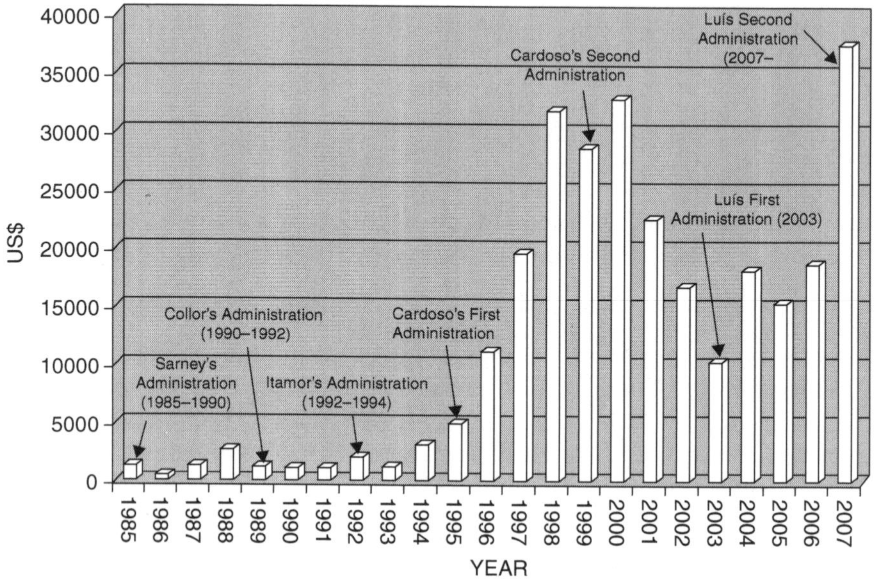

Figure 6.1. The evolution of Brazilian Foreign Direct Investure (FDI) 1985/2007. *Sources:* World Bank and UNCTAD.

Sarney administration, chiefly by the Foreign Trade Department (Cacex) of the Bank of Brazil. This period concurred with the GATT Uruguay Round and, more precisely, began with the Montreal Ministerial Conference, held in December, 1988 (Bresser Pereira, 1992; Campos Mello, 2000). A critical view of national-developmentalism prevailed in these studies, leading the way to a perspective in favor of a more open economy. This perspective later guided the enhanced foreign trade liberalization process of the Collor de Mello administration.

In the beginning, the integration process with Argentina[1] was based on the developmentalist logic, aiming to promote business competition with a view to the country's modernization and competitive insertion in the international economic system (Peña, 1991). During this phase, the perception that finding common ground would improve international insertion gained strength among part of the Brazilian elite, including business groups and top officials. Even when the Treaty of Integration, Cooperation and Development was signed (November 1988), laying the bases for Mercosur and providing stability and strength to the Argentina–Brazil alliance, the prevailing perspective was an inter-governmental one.

In the process of reviewing foreign policy and international economic relations—which was being conducted within government agencies such as the Ministry of Finance, the Bank of Brazil, the Central Bank and gradually by Brazil's diplomats—the approximation between Brazil and Argentina was seen as essential for Brazilian foreign policy. It gained advocates among part of the diplomatic corps and was linked to the universalist paradigm strategy (Flecha de Lima, 1989: 30–31). This approximation strengthened the idea of a better political and economic presence in the world and conferred greater agenda power to its members in the formulation of international regimes and institutions. For some, making progress in the regional integration process would enhance the ability of the alliance to engage with the powerhouses, especially with the United States (Amorim and Pimentel, 1996). These perspectives allowed the pro-integration alliance to make intra-bureaucratic agreements viable and to gain support from various segments of society. The alliance was made up of sectors of the nationalist tradition and also of those who wished to enhance Brazil's insertion in the liberal international order.

This is how the connection between regional integration, Mercosur and the alliance with Argentina, on the one hand, and the preservation of the values of partnership diversification and autonomy, on the other, was established. Regionalism would not diminish, but rather reinforce Brazil's universalist paradigm of international insertion. The notion of modernizing by internationalizing, which directly impacted the international insertion paradigm during the 1990s, did not clash with the notion of regionalism. The concept of open regionalism was used with the purpose of achieving full international insertion, taking advantage of the benefits of a free trade area and, as of 1995, of a customs union. The instruments required to achieve sustainable integration were not created, namely public actions aimed at social and economic development and measures to attenuate the large inequalities between and within States. The idea of autonomy remained deeply rooted in business and government, but now under the aegis of the autonomy through participation concept (Fonseca Jr., 1998). However, the initial business momentum, particularly in the export-oriented automotive industry, was not sustained.

Hence, the notion of autonomy was not ruled out by the Mercosur in the 1990s. Instead, it acquired different manifestations, in much the same way it did in relation to rich countries, with which Brazil sought to establish stronger ties—as they were considered economically and politically crucial—without putting aside essential national interests (Cardoso, 2001). Paradoxically, in Brazil–Mercosur relations, the idea of autonomy was expressed by insistently highlighting the country's potential to take action free from the constraints associated with institutionalized integration.

Lafer (1993b) talks about Brazil's need to engage more actively in the international scenery. From 1985 to the end of the 1990s, relations with Argentina gained prominence in Brazil's international agenda. At the same time, in the Cardoso administration, especially from 1999, there was increased concern for diversifying partnerships, by giving attention to other countries (such as China, India and South Africa) rather than focusing exclusively on the rich countries, Argentina and Mercosur.

Mercosur is clearly seen as an ambiguous option from the Brazilian perspective, which is not essentially different from the Argentinean point of view. Mercosur was a top international priority, according to the government's rhetoric,[2] and was presented as a very important instrument, but not as an end in itself. This was explicitly stated when Mercosur was founded:

> When the four presidents signed the Treaty of Asunción, they shared the same perception, namely that deepening the integration process could be the key to a more competitive insertion of their countries in a world divided into large consolidated economic blocs and where technological-industrial progress was becoming increasingly crucial for national economies (MRE, 1991: 279).

In fact, the instrumental logic became stronger and prevalent. According to Minister of Foreign Relations Luiz Felipe Lampreia (1995–2001):

> Mercosur is essentially an internationally open process. In the case of Brazil, developing Mercosur is part of a broad effort to open the economy, liberalize trade and better insert the country in the world economy. The integration process is not conceived of as an end in itself, but rather as an instrument to broaden Brazil's engagement in the global market (Lampreia, 1995: 135).

Mercosur did not develop evenly through time. Three distinct phases may be pointed out. The first one, which preceded President Cardoso's first term and went from 1991 to 1994 (from the Treaty of Asunción to the Ouro Preto Protocol), was characterized by the consolidation of the bloc's institutional design. The second phase, which went from 1995 to 1998, witnessed the ongoing expansion of trade within the bloc up to its maximum level. And finally, as of 1999, Mercosur entered a period of crisis because of the Brazilian currency (real) devaluation and the Argentinian recession that followed in 2001/2002. In addition to the temporary factors, which included frequent trade and political disputes, other reasons should be considered in the search for consistent explanations to the problems faced by the bloc: structural issues related to the economies of the countries involved and deep-rooted values in the States and societies, such as democracy, the self-perception of the country's position in the world, cultural affinities and others.

National crises were not seen as moments for adjustments in the integration process or to seek new opportunities. On the contrary, these crises weakened the integration process and reduced the efforts toward complementarity.

The difficulties faced by domestic economies enhanced objections to Mercosur among business groups and some sectors of the elites. Nevertheless, material elements alone do not explain the difficulties faced by the trade bloc to lay down its institutional underpinnings. The fact that Brazil and Argentina had alternated trade deficits between them contributed to the perception that regional integration could be detrimental to local economies. Each time a trade deficit appeared in any country, the advocates of protectionism would raise their voices. In the Brazilian case, the Argentinean foreign debt default in 2001 reignited the always latent and deep-rooted conception according to which Mercosur represented a narrow perspective for Brazil's economic and political potential. On the other hand, Brazil's surplus, after the devaluation of the real in January 1999, was pointed out in Argentina as one of the main causes of the country's own crisis at the end of 2001. Then, the devaluation of the peso, which had remained pegged to the US dollar from 1991 to 2001, made the Argentinean GDP fall by 10.9% (Kume and Piani, 2005), strengthening the Brazilian belief that macroeconomic instability does not offer a solid base for integration.

Mercosur experience suggests that the economic benefits of integration are necessary, but not enough to ensure its institutional consolidation. The perception that one of the partners stands to gain more from the integration process is detrimental to Mercosur consolidation efforts. If this is true for Argentina and Brazil, the same may be said for Paraguay and Uruguay. Therefore, elements of the realist perspective of international relations, which prevailed in South American relations for centuries, have not disappeared completely.

AUTONOMY AND DIVERSIFICATION: THE POSITION OF THE BRAZILIAN ELITES IN MERCOSUR

Brazilian diplomacy played a significant role in the integration model that was built through the years and was characterized by a low level of institutionalization. This position was shared in Brazil by different agencies and ministries, entrepreneurs, Congress, state governors, etc. As stated by Vaz (2002: 223), this Brazilian position was not essentially different from that of Argentina:

> Given its prevailing weight in the bloc, Brazil was not interested in giving up sovereignty to a supranational agency that would weaken its ability to make decisions and defend national interests within the bloc, whose importance for the country went well beyond trade. For Argentina, in terms of economic and trade policy, giving up sovereignty meant definitively losing any degree of freedom to conduct its own trade policy, which was precisely what the Argentinian government was trying to preserve at that moment.

For Mariano (2007: 194), Brazil showed a behavioral pattern that was "based on the search for autonomy, as an essential principle, and development, as a core objective." Vigevani et al (2004) and Wanderley and Vigevani (2005) have been able to measure how poorly state and municipal governments in Brazil adapted and were open to international and integration issues. Regional political and administrative elites were found to disregard these issues as pertaining to their scope of action. This has had major consequences for national policies and parliamentary representation. Matters clearly related to regional integration have not been linked to national issues, such as fiscal reform, for example. This strengthened those in Brazil who strived to maintain a certain degree of autonomy. Pinheiro (2000: 326–327) considers that the commitment of the Brazilian State to engage in international issues varies according to the power resources at hand. Brazil's position as to its geographical surroundings is thought to follow the logic of obtaining gains and advantages based on relatively asymmetric relations.

During the first years of the integration process, as one can see in the minutes of the Common Market Group,[3] there were signs of reasonable interest in enhancing Mercosur's institutionalization. In 1992, the Group approved the agenda of the Finance Ministers and Central Bank governors, which was intended to address the "economic situation and the analysis of the convergence of domestic economic policies" (GMC, 1992: 18). However, as of 1996 and 1997, specific trade problems, together with international insertion issues, bolstered the argument according to which Mercosur is a factor limiting the country's ability to diversify partnerships, especially within the Federation of Industries of the State of São Paulo (FIESP), the National Confederation of Industry (CNI), agribusiness organizations, top officials and the press. The objective reasons contributing to this inflection included the progress made in the negotiations for the creation of the FTAA (Free Trade Area of the Americas), the negotiations for the onset of a new WTO Round and the beginning of a discussion on the role of BRIC countries (Brazil, Russia, India and China). Although these negotiations or guidelines were not necessarily meant to weaken Mercosur, this was what they ended up doing because the notion of integration was never assimilated by Brazilian elites as a whole or by the general population.

The major international changes impacting States should be considered for one to understand the evolution of the Brazilian position in the regional integration process and in Mercosur. On the one hand, as clearly shown by the 2008 financial crisis, the economic power of the United States has diminished. On the other, the significance of other countries and regions has been enhanced, including that of South American countries. The dramatic growth of Asia in general and China in particular has had a dramatic impact, the dimension of which was unforeseeable in the early 1990s. Since 1985, when Argentina and Brazil strengthened relations, or since the creation of Mercosur in 1991, the international economic and political geography has changed profoundly. Waltz (2000: 30, 32) states: "Theory enables one to say that a new balance of power will form but not to say how long it will take. [. . .] In the meantime, the all-but-inevitable movement from unipolarity to multipolarity is taking place not in Europe but in Asia."

The restructuring of world power (Velasco e Cruz, 2007) in the 2000s—as shown by the above-average development of non-central countries such as India, Russia, South Africa and China—and the changes in the composition of Brazil's foreign trade contributed to a weakened role for regional integration in the international insertion project of the Brazilian elites and State. Both from the liberal and national-developmentalist perspective, Mercosur carries on being an important platform of Brazilian foreign policy. However, interests began to shift and corporate and government actions started to focus on other directions. According to Guimarães (2006: 275), "it is essential to work consistently and persistently in favor of a multipolar world system in which South America becomes one of the poles, rather than continuing to be just a sub-region of another economic and political pole."

As mentioned before, the evolution of trade within the bloc was highly significant from 1985 to 1998. Brazil's exports to future Mercosur countries increased from 3.86% of total exports in 1985 to 17.37% in 1998. In that same period, imports increased from 4.88% to 15.19% of the total (CEPAL, 2003). In addition to the evident importance of this evolution, the quality of Brazilian trade within the zone also evolved favorably, as the share of higher added-value products and services reached significant percentages.

Figures 6.2, 6.3, and 6.4 show the changes that took place in the composition of Brazil's foreign trade from 1989 to 2007; they show the evolution of imports and exports, as well as the trade balances achieved during that period. It is interesting to analyze trade data divided by country to see how Brazilian import and export percentages evolved for each Mercosur country, as well as for China and India, as shown in Tables 6.1 and 6.2. In the case of India, despite the efforts to strengthen international relations between both countries and their joint actions in the G-20 and IBSA, bilateral trade has not increased significantly. In contrast, trade between Brazil and China has taken a dramatic leap, which contributed to changing the economic profile of the country's international relations. In 2008, China was Brazil's second most important trade partner and continued to gain weight in 2009. Considering only its trade with China, Brazil is basically a commodity-exporting country.

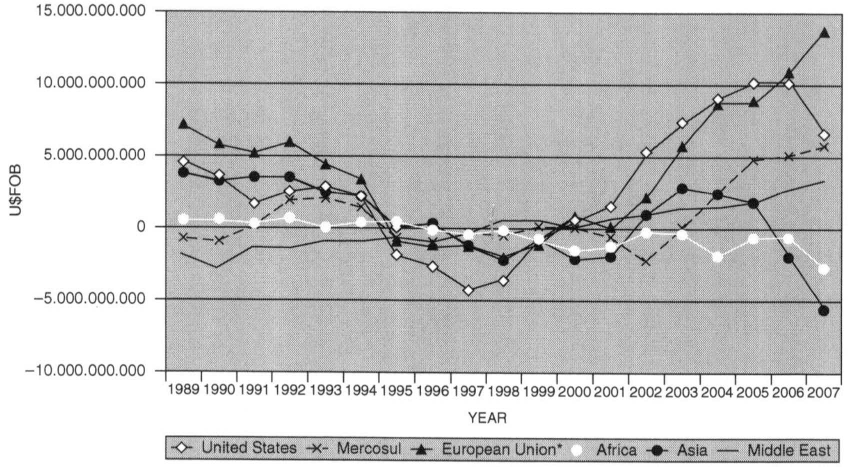

Figure 6.2. Share of Brazilian International Trade–Selected Country and Regions - 1989/2007.

The factors of international insertion are numerous, but the most important ones include capital, technology, values and cultural flows, as well as power relations. Trade is a factor of major importance, and the reasonably diversified destinations and origins of Brazil's foreign trade tend to underpin the arguments in favor of diversifying partnerships as part of the country's foreign policy. In 2007, Brazil's total foreign trade reached US$281 billion. The main individual trade partner was the United States, reaching a total of approximately US$44 billion in trade, that is, 16% of Brazil's total. The

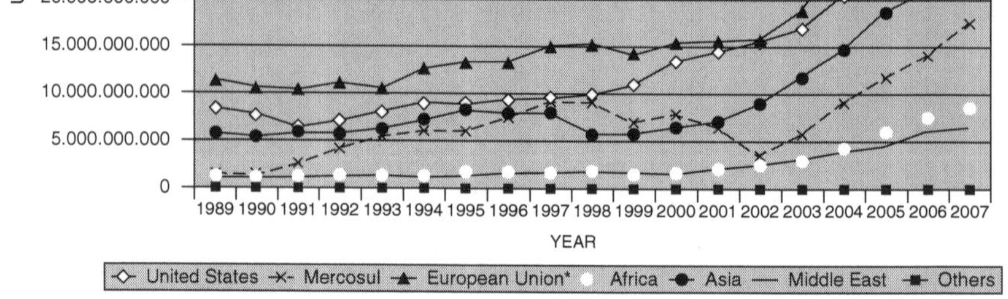

Figure 6.3. Brazilian Exports–Selected Country and Regions - 1989/2007.

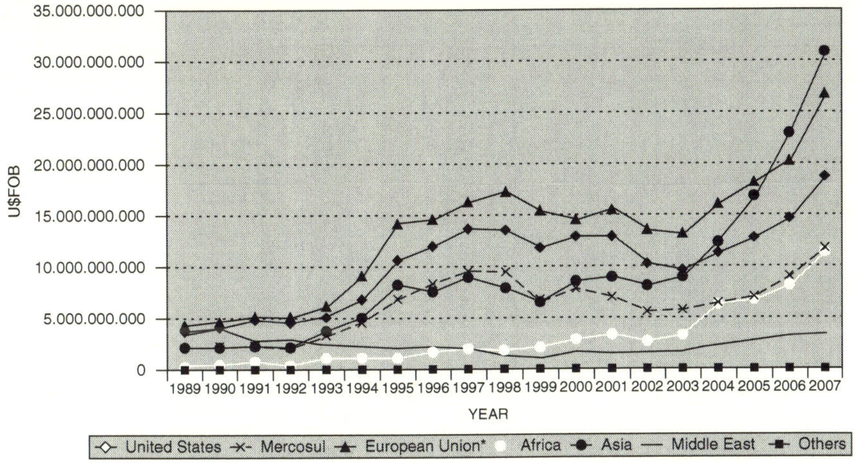

Figure 6.4. Brazilian Imports–Selected Country and Regions - 1989–2007.

second trading partner was Argentina, reaching a total of US$24.8 billion, almost 9%. Total trade flow between China and Brazil was US$23.3 billion, more than 8%. The long-term trade flows in Figure 6.4 show that imports from Asia have evolved most significantly. As shown in Table 6.2, the share of imports from China among total Brazilian imports increased from

Table 6.1. Brazil—Exports (% of Total)

Year (1989–2007)	*Argentina*	*Paraguay*	*Uruguay*	*China*	*India*
1989	2.10%	0.94%	0.97%	1.83%	0.58%
1990	2.05%	1.21%	0.94%	1.22%	0.53%
1991	4.67%	1.57%	1.07%	0.72%	0.52%
1992	8.49%	1.52%	1.44%	1.29%	0.42%
1993	9.49%	2.47%	2.01%	2.02%	0.32%
1994	9.50%	2.42%	1.68%	1.89%	1.43%
1995	8.69%	2.80%	1.75%	2.59%	0.69%
1996	10.83%	2.77%	1.70%	2.33%	0.39%
1997	12.77%	2.65%	1.64%	2.05%	0.31%
1998	13.20%	2.44%	1.72%	1.77%	0.28%
1999	11.17%	1.55%	1.39%	1.41%	0.65%
2000	11.32%	1.51%	1.22%	1.97%	0.39%
2001	8.60%	1.24%	1.11%	3.27%	0.49%
2002	3.89%	0.93%	0.68%	4.18%	1.08%
2003	6.25%	0.97%	0.56%	6.20%	0.76%
2004	7.66%	0.91%	0.70%	5.64%	0.68%
2005	8.39%	0.81%	0.72%	5.78%	0.96%
2006	8.52%	0.90%	0.73%	6.10%	0.68%
2007	8.97%	1.03%	0.80%	6.69%	0.60%

Source: Banco Central, 2008

Table 6.2. Brazil—Imports (% of Total)

Year (1989–2007)	*Argentina*	*Paraguay*	*Uruguay*	*China*	*India*
1989	6.78%	1.96%	3.25%	0.70%	0.19%
1990	6.62%	1.56%	2.83%	0.83%	0.08%
1991	13.88%	2.54%	4.57%	1.40%	0.23%
1992	8.42%	0.95%	1.47%	0.57%	0.14%
1993	10.76%	1.09%	1.53%	1.21%	0.36%
1994	11.07%	1.07%	1.72%	1.40%	0.27%
1995	11.19%	1.03%	1.48%	2.08%	0.34%
1996	12.76%	1.04%	1.77%	2.12%	0.35%
1997	13.29%	0.87%	1.62%	1.95%	0.36%
1998	13.90%	0.61%	1.81%	1.79%	0.37%
1999	11.81%	0.53%	1.31%	1.76%	0.35%
2000	12.27%	0.63%	1.08%	2.19%	0.49%
2001	11.17%	0.54%	0.91%	2.39%	0.98%
2002	10.04%	0.81%	1.03%	3.29%	1.21%
2003	9.68%	0.98%	1.11%	4.45%	1.01%
2004	8.86%	0.47%	0.83%	5.91%	0.88%
2005	8.48%	0.43%	0.67%	7.27%	1.63%
2006	8.82%	0.32%	0.68%	8.75%	1.61%
2007	8.63%	0.36%	0.65%	10.46%	1.79%

Source: Banco Central, 2008

0.7% in 1989 to 10.46% in 2007. On the other hand, the share of exports to China grew from 1.83% to 6.69%. The political and strategic impact of such evolution could not be negligible. In Figure 6.2, we can see that Brazil's trade surplus was especially due to its balance of trade with the European Union, the United States and Mercosur. Trade with Argentina, which had recovered after the acute 1999–2002 crisis, does not reach again the 1998 peak, in relative terms. As shown in Figure 6.3 and 6.4, trade relations with Mercosur grew. As previously stressed, the region contributed significantly to the Brazilian surplus, especially considering the share of higher added-value products. Even so, the regional bloc lost market share in Brazil's total foreign trade.

The following items contributed to a shift in the interests of major private and public sector groups: global economic growth as of 2001 (in which Asia, and China in particular, played an essential role), Brazil's active engagement in WTO negotiations (using this organization to strengthen its positions) and the high price of commodities as of 2003 (Prates, 2005/2006). Brazil's behavior in the face of the 2008 financial and economic crisis suggests that the emphasis given to creating a multipolar global system and to ending unilateralism is supported by the perception that maximizing capabilities requires participating in various regional and multilateral fora. Brazil's active engagement in the financial G-20 talks and, at the same time, the difficulties to coordinate policies regionally have made this evident. At the close of the financial G-20 summit on Global Economy and Financial Markets that took place in Washington in November 2008, President Lula concluded: "given the political strength, the representation of the countries in the G-20, [. . .] there is no logic in making [global] decisions regarding the economy and politics without taking this forum into consideration" (*Gazeta Mercantil,* 2008a).

Although the emphasis on a universalist worldview was expected to generate positive externalities in terms of converging positions both in multilateral and regional fora, this has only been partially true. In the transition from the Cold War to an emerging world order, the decoupling of political and military supremacy from economic competitiveness has transformed foreign policy options into complex calculations, as trade and financial alliances do not necessarily coincide with the convergence of political views. Mercosur, the Union of South American Nations (UNASUR) and the relations with associate countries would be strengthened by the end of unilateralism and the establishment of multilateralism. Brazilian politics are strongly interested in regional integration, but moving forward in this process, especially in the case of Mercosur, is linked to the global setting.

Once the overall guidelines and perceptions underpinning the Brazilian regional integration policy have been understood, it is important to explain the political significance of relations with China, as they are economically and commercially important for the entire region. According to Vadell (2008), the weight of China in South American investments and trade has changed the expectations of domestic actors, as indicated by the change of direction in Brazil's foreign trade. A similar phenomenon is taking place in Argentina and other countries. León-Manríquez (2006) considers that expectations of these stakeholders with regard to China are high because now they see this country as an important option for national development. The type of economic relations that are taking place has also led to a certain degree of perplexity. Vadell (2008) points out the need to be attentive to the risk of specializing production in line with a center-periphery model. These risks may emerge both in a growth scenario—given the Chinese economy's enormous appetite for commodities—and in a global recession, like the one that began in 2008, in which the EU and US economies are contracting. In the latter scenario, important Brazilian business organizations such as Abicalçados (shoe manufacturers), Abimóvel (furniture manufacturers) and Sindivestuário (clothing manufacturers) fear an Asian move in search of new markets for their products, triggered by the economic recession and decreased demand in developed countries (*Gazeta Mercantil,* 2008b). Argentina is experiencing a similar situation, which is leading to protectionist actions with potential consequences for Mercosur itself.

Despite the risks pointed out, the opportunities that corporate and social groups may derive from engaging with China have consolidated a movement which does not converge directly with regional integration, as its benefits do not depend on complementary regional production systems. In some cases, trade surpluses with China, which are important for Argentina, may feed a phenomenon classified as a modern form of national-developmentalism (Godio, 2006). In the Brazilian case, the balance of trade has altered between surpluses and deficits. By means of its unrivaled growth, China encourages strategic reorientations in others, be it in the high technology industry (for example, Embraer's airplanes, satellite launching) or in the commodity sector (for example, iron ore—Vale do Rio Doce Company).

As shown in Figures 6.2, 6.3 and 6.4, the increased trade balance of non-traditional markets (Africa, Asia, Eastern Europe, the Middle East and others) has not yet suffered a drastic change in recent years if compared with Mercosur. However, some countries in the South are receiving increasing attention from the elites and the Brazilian government for the reasons detailed above.

The perspective of benefits of scale for the economy and trade has encouraged stakeholders to focus resources on achieving access to major markets, which in turn fueled discussions about autonomy and diversifying partnerships that limited the progress of Mercosur process. The Lula da Silva administration has consolidated this focus on major markets without disregarding regional integration. The efforts deployed for Venezuela's full engagement in the trade bloc are explained by this perspective, which may potentially revitalize the regional integration process.

In the beginning of the twenty first century, the Nestor and Cristina Kirchner and Lula administrations held similar ideological positions (all presented themselves as reformist politicians with left-wing traits). Despite the shared political views, the deepening of Mercosur process has not materialized. Even though common policies were possible in specific cases, the overall level of identity has been insufficient to make irreversible progress in the regional integration process. In the Brazilian State's conceptual frame of reference, there is a concern about deepening regional integration, which is clearly visible in the Lula administration, but it has been unable to take on a more intense dynamic of its own.

> The cornerstone [of regional integration] is the bilateral relation with Argentina. The strong convergence between the viewpoints of presidents Lula and Kirchner in the most pressing matters we have faced was expressed in the "Buenos Aires Consensus," adopted in October, 2003. This document reflects our common

> aspiration for economic growth with social justice and manifests our determination to transform the Mercosur trading bloc [. . .] into a catalyst for building a shared future (Amorim, 2004: 158).

At the 2005 Summit of Heads of State of the Americas in Mar del Plata, Brazil and Argentina advocated postponing the FTAA negotiations, going against what seemed to be the interest of the United States. In the Brazilian case, regional integration difficulties cannot be attributed exclusively to the government. Society has shown little interest in strengthening Mercosur and, in some cases, has been openly against it. For example, at a meeting held in November 2004, during which business leaders from various industries and organizations such as FIESP, Abicalçados, Eletros (electronic consumer product manufacturers) and the Brazilian Foreign Trade Association (AEB), questioned in various ways the importance for Brazil of deepening the trade bloc. Among the business community, there is heated debate about the need to shift away from a still imperfect customs union back to a free trade area. According to the representatives of the above-mentioned organizations, Mercosur is an anchor that limits Brazil's ability to engage in international negotiations, hindering bilateral agreements with the United States and the European Union (*Valor Econômico,* 2004).

The analyses that resulted from the concerns of the private sector confirmed this tendency to assign declining significance to the integration process in Brazil. Some business groups are interested in weakening the role of Mercosur in the country's foreign policy and economic and international trade strategy. When society faces the problems that are inherent to the integration process, different types of resistance against Mercosur emerge, but few actions to improve it are proposed. The administration's position of maintaining Mercosur with a weak institutional framework seems to meet the average expectations and needs of the Brazilian elites, within and without the State.

MOTIVATIONS OF BRAZILIAN POLICY TOWARD SUPRANATIONALITY

As pointed out before, the concepts of autonomy and diversification of partnerships, defended by part of the elites and present in the institutional memory of the Ministry of Foreign Relations, lead to a certain questioning of Mercosur. Wendt (1994: 386) states that "collective identity is neither essential nor equivalent to such a multilateral institution but provides an important foundation for it by increasing the willingness to act on 'generalized principles of conduct' and diffuse reciprocity." The perception that Brazil will lose sovereignty and autonomy as the integration of the bloc is deepened continues to guide the actions of part of the State bureaucracy. Therefore, this option is rejected because it is thought to limit Brazil's room for maneuver in international negotiations around the globe, hindering its ability to diversify partnerships. Lima (1994; 2003) states that the pattern of Brazilian foreign policy is contrary to a deepening institutionalization of Mercosur, as the prevailing aspiration is to transform the country into a significant international player. There is also a belief in the specificity of the country (an idea also present in Argentina) in the Southern Cone context.

Given the objective of discussing the structural reasons underpinning the Brazilian integration policy, it is interesting to show the rationale underlying the Brazilian position, which advocates the principles of national autonomy and sovereignty. Pierson (1998) considers that national governments, when delegating specific functions to regional community institutions or agencies, over time, tend to lose control over the integration process to these institutions. Regional institutions or agencies may potentially open space to allow new domestic players to take part in the decision-making process without the intermediation of governments. This may tend to strengthen these regional entities and provide them with new sources of legitimacy. Once these institutions gain some authority in the integration process, member States find it difficult to roll back such changes, in order to recover their original power. Regaining power is unfeasible because the cost is too high. Gradually the dynamics of decision making in regional integration tend to become increasingly independent vis-à-vis nation-States. This is why the Brazilian government is not very willing to strengthen the trade bloc institutionally, that is, the State does not wish to lose control over the integration process.

The structure of the bloc, as defined by the 1991 Treaty of Asunción, centralizes decision-making power in the Common Market Council. This council is made up of member countries' presidents and ministers of finance and foreign affairs. On the other hand, the Common Market Group, which is made up of the deputy ministers or under-secretaries of foreign affairs, is in charge of the executive management of the integration process. This institutional engineering has been unsuitable to build an integrationist identity among member countries.

A more institutionalized Mercosur does not seem to interest a considerable part of the social, economic and regional elites, or the political world in Brazil, as the current structure seems to fully meet their needs. Although Mercosur objectives have been re-dimensioned, there is still an interest in expanding trade and, in some cases, increasing cross-border investments, as is the case with Petrobras, Itaú Bank, Bunge, Gerdau, AmBev, Techint and other national and multinational companies, especially from the automotive and food industries. The bloc continues to be significant in some important circumstances. It is useful in some relations with the United States, it is important to engage with the European Union, especially in the case of the WTO and in some negotiations with emerging countries, particularly in dialogues between trade blocs. Nonetheless, positions that some believe limit the options made possible by increased autonomy and a greater number of trade partners are avoided. Therefore, "The major obstacle for Brazil and Argentina to actually 'invest' in the Mercosur project is the ambiguity with which various sectors of both societies and governments assess the trade bloc, regardless of the pro-integration rhetoric" (Gonçalves and Lyra, 2003: 14).

FINAL REMARKS

Brazilian elites' aspirations of playing a leading and universalist role entail the need to be free to act at will in the international scene and not be restricted by regional agreements and obligations deriving from concessions that have to be made to minor partners (see Appendix 3). Regional integration is not rejected, on the contrary, it is believed to be beneficial, but without the costs of what Burges (2009) refers to as "cooperative economic growth." Our analysis suggests that there is not enough critical mass in Brazilian society to intensify the integration process. In the Lula administration, efforts have been made to offset this situation by trying to understand the drivers underpinning the interests of some of Brazil's neighbors. The Brazilian government has been able to maintain a balance between good international relations, based on democratic stability and national development, and the defense of national interests, as was seen in the negotiations with Bolivia as of 2006, because of the intervention of the Evo Morales administration in the gas industry. The same applies to Paraguay as of 2008, when the Fernando Lugo administration presented an agenda to renegotiate the Itaipú hydroelectric power plant treaty, to President Rafael Correa of Ecuador, and even to President Hugo Chavez of Venezuela. We believe that both the private and public sectors have hesitated to take on the costs of regional integration and to deal with the obstacles imposed by power asymmetries between Mercosur countries, even though the bloc is referred to as a priority of the foreign trade policy in official statements of the Presidency of the Republic and of the Ministry of Foreign Relations. According to Marcelo Mariano:

> Expansion combined with the government's low commitment to overcome the existing asymmetries led to an integration process that could not be very ambitious in terms of how deeply rooted it would be. Simultaneously, the limits imposed by a non-consolidated customs union and the inherent difficulties in

> managing the new demands arising from this situation may make the integration process unattractive to governments and major domestic stakeholders, creating a situation of deadlock that may strengthen anti-integration social forces. This seems to be the stage at which the bloc is at present (Mariano, 2007: 194).

In Brazil, there is little sensitivity to regional matters. This is owed, firstly, to the dimension that domestic problems acquire in a country of continental proportions; secondly, to the increasing importance attributed to global issues and agendas during the Cardoso administration and even more under Lula. "In Argentina, for worse or for better, Brazil is an issue: it is present in day-to-day life, a permanent subject in the press. In Brazil, however, Argentina arouses much less interest, except in moments of acute crisis" (Gonçalves and Lyra, 2003: 21).

For Brazilian society and local elites, understanding the prospects of the Mercosur has to do with the debate about Brazil's future position in the world. The need to better define whether regional integration is useful and important for Brazil has been strongly debated in the Lula da Silva administration. But what remains to be defined is the willingness to take on its costs. Normally a highly asymmetric integration process requires a paymaster (Mattli, 1999). In this case, Brazil would have to play such a role in South America. Therefore, it would be essential to analyze another topic: whether the country has the ability to play such a role. Poor countries face objective limitations to take on the costs of regional integration; they may not have the capacity to do so. Mattli (1999) states that the role of the paymaster is not only related to the economy, but also to delegating some functions to community institutions. This means accepting and trusting regional integration, by considering it a part of domestic policies. Some actions, such as the creation of the Mercosur Structural Convergence Fund (FOCEM),[4] initially with US$100 million, increased to US$250 million in 2008, were intended to strengthen regional integration, as was the creation of the Mercosur Parliament on May 7, 2007, replacing the Joint Parliamentary Commission. Nevertheless, the shyness of the economic and political actions, as shown by the scant resources of the FOCEM fund, seem to confirm the conclusion that the bloc is making very slow progress in terms of building an institutional framework. Differently from the analysis by Burges (2009), this is probably not merely owed to Brazil's selfish interest in being the leader with no compensation for the other countries involved. In the Lula da Silva administration, domestic criticism is more often made in precisely the opposite direction, highlighting Brazil's economic and political limitations.

A potential step back by Mercosur toward becoming a free trade area, a position advocated by significant social sectors in Brazil, would weaken the power of negotiation of both the country and the bloc in the international system. Greater institutionalization, as previously discussed, would entail costs for Brazil (for example, reduced international autonomy), but it is essential to consider the disadvantages of non-institutionalization and of an undefined situation that has prevailed since at least 1997, in the name of short-term economic and tariff-related interests.

Our analysis shows the need for agreements capable of making some degree of supranationality feasible (i.e., actions, rules and norms to ensure the deepening of the bloc). The Lula administration has shown that it is not against certain actions in this direction. This implies re-processing the concepts underpinning Brazilian policy, namely autonomy and diversification of partnerships, to enable them to absorb the principles of integration, including the notion of association of objectives (Nardin, 1987). This entails creating and promoting a culture that values long-term gains and accepts some short-term costs. If, as stated in official documents and statements, Mercosur is the basis of Brazil's international insertion strategy, the bloc would need to achieve higher levels of institutionalization.

Industrial and sectoral integration policies, actions to support regional production chains and improvements in institutional instruments—conceived in the 1980s when the 24 sector protocols were signed within the remit of the 1986 Economic Integration and Cooperation Program (PICE)[5]—would attenuate asymmetries and favor the allocation of resources where there is greater market potential.

NOTES

1. Iguaçu Declaration, November 1985; Economic Integration and Cooperation Program (PICE), June 1986; the 24 resulting Protocols; Treaty of Integration, Cooperation and Development, November 1988.

2. Andrés Malamud (2005), for example, tries to demonstrate that the rhetoric of intergovernmentalism is distant from the concrete achievements of Mercosur.

3. The Common Market Group is the executive body of Mercosur. Its basic duties are to enforce the Asunción Treaty and to pass resolutions required to implement the decisions made by the Council.

4. Mercosur Structural Convergence Fund was created by Mercosur Council to fund programs aimed at promoting the structural convergence, competitiveness and integration of South American countries.

5. The objective of the PICE was to provide a common economic space, with the selective opening of markets and incentives to the economic complementation of certain sectors in each country.

Chapter 7

Two Contrasting Types of Autonomy

Brazil–Venezuela Relations

INTRODUCTION

In this chapter, we examine Brazil's relations with Venezuela. This country is important to Brazilian foreign policy since it has great energy potential and is presided by a controversial figure, Hugo Chávez, who has been in office throughout Lula's two terms. Chávez has come closer to and diverged from Brazil at several points. Nevertheless, the friendly relations between the two countries do not mean the inexistence of differences. The analysis of these relations is important since it makes the specific foreign policy characteristics of President Lula's government more evident. The differences in interests and styles of the Brazilian and Venezuelan foreign policies could affect the strategy of autonomy by diversification initiated by Lula, since Chávez has presented different political alternatives that influence certain governments in Latin America. In Hugo Chávez's administration, Venezuela practices a foreign policy that, according to his own interpretation, promotes "a socialism of the twenty first century" (Urrutia, 2006: 159). Although the meaning of this catchphrase remains unclear, Chávez adopts an extreme rhetoric of autonomy through distance in relation to the United States (Zúquete, 2008). With regard to Brazil, due to aspects that may seem a partial and limited ideological identification between Chávez and Lula, there was an approximation over the last few years between the two countries, although there are differences in terms of their foreign policies. Economic relations have become more intense both in the trade and the investment aspect.

THE FIVE PHASES OF VENEZUELAN FOREIGN POLICY

Lima and Kfuri (2007) divide the history of Venezuelan foreign policy into five distinct phases. The first phase, from 1958 to 1967, was a period of democratic consolidation and establishment of the Betancourt Doctrine, which defined the non-recognition by the Venezuelan government of non-democratic governments resulting from *coups d'état*. During this period, diplomatic relations were interrupted with Brazil, Bolivia, Colombia, Argentina and Peru. This political posture, added to the economic demands of the oil trade, led Venezuela to establish a special relationship with the United States.

The next phase, from 1967 to 1980, marks the beginning of the reversal of the Venezuelan isolationist policy in relation to Latin America. Brazil cooperated with Venezuela by supporting the high oil price policy, which strengthened the Venezuelan diplomatic discourse of revaluation of the Third World's raw materials. This happened throughout Ernesto Geisel's government, from 1974 to 1978. On the other hand, Venezuela signed cooperation agreements with Brazil in April 1978 in the oil, petrochemical, mining and steel industry areas. Also in 1978, Venezuela accepted that the existence of regional agreements with the Andean Pact (of an economic nature) were not incompatible with agreements of a political character on the administration of natural resources, creating the conditions necessary for the signing of the Amazon Cooperation Treaty, a Brazilian initiative.

Venezuelan governments have long used oil to influence Andean countries, Central America and the Caribbean (Villa, 2007; Villa, 2006; Serbin, 2006). This policy was implemented in the first term of President Carlos Andrés Pérez (1974–1979) of Democratic Action (AD), a party with close ties to international Social Democracy. This was a period during which oil prices reached very high levels. The so-called "Brazilian economic miracle," a period of rapid economic growth particularly during the Emílio Garrastazu Médici (1969–1973) government, had led to suspicion on the part of Venezuelan elites, which foresaw disputes with Brazil over leadership in these regions. Unlike the Brazilian government project of political autonomy in relation to the United States, Venezuelan foreign policy over the course of practically the whole twentieth century defined as strategic the political partnership with the United States. This partnership characterized the third phase of Venezuelan foreign policy, from 1980 to 1988. At international forums, some Venezuelan governments, especially those of AD, stood out on account of third-worldist positions, without confronting directly the interests of central countries, particularly the United States.

Cooperation and reciprocity actions with Latin America were implemented in the 1980s. Brazil responded positively to an old Venezuelan proposal of creating a Latin American oil multinational, Petrolatina (Villa, 2006: 70). In Caracas, in 1981, Brazil signed a protocol to initiate the idea with Venezuela and Mexico. However, the Petrolatina project remained shelved until the Hugo Chávez administration, which began on February 2, 1999.

With Brazil's re-democratization, beginning in 1985 under President José Sarney, a new idea came into play: competitive international insertion would only be possible with South American regional integration, as analyzed in chapter 2. According to the Brazilian president, integration was the best route to three objectives: national development, defense of democracy and competitive international insertion. During the Sarney administration, the Brazilian government signed Cooperation Protocols with Argentina in 1986 and the Caracas Protocol with Venezuela in 1987, during the administration of AD President Jaime Lusinchi (1984–1988) (Villa, 2006: 71). During the administrations of Itamar Franco in Brazil and Rafael Caldera in Venezuela—the latter from the Committee of Independent Electoral Political Organization (COPEI) party, of Christian Democratic leanings—some of the bases for Brazil's South American integration project were laid. On Venezuela's part, Andean sub-regional integration and the national development project were strengthened, characterizing the fourth phase of Venezuelan foreign policy. This phase coincided with the crisis of the political system. Signs started appearing that the predominance of AD and COPEI was coming to an end, as Venezuela started oil exploration on the Orinoco Strip (Lima and Kfuri, 2007). These changes in foreign policy signaled that South American countries would turn away from national development models focused on expanding the domestic market and begin regional cooperation guided by the logic of autonomy through participation.

With regard to the debate on regional integration, particularly directed at the common Amazon border area, the Brazil–Venezuela project had three main goals:

1. developing border and energy integration actions
2. developing bilateral trade flows, and
3 increasing investments between the two countries with the creation of a South American free trade zone

To the Brazilian initiative "Development and Security in the Region to the North of the Solimões and Amazonas Rivers—Calha Norte Project," Venezuela would respond, in the mid 1990s, with the "Project for the Sustainable Development of the South" (Prodesur). The two had common objectives, such as improving the quality of life of local populations, environmental protection and the development of the economic potential of border regions (Villa, 2006:

72). In the Brazilian case, there was also a security concern. In Fernando Henrique Cardoso's second term, the BR-174 highway was reopened, with its Manaus–Santa Helena de Uairén (first Venezuelan border town) stretch connecting the two countries. Venezuela had already done its part by inaugurating the BC-8, by means of which electricity from the Venezuelan River Caroní power stations is supplied to Boa Vista. At that moment, Brazil already aimed at using regional integration as a tool for greater international insertion, characteristic of the autonomy through participation strategy that aimed at increasing cooperation and Brazil's South American presence. Since 1995, trade relations between Brazil and Venezuela have been intensifying significantly. Commercial flows increased between 1988 and 1995 (Cisneros *et al.*, 1998: 9). On the other hand, attracting Brazil as an investment partner for the Andean Development Corporation (financing body of the Andean Community of Nations) was part of the Venezuelan strategy.

The fifth and current phase of Venezuelan foreign policy, inaugurated by Hugo Chávez's "Bolivarian revolution," is a reaction to the policies prevailing throughout the second half of the twentieth century, deepened since the 1980s, and to the frustrations with the country's great dependence on the US oil market (Lima and Kfuri, 2007). The guidelines of Venezuelan foreign policy were set out by the 2001/2007 National Development Plan. This plan aims to promote the democratization of international society, Latin American and Caribbean integration, the strengthening of South–South relations and Venezuela's position in the world economy. In order to implement these policies, oil would be used as the basis for a "socialist" regional integration project (Lima and Kfuri, 2007). This project has three specific goals: (1) confronting the United States with an anti-hegemonic movement; (2) strengthening regional relations to build Latin American integration; and (3) creating the Bolivarian Alternative for the Americas (ALBA), a regional integration proposal with a socialist character, which appeared to counteract the FTAA.

An important instrument for the Chávez government to reach its objectives is the wide-ranging use of the media; the other important instrument is oil. Communication media are Hugo Chávez's worldwide political promotion instruments. They make his acts resonate both positively and negatively, consolidating him as a political character of the international system (Santoro and Valente, 2006). In the Brazilian case, the Lula administration has been accused by opposition parties of acting in the international system with positions that do not correspond to its economic and political realities. They see certain positions as unsustainable, such as seeking a permanent seat on the UN Security Council. To the Venezuelan opposition, and especially to the opponents of Chávez's policy, his words and actions do not always converge: "We know, for example, that the ease with which Chávez verbally attacks the United States is inversely proportional to the difficulty he would have in ceasing to supply oil to that country" (Santoro and Valente, 2006). The 2008–2009 financial crisis, when oil prices on the international market fell sharply, could make a more assertive foreign policy more difficult. The articulations of the Venezuelan government, especially as of 2001, demonstrate some influence, particularly ideological, over certain countries in the region, such as Cuba, Bolivia, Ecuador and more recently Paraguay and Nicaragua. Brazil's action, with the impediments discussed in chapter 6 is buttressed by economic formulations that aim at the rational use of resources, as has been visible in the discussions on the creation of a Bank of the South to fund South American development.

The creation of a South American free trade zone, including Central America and the Caribbean, has gained prominence for the Chávez administration. In this sense, Brazil started taking up a strategic place in Venezuelan foreign affairs, contributing to the process of approximation to Mercosur. Venezuelan trade diplomacy in the Chávez administration—continuing policies initiated in Rafael Caldera's second presidential term (1994–1998)—shifted its integration interests in the Amazon region, especially in relation to deepening commercial, energy and political ties with Brazil and Mercosur. The relationship between Venezuela and Brazil is favored by the Chávez administration's interest in joining Mercosur (Ministério de Relaciones Exteriores de Venezuela, 2005). At the July 2004 Mercosur Summit, Venezuela became the fourth associate member of the Mercosur (after Bolivia, Chile and Peru) from the Andean Community of Nations (CAN). Then, Venezuela signed the Protocol of Adhesion to Mercosur on July 4, 2006, becoming a member of the economic block that accounts for approximately 75% of Latin America's GDP. As a result, the country undertook to adopt the Mercosur Common External Tariff (TEC) by January 2010, with exceptions made for sensitive products (Sennes and Barbosa, 2007).

APPROXIMATION AND DIVERGENCES BETWEEN VENEZUELA AND BRAZIL

Brazil's attitude in condemning the coup d'état that tried and failed to overthrow Chávez in April 2002 (therefore still during the Cardoso government) strengthened the relations between the two countries. This gesture should be considered normal, reflecting the tradition of respect for the sovereignty of all States. Deepening the Cardoso government's line, the proposal of the Friends of Venezuela Group, that originated precisely at the moment of transition to the Lula administration in December 2002, helped transform three negative ideas regarding Brazil, deeply rooted among Venezuela's elites—namely, expansionism, distrust of the Brazilian regional integration plan and a peripheral view of Brazil in Venezuelan foreign policy—, into a positive image of the country. For Chávez's Venezuela, a prominent position means more than the quest for ideological confrontation with the United States and for domestic development. It is an attempt to build in the region the project of the Bolivarian revolution. In this sense, Chávez's strategy of insertion in Latin America is based on providing assistance to certain countries. An initiative along these lines was the agreement with Cuba whereby Venezuela undertook to supply oil in exchange for the services of Cuban doctors for its hospitals. According to the Venezuelan ambassador at the Organization of American States (OAS), "Oil can be, as our government realizes, a powerful lever to drive development, integration, cooperation, solidarity, and the economic complementary of our countries." (Valers, 2005) Through PetroCaribe, founded in 2005, Venezuela committed to supplying US$17 billion worth of subsidized oil over the following 10 years to member-countries in Central America and the Caribbean. This program put Venezuelan aid on the same level as that of OECD countries such as Australia, Belgium, Denmark, Norway, Portugal, Spain and Switzerland (Burges, 2007: 1347). For its part, PDVSA (Petróleos de Venezuela SA, the Venezuelan State oil company) sought a partnership with Petrobras (Brazilian State oil company), one of the largest multinationals in the Western Hemisphere.[1] Although the partnership between these two companies is an aspect of potential cooperation between Brazil and Venezuela, the ambitious project to create a "gas pipeline linking all countries in South America," with a "minimum price tag of $20 billion" made many industry insiders consider the project too big and of doubtful feasibility (Burges, 2007: 1348). With its oil money, Venezuela also sought to support Argentina, buying US$1.3 billion worth of its bonds soon after President Nestor Kirchner completely restructured his country's debt (*The Economist,* October 26, 2006). Brazil–Venezuela relations in the oil sector became stronger with the maintenance of Petrobras investments in Venezuelan oil fields and the continuation of negotiations aimed at different forms of cooperation. Other Brazilian companies operate in Venezuela, especially large construction companies.

The relationship between Brazil and Venezuela is strengthened by the positive identities between the two countries built up over the last few decades. The interest of the Brazilian business community, especially the industrial sector, is very important. It sees the Venezuelan market as a promising destination for its products, and is thus in favor of the definitive incorporation of Venezuela as a full member of Mercosur. This, in turn, is combated in the political and ideological spheres by some political forces and sections of the media in Brazil. The ideological affinity between Chávez and Lula contributes to the two countries' relationship, but this partnership is not merely circumstantial. Among the Venezuelan elite, there has developed an interest in ties with Brazil that probably goes beyond the current political scenario.

The Lula government has sought to promote a certain diplomatic balance, taking into account existing asymmetries and seeking, within the perspective of autonomy through diversification (Naím, 2009), to contribute to the rebalancing of the international system, weakening unilateralism and hegemonic policies. Hence, Brazil seeks to defend multilateralism and the reform of international organizations, whilst Venezuela promotes an anti-hegemonic action and puts forward as the core objective the articulation of a counter-power in the face of the United States. In other words, Brazil's perspective under Lula has been the search for deep changes within the system, whilst Venezuela wants to change the system itself.

FINAL REMARKS

In chapter 6, we discussed Brazil's relations with Argentina, considered its most important partner in the region in the political, economic and strategic aspects. However, this does not mean relations with other neighbors are not important. Brazil will probably look with increasing interest to another important neighbor, Venezuela. Relations with Venezuela, although very close, have been marked in the Chávez government by difficulties on specific matters generated by his strategy of confrontation with countries such as Peru and Colombia. The Venezuelan president uses confrontational rhetoric against the United States and often acts in the regional sphere motivated by strong ideological positions. His action apparently lacks long-term, rational planning. Chávez's support for the nationalization of Bolivian gas at the start of the Evo Morales presidency harmed Petrobras' interests, which led to a highly negative image in the eyes of the Brazilian elites and government. The above factors notwithstanding, the approximation of the two States does not seem to be a circumstantial movement consequent on political affinities, but rather the result of a historic tendency with origins in a convergence of interests that go beyond the two governments.

NOTE

1. At the end of the first quarter of 2008, Petrobras' market value was estimated at US$235 billion, only behind ExxonMobil and Royal Dutch/Shell within the oil sector (*Folha de S. Paulo*, July 26, 2008).

General Conclusions

The central thesis of this book is that Brazil, at least from the mid-1980s to 2009, has given priority to maintaining its external autonomy, though promoting important changes in pursuit of this goal. Therefore, autonomy would take on three ideal forms: through distance, through participation and through diversification. These instruments for attaining autonomy—like autonomy itself—are never found as pure forms in the real world. They are analytical categories that merely signal tendencies. Even if Brazilian foreign policy makers could establish their guidelines accurately, reality imposes concrete obstacles to their exact implementation. These obstacles may be imposed by other countries or even by domestic segments opposed to those that formulate Brazilian foreign policy. This is a classic situation that may be found just about anywhere, be it in stronger or weaker States. Deutsch states this clearly in his classic book, *The Analysis of International Relations* (1968).

In chapter 1, we demonstrated that Latin Americans conceive of the concept of autonomy differently from scholars of the realist and neorealist traditions. The latter understand autonomy as the notion that States, placed within an anarchical international order, are legally recognized as equals. For this reason, they privilege the notion of sovereignty. For their part, Latin American authors understand it as the capacity of a certain State to practice a foreign policy with few constraints imposed by the global powers. In their eyes, autonomy is a polar concept within a continuum that goes from full autonomy to an automatic alignment to the major international powers. In this sense, there are three instruments for striving for autonomy, as has been amply discussed: distance, participation and diversification. Brazilian authors have developed the concepts within this perspective. Fonseca Jr. (1998, 2008) argued that the Cardoso administration (1995–2002) consolidated a change in Brazilian foreign policy that had been taking place since the 1980s, with the democratic transition period and the end of the Cold War. In other words, Cardoso adopted autonomy through participation instead of autonomy through distance, the latter having prevailed in Brazil since the 1930s, including during the military governments, with the partial exception of the Castello Branco presidency (1964–1967), which drew closer to the United States on issues of international politics.

Autonomy through distance is based on economic development geared to expanding the domestic market, on protectionist practices and on a relative distancing from the major international issues and hegemonic regimes, and endeavors to strengthen South–South alliances. Autonomy through participation involves greater international insertion, a certain approximation to rich countries' agenda and a negotiated acceptance of liberal norms and regimes. Lastly, autonomy through diversification implies an approximation to the Southern countries in order to obtain greater involvement in international regimes (even liberal ones), whilst betting on multilateral solutions and condemning the unilateral policies practiced by powerful countries, particularly the United States.

In chapter 2, we ascertained that during the Sarney administration Brazil was submitted to strong pressures by the US government and corporations. These pressures, together with changes in the international system (end of the Cold War and acceleration of economic globalization) and also at domestic level (democratic transition), made the country gradually shift from a strategy guided by autonomy through distance to one guided by autonomy through participation. In chapter 2, we used four important cases to exemplify the pressures Brazil was under at that time: the foreign debt negotiation, the dispute over IT and patents and the negotiations on the inclusion of "new issues" (intellectual property and services) in the GATT/WTO Uruguay Round.

In chapter 3, we showed that the Collor de Mello and Itamar Franco years constituted a transitional phase, during which a "paradigm" of Brazilian foreign policy was not fully exhausted and another was not yet defined. Although Collor de Mello did not abandon the autonomist tradition, the plurality of guidelines adopted (Cruz Jr., Cavalcante and Pedone, 1993) suggests that the direction of his foreign policy was not clear. In his first year as president, Collor de Mello wished to break the autonomist logic, aligning with the USA and other rich countries, since he believed modernization would be achieved by means of economic openness. However, the Ministry of Foreign Relations (MRE) would seek to minimize the president's more radical actions. With Celso Lafer's assumption of command at the ministry, foreign policy went back to being formulated by the diplomatic corps. After Collor de Mello's impeachment, Itamar Franco continued delegating the foreign policy decision-making process to the MRE, headed by Cardoso. When Amorim took over at the MRE (whilst Cardoso became finance minister), traditional themes of

Brazilian diplomacy were taken up again. A more autonomous posture was put in place, symbolized by the aim of taking up a permanent seat on the UN Security Council. Three central characters—Lafer, Cardoso and Amorim—were to occupy key positions in the country's political setting in the near future, thus having a second chance to refine the "paradigms" sketched during the few years that each conducted Brazilian foreign policy prior to 1995.

In chapter 4, we indicated that the Clinton administration, which coincided with six years of the Cardoso presidency (1995–2000) and its foreign policy guided by the logic of autonomy through participation, left the door open to the Brazilian expectation of building multilateral rules and institutions of a liberal type, even though this expectation was not confirmed in many aspects. After September 11, 2001, already under President George W. Bush, US unilateralism gained a renewed impetus. The focus shifted to the security question in different parts of the world, particularly the Middle East, making actions in line with the strategy of autonomy through participation more difficult. The concept of autonomy through participation was not totally invalidated during the Cardoso government, but it did take on new characteristics. As a reaction, his administration deepened relations with China, India and South Africa, but maintained the dialogue with the USA over the Free Trade Area of the Americas (FTAA), particularly between the Santiago (1998) and Quebec (2001) Summits Meetings of Heads of State and Government of the Americas, and encouraged the Mercosur–European Union relationship. In other words, the concept of autonomy through participation, refined and put into practice in fuller fashion by the Cardoso administration, was already displaying signs of wear and tear toward the end of his eight years in office. This permitted adjustments and changes in Brazilian foreign policy that ended up taking place in the following administration, reaching a level slightly above program changes and coming close to problem and goal changes, according to Hermann's (1990) classification.

In chapter 5, we argued that the foreign policy of President de Luiz Inácio Lula da Silva, in comparison with Cardoso, has elements of change with continuity, but also of adjustments and new programmatic orientations. It is characterized by a strategy of autonomy through diversification. This incremental change—therefore, without rupture—is characterized by problem and goal changes. As a key mark of his government, President Lula aims for the multilateralization of the international system, reducing the asymmetries of power and making it more democratic. His administration is resistant to the hegemonic logic and to unilateralism, maintaining dialogue and cooperation with the rich countries nonetheless. The Lula government has not distanced itself from the historical principle of Brazilian diplomacy, which sees itself as an instrument of economic development and of the preservation of the country's autonomy. Analyzing the two governments' positions, we notice that

President Lula seeks to institutionalize the partnerships with countries of the South (e.g., IBSA and the G-20) in order to increase the country's bargaining power in international negotiations. Therein lies the difference in relation to Cardoso, who sought to establish a dialogue with a view to enhancing trade, but not to institutionalizing partnerships with China, India and South Africa, among others. The attempt to build a new geometry of world power, in which relations are less asymmetrical, does not imply a confrontation with rich countries, especially with the United States, for Brazilian diplomacy has differential strategies for different issue areas (security, trade, etc.). Therefore, the effort to diversify partnerships—and not just to participate in international institutions where developed countries' values prevail—is an important differentiating element of Lula's foreign policy, though not a totally consensual one among Brazilian elites and foreign policy makers.

It is hard to say for sure what direction Brazilian foreign policy will take over the next few years, but there will probably be a reasonable level of continuity. The international economic crisis that began in 2008 and continues affecting the world economy as we write in 2009, is one of the elements of uncertainty. The election of Democrat Barack Obama to the US presidency in the wake of the public's dissatisfaction with George W. Bush's policies makes it difficult to make accurate prognoses regarding Brazil's performance on the world stage. Changes of course in the United States, the most powerful country on the planet, will bring on global changes with which Brazil must deal. Moreover, there will be presidential elections in Brazil in 2010 and it is impossible to foresee the result. If President Lula manages to get his candidate elected, Brazilian foreign policy will probably retain its main guidelines of autonomy through diversification, with whatever adaptations required by new international scenarios. If, on the other hand, the opposition led by the Brazilian Social Democratic Party (PSDB) wins, the path that the country's foreign policy takes may change a little more. However, in the light of President Lula's high approval ratings in his second term,[1] it is hard to imagine that the new president would completely undo the eight-year legacy of the previous government. Although some argue that President Lula's popularity is owed solely to his domestic policies of poverty reduction and income redistribution, several facts demonstrate that the country's external activity has been successful in recent years. For example, Brazil has intensified its participation in international fora like the financial G-20 (which aims to reform international financial institutions and seek solutions for the current global economic crisis), is one of the countries least affected by the crisis, is considered one of the most promising emerging economies (possibly after China and India) and is part of the BRIC (Brazil, Russia, India, and China) a group of developing countries likely to play a major role in the future international setting. President Lula has also managed to stand out considerably on the world stage. At the end of 2008, *Newsweek* ranked him 18th among the most powerful people on the planet. He is seen as possibly the world's most popular president, according to the magazine's international editor Fareed Zakaria and to President Barack Obama himself. He is considered a possible candidate for president of the World Bank after leaving the Presidency of the Republic. This would be a first, since the institution has traditionally been presided by US Americans and Europeans.

In chapter 6, we contend that Brazil's global player and global trader aspirations, the strong emphasis on autonomy, the intense quest for the diversification of partnerships, with an interest in the major developing countries such as China, India, South Africa and Russia, among others, constitute potential obstacles to agreements that might deepen Mercosur and to concessions to regional bloc partners Paraguay, Uruguay and Argentina. From the point of view of different Brazilian governments, an enhanced institutionalization of regional integration would lead to loss of sovereignty and international autonomy. With the diversification of partnerships, the country would concentrate its resources and efforts toward actors considered strategic. Mercosur and South American integration carry on being important, the latter receiving more of an emphasis. But these objectives are not the only focus of interest. This does not mean that regional integration is not considered beneficial. But there is a certain hesitation among important Brazilian political and business leaders with regard to shouldering the costs of integration. We believe the chief obstacle to the advance of integration is not Brazil's selfish interest (i.e., a wish to establish leadership without matching measures to the benefit of other countries in the region). Rather, the obstacles derive from Brazil's own economic and political limitations, consequences of its condition as a developing country.

In chapters 6 and 7, we suggest that the strategies set out by Brazil over the years—autonomy through diversification, mainly—face challenges often placed before it by other countries of the region. We analyzed the cases of Argentina and Venezuela, but the same may be said of Paraguay and Bolivia. Successive Brazilian governments have argued that they seek to respond with more cooperation. But this response faces serious obstacles to become concrete. One of the biggest obstacles to South American integration is that the region is made up of poor countries with economic structures that are not mutually complementary and almost always are directed at developed markets, which are the buyers of commodities produced by less developed nations. China is a new actor of great importance, though also a buyer of commodities, hence not altering the pattern normally associated with North–South relations.

We also saw that Brazil's capacity and will to become the paymaster of South American regional integration, or even of just Mercosur, are limited. The Brazilian strategy finds obstacles before it that are linked with the structure of the international system. The autonomy through diversification strategy developed during the Lula government aims to maximize the country's capabilities. Success, as in any political situation, is not predetermined; neither is it always totally clear a posteriori. There are important changes in comparison with the policy pursued in the 1990s by the Cardoso government. These result from domestic political relations, with forces from the Left having more weight, and also due to the fact that the economy seems to have become reasonably stable and able to sustain itself in the long term. The changes also result from the large-scale reconfiguration of the international system, as we have seen over the course of this book. Strong US unilateralism under Bush, China's growing weight and the access won to relevant fora—such as the commercial G-20, the financial G-20, the G-8+5, etc.—all meant that it made sense for Brazil to want to take part in the attempt to reorganize the international system, strengthening multilateralism in its political, economic, strategic and cultural dimensions. This was done without political ruptures, keeping up the dialogue with the most varied interlocutors, both from developed and from developing countries.

From a theoretical point of view, the three notions of autonomy (distance, participation and diversification) counterposed to a foreign policy aligned with the interests of the great powers, may serve as an analytical framework for studying the foreign policies of a range of countries, especially developing nations. Although this was not an effort made in this book, a series of countries may fit into one of these analytical types. Focusing on certain strategies helps countries have a clearer roadmap for their future actions (which is good for policy makers) and a clearer analysis of their past positions (which is advantageous for academics). Countries often adopt foreign policies that mix typologies (for example, having elements of autonomy through distance with autonomy through participation), since they have differential actions in distinct issue areas (security, trade, human rights, etc.). In other situations, the foreign policy of a given country does not fit into all the typologies developed here—just autonomy through distance, but not through participation or through diversification, for instance. However, we suggest that the framework of this book may be useful for analyzing other country case studies, even if it requires adjusting to different realities and trajectories.

NOTES

1. His government was evaluated as "excellent" or "good" by some 70% of voters in 2008 and 2009, according to opinion polls conducted by the *Datafolha* research institute—http://datafolha.folha.uol.com.br/.

Bibliography

Abdenur, Roberto. "A política externa brasileira e o 'sentimento de exclusão'". In: Fonseca Jr., Gelson and Castro, Sérgio Henrique Nabuco de (orgs.). *Temas de política externa brasileira II*, vol. 1. São Paulo: Paz e Terra, 1994.

Abreu, Marcelo de Paiva. "O Brasil e a ALCA: interesses e alternativas". Rio de Janeiro: Departamento de Economia da PUC-Rio, 1997 (*Working Papers*, n. 371).

Abreu, Marcelo de Paiva. "O Brasil, o GATT e a OMC: história e perspectivas". *Política Externa*, vol. 9, n. 4, 2001: 89–119.

Adler, Emanuel. "Ideological 'guerrillas' and the quest for technological autonomy: Brazil's domestic computer industry". *International Organization*, 40, n. 3, 1986: 673–705.

Adler, Emanuel. *The power of ideology: the quest for technological autonomy in Argentina and Brazil*. Berkeley: University of California Press, 1987.

Albuquerque, José Augusto Guilhon. "De novo na encruzilhada: as relações internacionais do Brasil às vésperas do século 21". *Carta Internacional*, n. 94/95, 2000: 13–17.

Alden, Chris and Vieira, Marco Antonio. "The new diplomacy of the South: South Africa, Brazil, India and trilateralism". *Third World Quarterly*, vol. 26, n. 7, 2005: 1077–1095.

Almeida, Paulo Roberto de. "Uma política externa engajada: a diplomacia do governo Lula". *Revista Brasileira de Política Internacional*, Brasília: IBRI, vol. 47, n. 1, 2004: 162–184.

Amado, Rodrigo (org.). *Araújo Castro*. Brasília: Editora Universidade de Brasília, 1982.

Amaral, Ricardo. Brazil bypasses patent on Merck AIDS drug. *Washington Post*, 5 May, 2007.

Amorim, Celso. "Uma diplomacia voltada para o desenvolvimento e a democracia". In: Gelson Fonseca Jr. and Sérgio Henrique Nabuco de Castro (orgs.). *Temas de política externa brasileira II*, vol. 1. São Paulo: Paz e Terra, 1994.

Amorim, Celso and Pimentel, Renata. "Iniciativa para as Américas: o acordo do Jardim das Rosas". In: José Augusto Guilhon Albuquerque. *Sessenta anos de política externa brasileira (1930–1990)*. São Paulo: Cultura/Nupri – USP/ FAPESP, vol. II, 1996.

Amorim, Celso. Interview with Alexandra de Melo e Silva. Rio de Janeiro: Fundação Getúlio Vargas - CPDOC, 1997.

Amorim, Celso. Speech of the Minister of Foreign Relations, Ambassador Celso Amorim, due to the transfer of the Foreign Relations Secretary General's post. In: Luiz Inácio Lula da Silva, Celso Amorim and Samuel Guimarães. *A política externa do Brasil*. Brasília: Funag, 2003.

Amorim, Celso. Interview with *Revista CNI – Indústria Brasileira*, 2004. Available at: http://www.mre.gov.br/portugues/politica_externa/discursos/discurso_detalhe .asp?ID_DISCURSO=2175.

Amorim, Celso. Política externa do Governo Lula: os dois primeiros anos, 2005. Available at: <observatorio.iuperj.br/artigos_resenhas/Artigo%20Celso%20Amorim.pdf>.

Amorim, Celso. Brasil e EUA: o sentido de uma visita. *Folha de S. Paulo*, 8 April 2007.

Ayoob, Mohammed. "Inequality and theorizing in international relations: the case for subaltern realism". *International Studies Review*, vol. 4, n. 3, 2002: 27–48.

Azambuja, Marcos Castrioto de. A política externa do governo Collor. Lecture at the Institute of Advanced Studies of the University of São Paulo, 19 Oct 1990.

Batista, Paulo Nogueira. "A política externa de Collor: modernização ou retrocesso?". *Política Externa*, vol. 1, n. 4, 1993: 106–135.

Belluzzo, Luiz Gonzaga. Interview with Tullo Vigevani, 4 Jun 1991.

Bresser-Pereira, Luiz Carlos. "A Brazilian approach to external debt negotiation". *Lasa Forum*, vol. 19, n. 4, 1989.

Bresser-Pereira, Luiz Carlos. "Contra a corrente no Ministério da Fazenda". *Revista Brasileira de Ciências Sociais*, vol. 19, n. 7, 1992: 5–30.

Buck, Ralph. Interview with Tullo Vigevani, 23 May 1991.

Bueno, Clodoaldo. *Política externa da Primeira República: os anos do apogeu – de 1902 a 1918*. São Paulo: Paz e Terra, 2003.

Burges, Sean W. "Bounded by the reality of trade: practical limits to a South American region". *Cambridge Review of International Affairs*, vol. 18, n. 3, 2005: 437–454.

Burges, Sean W. "Building a global Southern coalition: the competing approaches of Brazil's Lula and Venezuela's Chávez". *Third World Quarterly*, vol. 28, n. 7, 2007: 24–64.

Burges, Sean W. *Brazilian foreign policy after the Cold War*. Gainesville: University Press of Florida, 2009.

Campos Mello, Flávia de. *Regionalismo e inserção internacional: Continuidade e transformação da política externa brasileira nos anos 90*. São Paulo: FFLCH/USP, 2000 (Ph.D. Dissertation).

Canani, Ney. *Política externa no governo Itamar Franco (1992–1994): continuidade e renovação de paradigma nos anos 90*. Porto Alegre: Editora UFRGS, 2004.

Cardoso, Fernando Henrique. "Política externa: fatos e perspectivas". *Política Externa*, vol. 2, n. 1, 1993.

Cardoso, Fernando Henrique. "Política externa em tempos de mudança: a gestão do Ministro Fernando Henrique Cardoso no Itamaraty". Brasília: Funag, 1994.

Cardoso, Fernando Henrique. Pronouncement of the President of Republic–1995. Brasília, 1996.

Cardoso, Fernando Henrique. Interview with Brasilio Sallum Jr. "Estamos reorganizando o capitalismo brasileiro". *Lua Nova*, n. 39, 1997.

Cardoso, Fernando Henrique. Speech of the President of Republic, Fernando Henrique Cardoso, in the Brazilian Center for International Relations (Cebri). Rio de Janeiro, 2000. <http://ftp.unb.br/pub/UNB/ipr/rel/discpr/2000/2929.pdf>.

Cardoso, Fernando Henrique. Speech of the President of Republic, Fernando Henrique Cardoso, in the opening of the III Summit of the Americas. Québec, 20 Apr 2001.

Cardoso, Fernando Henrique. *A arte da política: a história que vivi*. Rio de Janeiro: Civilização Brasileira, 2006.

Cardozo, Sandra Aparecida and Miyamoto, Shiguenoli. Política externa brasileira em dois momentos: uma análise comparativa entre a política externa do governo Geisel e do governo Lula. Paper presented at the V Conference of the Brazilian Political Science Association (ABCP), UFMG, Belo Horizonte, 26–29 Jul 2006.

Cepal (Comisión Económica para América Latina y el Caribe). *Panorama de la inserción internacional de América Latina y el Caribe, 2000–2001*. Santiago: Cepal, 2003.

Cervo, Amado and Bueno, Clodoaldo. *História da política exterior do Brasil*. 2nd ed. Brasília: Editora da Universidade de Brasília, 2002.

Cisneros, Imelda *et al*. *El desarrollo del comercio y las inversiones entre Brasil y Venezuela*. Brasília: Fundação Alexandre de Gusmão, 1998.

Conca, Ken. "Technology, the military and democracy in Brazil". *Journal of Interamerican Studies and World Affairs*, vol. 34, n. 1, 1992: 141–177.

Cruz Jr., Ademar Seabra de; Cavalcante, Antonio Ricardo F. and Pedone, Luiz. "Brazil's foreign policy under Collor". *Journal of Interamerican Studies and World Affairs*, vol. 35, n. 1, 1993: 119–144.

Danese, Sérgio. *Diplomacia presidencial*. Rio de Janeiro: Topbooks, 1999.

Deutsch, Karl W. *The analysis of international relations*. New Jersey: Prentice-Hall, 1968

Escudé, Carlos. "An introduction to peripheral realism and its implications for the interstate system: Argentina and the Cóndor II Missile Project". In: Stephanie G. Neuman (ed.). *International relations theory and the Third World*. New York: St. Martin's Press, 1998.

Estado de S. Paulo, O. EUA são o parceiro fundamental, diz Fernando Henrique Cardoso. *O Estado de S. Paulo*, 24 Sep 1995.

Estado de S. Paulo, O. FH fala das aspirações brasileiras. *O Estado de S. Paulo*, 1 Sep 1996.

Estado de S. Paulo, O. FHC propõe eixos estratégicos para o País. *O Estado de S. Paulo*, 30 Jan 2000.

Evans, Peter. B. "Declining hegemony and assertive industrialization: U.S.-Brazil conflicts in the computer industry". *International Organization*, vol. 43, n. 2, 1989: 207–238.

Evans, Peter B. *Embedded autonomy: states and industrial transformation*. Princeton, NJ: Princeton University Press, 1995.

Flecha de Lima, Paulo Tarso. "Dados para uma reflexão sobre a política comercial brasileira". In: Gelson Fonseca Jr. and Valdemar Carneiro Leão (orgs.). *Temas de política externa brasileira*. Brasília: Funag/Ed. Ática, 1989.

Fonseca Jr., Gelson. *A legitimidade e outras questões internacionais*. São Paulo: Paz e Terra, 1998.

Fonseca Jr., Gelson. *O interesse e a regra: ensaios sobre o multilateralismo*. São Paulo: Paz e Terra, 2008.

Folha de S. Paulo. Na Bolsa, ação da Petrobras pode ter perda indireta, 26 Jul 2008.

Garcia, Marco Aurélio. Interview with Luiz Antônio Araujo and Rosane de Oliveira. *Zero Hora*, 13 Mar 2004.

GATT (*General Agreement on Tariffs and Trade*). United States – Import restrictions on certain products from Brazil. Request by Brazil, Document L/6386, 24 Aug 1988.

Gazeta Mercantil. Brasil e EUA retomam o diálogo, 11 Sep 1986.

Gazeta Mercantil. EUA ainda estudam represálias, 20 Jun 1987.

Gazeta Mercantil. Brasil negocia na Rodada Uruguai em situação desfavorável, 10 Sep 1988.

Gazeta Mercantil. Brasil volta da reunião com trunfos nas mãos, 17 Nov 2008a.

Gazeta Mercantil. Crise põe o Brasil na mira da China, 21 Nov 2008b.

Geddes, Barbara and Ribeiro Neto, Artur. "Fontes institucionais da corrupção no Brasil". In: Keith S. Rosenn and Richard Downes (orgs.). *Corrupção e reforma política no Brasil: o impacto do impeachment de Collor*. Rio de Janeiro: Editora FGV, 1999.

Genoíno, José. "O declínio da diplomacia presidencial". *Carta Internacional*, n. 71, 1999. Available at: <http://143.107.80.37/nupri/carta717.htm>.

Giannetti, Roberto and Marconini, Mário. "Inserção internacional e comércio exterior brasileiro". *Revista Brasileira de Comércio Exterior*, vol. 87, 2006: 43–17.

Godio, Julio. *El tiempo de Kirchner: el devenir de una revolución desde arriba*. Buenos Aires: Ediciones Letra Grifa, 2006.

Goertz, Gary. *Social Science concepts: a user's guide*. Princeton and Oxford: Princeton University Press, 2006.

Gonçalves, José Botafogo and Lyra, Maurício Carvalho. *Aliança estratégica entre Brasil e Argentina: antecedentes, estado atual e perspectivas*. Rio de Janeiro: Centro Brasileiro de Relações Internacionais (Cebri), ano 2, vol. 2. Available at: <www.cebri.org.br>.

GMC (Grupo Mercado Comum). V Reunión. *Boletim de Integração Latino-Americana*. Brasília: Ministério das Relações Exteriores, n. 4, Jan/Mar 1992.

Guimarães, Samuel Pinheiro. *Quinhentos anos de periferia*. 3rd ed. Porto Alegre: Editora da Universidade/Contraponto, 1999.

Guimarães, Samuel Pinheiro. Los tres años del Gobierno del Presidente de Brasil Luiz Inácio Lula da Silva. *La Onda Digital*, 12 May 2006. Available at: <http://www.uruguay2030.com/LaOnda/LaOn da/277/Recuadro2.htm>.

Hermann, Charles F. "Changing course: when governments choose to redirect foreign policy". *International Studies Quarterly*, vol. 34, n. 1, 1990: 3–21.

Hirst, Monica and Pinheiro, Leticia. "A política externa do Brasil em dois tempos". *Revista Brasileira de Política Internacional*, vol. 38, n. 1, 1995.

Hurrell, Andrew. *The quest for autonomy: the evolution of Brazil's role in the international system, 1964–1985*. University of Oxford, 1986 (PhD. Dissertation).

Hurrell, Andrew. "The politics of Amazonian deforestation". *Journal of Latin American Studies*, vol. 23, n. 1, 1991: 197–215.

Intal (Institute for the Integration of Latin America and the Caribbean). "Informe Mercosul: período 2001–2002". *Informe Mercosul*, Buenos Aires: Intal/BID, year 7, n. 8, 2003.

Jaguaribe, Hélio. "Autonomía periférica y hegemonía céntrica". *Estudios Internacionales*, n. 46, 1979: 91–130.

Jaguaribe, Hélio. "Introdução geral". In: J. A. G. Albuquerque (org.). *Sessenta anos de política externa brasileira (1930–1990): crescimento, modernização e política externa*. vol. 1. São Paulo: Cultura Editores Associados/Nupri, 1996.

Jank, Marcos S. Revendo a política comercial brasileira. *O Estado de S. Paulo*, 18 Oct 2006.

Jornal do Brasil. Resek nos EUA defende política de não-confrontação, 13 May 1990.

Jornal do Brasil. Retórica do 1° Mundo é abandonada, 26 Aug 1991.

Keohane, Robert O. and Nye, Joseph S. *Power and interdependence*. Boston: Scott, Foresman and Company, 1989.

Keohane, Robert O. and Goldstein, Judith E. *Ideas and foreign policy: beliefs, institutions, and political change*. Ithaca and London: Cornell University Press, 1993.

Krasner, Stephen D. *Structural conflict: The Third World against global liberalism*. Berkeley, Los Angeles, London: University of California Press, 1985.

Krasner, Stephen D. "Compromising Westphalia". *International Security*, vol. 20, n. 3, 1995/96: 115–151.

Krasner, Stephen D. *Sovereignty: organized hypocrisy*. Princeton: Princeton University Press, 1999.

Kume, J. A. and Piani, Guida. "Mercosul: o dilema entre união aduaneira e área de livre comércio". *Revista de Economia Política*, vol. 25, n. 4(100), 2005: 370–390.

Lafer, Celso. Política externa brasileira: três momentos. São Paulo: Konrad-Adenauer Foundation, 1993a (Papers, n. 4).

Lafer, Celso. "A política externa brasileira no governo Collor". *Política Externa*, vol. 1, n. 4, 1993b: 95–105.

Lafer, Celso. *A OMC e a regulação do comércio internacional: uma visão brasileira*. Porto Alegre: Livraria do Advogado, 1998.

Lafer, Celso. *A identidade internacional do Brasil e a política externa brasileira: passado, presente e futuro*. São Paulo: Editora Perspectiva, 2001a.

Lafer, Celso. ALCA não é destino, é opção. *O Estado de S. Paulo*, 3 Mar 2001b.

Lafer, Celso. Swearing-in speech of the Brazilian Ministry of Foreign Relations. Brasília, 29 Jan 2001c.

Lafer, Celso. *Mudam-se os tempos. Diplomacia brasileira 2001–2002*. vols. I e II. Brasília: Funag, 2002.

Lafer, Celso. *A identidade internacional do Brasil e a política externa brasileira: passado, presente e futuro*. São Paulo: Perspectiva, 2004.

Lampreia, Luiz Felipe. "Seminário sobre Mercosul". Resenha de *Política Exterior do Brasil*, vol. 21, n. 76, set. 1995.

Lampreia, Luiz Felipe. "O consenso brasileiro em torno da ALCA". *Política Externa*, vol. 5, n. 4, 1997: 4–6.

Lampreia, Luiz Felipe. *Diplomacia brasileira*. Rio de Janeiro: Lacerda Editora, 1999.

Lampreia, Luiz Felipe. Farewell address and transfer of the Ministry of Foreign Relations' post to Celso Lafer. Brasília, 2001. Available at: <http://www.radiobras.gov.br/integras /01/integra_2901_6.htm. 2001>.

Lehman, Howard P. and McCoy, Jennifer L. "The dynamics of the two-level bargaining game – The 1988 Brazilian debt negotiations". *World Politics*, vol. 44, n. 4, 1992: 600–644.

León-Manríquez, José Luís. "China-América Latina: una relación económica diferenciada". *Nueva Sociedad*, n. 203, 2006: 28–47.

Lima, Maria Regina Soares de. "A economia política da política externa brasileira: uma proposta de análise". *Contexto Internacional*, ano 6, n. 12, 1990: 7–28.

Lima, Maria Regina Soares de. "Ejes analíticos y conflicto de paradigmas en la política exterior brasileña". *América Latina/Internacional*, vol. 1, n. 2, 1994: 27–46.

Lima, Maria Regina Soares de. "Política doméstica determina atuação diplomática". *Carta Internacional*, n. 35, 1996.

Lima, Maria Regina Soares de. "Brazil's alternative vision". In: Gordon Mace and Louis Béranger (orgs.). *The Americas in transition*. Boulder/London: Lynne Rienner, 1999.

Lima, Maria Regina Soares de. "Na trilha de uma política externa afirmativa". *Observatório da Cidadania*, Rio de Janeiro: Ibase, 2003.

Lima, Maria Regina Soares de. "A política externa brasileira e os desafios da cooperação sul-sul". *Revista Brasileira de Política Internacional*, vol. 48, n. 1, 2005: 24–59.

Lima, Maria Regina Soares de and Hirst, Mônica. "Brazil as an intermediate State and regional power: action, choice and responsibilities". *International Affairs*, vol. 82, n. 1, 2006: 21–40.

Lima, Maria Regina Soares de and Kfuri, Regina. "Política externa da Venezuela e relações com o Brasil". Rio de Janeiro: Observatório Político Sul-Americano, 2007 (Papéis Legislativos, n. 6).

Lula da Silva, Luiz Inácio. Speech of the President of the Republic at the National Congress, swearing-in session for the 2003–2006 mandate. In: Luiz Inácio Lula da Silva; Celso Amorim and Samuel Guimarães. *A política externa do Brasil*. Brasília: Funag, 2003.

Lula da Silva, Luiz Inácio. Speech of the President of the Republic at the National Congress, swearing-in session for the 2007–2010 mandate. Presidência da República, 1 Jan 2007.

Lyrio, Maurício Carvalho. *O contencioso das patentes farmacêuticas e as relações entre Brasil e Estados Unidos*. Rio de Janeiro: IRI-PUC/RJ, 1994 (Master Thesis).

Malamud, Andrés. "Mercosur turns 15: between rising rethoric and declining achievement". *Cambridge Review of International Affairs*, vol. 18, n. 3, 2005: 36–421.

Mariano, Marcelo Passini. *A política externa brasileira, o Itamaraty e o Mercosul*. Araraquara: UNESP, 2007 (Ph.D. Dissertation).

Mattli, Walter. *The logic of regional integration: Europe and beyond*. Cambridge: Cambridge University Press, 1999.

Ministério de Relaciones Exteriores de Venezuela. Inserción protagónica de Venezuela, 2005.

Moura, Gerson. *Autonomia na dependência*. Rio de Janeiro: Nova Fronteira, 1980.

Moura, Gerson; Kramer, Paulo and Wrobel, Paulo. "Os caminhos (difíceis) da autonomia: as relações Brasil-EUA". *Contexto Internacional*, ano 1, vol. 2, 1985.

MRE (Ministério das Relações Exteriores). "Brasil, Argentina, Uruguai e Paraguai criam Mercado Comum do Sul (Mercosul)". *Resenha de Política Exterior do Brasil*, Brasília, n. 68, 1991.

MRE (Ministério das Relações Exteriores). *A inserção internacional do Brasil: A gestão do Ministro Celso Lafer no Itamaraty*. Brasília: Funag, 1993a.

MRE (Ministério das Relações Exteriores). *Reflexões sobre a política externa brasileira*. Brasília: Funag, 1993b.

MRE (Ministério das Relações Exteriores). *A palavra do Brasil nas Nações Unidas: 1945–1995*. Brasília: Funag, 1996.

Naím, Moisés. "The 'axis of Lula' vs. the 'axis of Hugo'". *Foreign Policy*, March, 2009. Available at: < http://www.foreignpolicy.com/story/cms.php?story_id=4780>.

Nardin, Terry. *Lei, moralidade e as relações entre os Estados*. Rio de Janeiro: Forense-Universitária, 1987.

Narlikar, Amrita. *International trade and developing countries: bargaining coalitions in the GATT and WTO*. London: Routledge, 2003.

Neuman, Stephanie G. "International relations theory and the Third World: an oxymoron?". In: Stephanie G. Neuman (ed.). *International relations theory and the Third World*. New York: St. Martin's Press, 1998.

Novaes de Almeida, João Lucas Quental. *A política externa brasileira nas negociações de propriedade intelectual no GATT*. Rio de Janeiro: PUC-RJ, 1994 (Master Thesis).

O'Donnell, Guillermo. *Delegative democracy?*. Notre Dame, IN: Kellogg Institute, 1992 (Working Paper, 172). Available at: <http://kellogg.nd.edu/publications/workingpapers/WPS/172.pdf>.

Peña, Félix. O Mercosul e suas perspectivas: uma opção pela inserção competitiva na economia mundial. Bruxelas, 1991 (mimeo).

Pereira, Analúcia Danilevicz. *A política externa do governo Sarney: A Nova República diante do reordenamento internacional (1985–1990)*. Porto Alegre: Editora UFRGS, 2003.

Pierson, Paul. "The path to European integration: a historical-institutionalist analysis". In: Sandholtz Wayne and Alec Stone Sweet (eds.). *European integration and supranational governance*. New York: Oxford University Press, 1998.

Pinheiro, Letícia. "1997: O ano que não terminou". *Carta Internacional*, n. 59, 1998: 2.

Pinheiro, Letícia. "Traídos pelo desejo: um ensaio sobre a teoria e a prática da política externa brasileira contemporânea". *Contexto Internacional*, vol. 22, n. 2, 2000: 305–335.

PMA (Pharmaceutical Manufacturers Association). Petition for relief pursuant to Section 301 of the Trade Act of 1974, as amended – Denial by the Government of Brazil of fair and equitable provision of adequate and effective protection of intellectual property rights. 1987.

Prates, Daniela Magalhães. "A inserção externa da economia brasileira no governo Lula". *Política Econômica em Foco*, n. 7, 2005/2006: 112–151.

Presidential Documents. Proclamation 5885: Increase in the rates of duty for certain articles from Brazil. *Federal Register*, vol. 53, n. 205, 24 Oct. 1988.

PT. *Programa de Governo 2002*. Available at: <http://www.lula.org.br/assets/programadegoverno.pdf>.

Puig, J. C. *Doctrinas internacionales y autonomía latinoamericana*. Caracas: Universidad Simon Bolıvar, 1980.

Puig, J. C. "Introducción". In: Juan Carlos Puig (ed.). *América Latina: políticas exteriores comparadas*. Buenos Aires: GEL, 1984.

Reagan, Ronald. Presidential Radio Address - 7 September 1985. Available at: <http://en.wikisource.org/wiki/Presidential_Radio_Address_-_7_September_1985>.

Ricupero, Rubens and Didonet, Evandro. "A abertura comercial brasileira". In: MRE/SGIE/GETEC. *Boletim de Diplomacia Econômica*, n. 19, 1995.

Rosati, Jerel. "A cognitive approach to the study of foreign policy". In: Jeanne A. K. Hey and Patrick J. Haney (eds.). *Foreign policy analysis: continuity and change in its second generation*. New Jersey: Prentice Hall, 1995.

Rosenberg, Justin. *The empire of civil society. A critique of the realist theory of international relations*. Verso: London, 1994.

Russell, Roberto and Tokatlian, Juan Gabriel. "From antagonistic autonomy to relational autonomy". *Latin American Politics and Society*, vol. 45, n. 1, 2003: 1–24.

Santoro, Maurício and Valente, Leonardo. "A diplomacia midiática do Governo Hugo Chávez". Rio de Janeiro: Observatório Político Sul-Americano, 2006. Available at: <http://observatorio.iuperj.br/artigos_resenhas/Diplomacia_Midiatica_Governo_Chavez.pdf>

Sarney, José. "Brazil: a president's story". *Foreign Affairs*, vol. 65, n. 1, 1986a: 6–105.

Sarney, José. Speech delivered at the sanctioning ceremony of the First Plan for Informatics and Automation. Planalto Palace, 17 April 1986b.

Schmitter, Philippe C. "Still the century of corporatism?" In: Philippe Schmitter C. and Gerhard Lehmbruch (orgs.). *Trends toward corporatist intermediation*. Berverley Hills: Sage Publications, 1979.

Secex (Secretaria de Comércio Exterior). *Boletim Informativo*, Brasília, 2007.

Seixas Corrêa, Luiz Felipe de. *A palavra do Brasil nas Nações Unidas*. Brasília: Funag, 1995.

Seixas Corrêa, Luiz Felipe de. "A política externa de José Sarney". In: José Augusto Guilhon Albuquerque (org.). *Sessenta anos de política externa brasileira. Crescimento, modernização e política externa*. São Paulo: Cultura Editores Associados, 1996.

Sell, Susan. "The origins of a trade-based approach to intellectual property protection: the role of industry associations". *Science Communication*, vol. 17, n. 2, 1995: 163–185.

Sell, Susan. "Intellectual property rights". In: David Held and Anthony McGrew (eds.). *Governing globalization: power, authority and global governance*. Cambridge: Polity Press, 2002.

Sennes, Ricardo and Barbosa, Alexandre Freitas. "Avaliação do potencial econômico da relação Brasil-Venezuela". Rio de Janeiro: Observatório Político Sul-Americano, 2007 (Papéis Legislativos, n. 5).

Serbin, Andrés. "Cuando la limosna es grande: el Caribe, Chávez y los limites de la diplomacia petrolera". *Nueva Sociedad*, n. 205, 2006: 75–91.

Shukla, S. P. "From the GATT to the WTO and beyond". In: Deepak Nayyar (ed.). *Governing globalization: issues and institutions*. Oxford: Oxford University Press, 2002.

Silva, Carlos Eduardo Lins da. "Política e comércio exterior". In: Bolivar Lamounier and Rubens Figueiredo. *A era FHC: um balanço*. São Paulo: Cultura Editores Associados, 2002.

Souto Maior, Luiz Augusto P. "Dois anos de 'presença soberana': uma reflexão sobre a política externa do Governo Lula". *Cena Internacional*, vol. 6, n. 2, 2004: 53–72

Souza, Amaury de. A agenda internacional do Brasil: um estudo sobre a comunidade brasileira de política externa. Rio de Janeiro: Centro Brasileiro de Relações Internacionais (Cebri), 2002. Available at: <http://www.wilsoncenter.org/events/docs/brazil.agendainternacionaldobrasil.pdf>

Suns On-line. Third World dissatisfied with Uruguay Round Processes. 29 Sep 1988. Available at: < http://www.sunsonline.org/trade/process/during/uruguay/tnc/09290088.htm>

Tachinardi, Maria Helena. *A guerra das patentes: o conflito Brasil x Estados Unidos sobre propriedade intelectual*. São Paulo: Paz e Terra, 1993.

The Economist. The Chávez play, 26 Oct 2006.

Tickner, Arlene. "Seeing IR differently: notes from the Third World". *Millenium – Journal of International Studies*, vol. 32, n. 2, 2003: 295–324.

United States. "Trade Act of 1974". In: John H. Jackson; William J. Davey and Alan O. Sykes Jr. Documents Supplement to *Legal problems of international economic relations*. Minnesota: West Group, 2002a.

United States. "Omnibus Trade and Competitiveness Act of 1988". In: John H. Jackson; William J. Davey and Alan O. Sykes Jr. Documents Supplement to *Legal problems of international economic relations*. Minnesota: West Group, 2002b.

Urrutia, Edmundo González. "Las dos etapas de la política exterior de Chávez". *Nueva Sociedad*, n. 205, 2006: 158–171.

Vadell, Javier. South America welcomes the Asian dragon. Paper presented at 49th annual International Studies Association (ISA) Convention, 2008.

Valadão, Alfredo. "A autonomia pela responsabilidade: o Brasil frente ao uso legítimo da força". *Res-Publica*, vol. 1, 2005: 117–135.

Valero, Jorge. "Petróleo, democracia y cooperación hemisférica". Washington DC, OAS/Ser. G CP/INF. 5252/05, 29 Sep 2005.

Valor Econômico. Empresários defendem um passo atrás no Mercosul, 16 Nov 2004.

Valor Econômico. Apoio à entrada da Rússia na OMC em troca de nada, 19 Oct 2005.

Vaz, Alcides C. *Cooperação, integração e processo negociador: a construção do Mercosul*. Brasília: IBRI, 2002.

Veiga, João Paulo Candia. *Dívida externa e o contexto internacional: os limites à formulação de política para a dívida externa na gestão da ministra Zélia Cardoso de Mello*. São Paulo: Universidade de São Paulo, 1993 (Master Thesis).

Velasco e Cruz, Sebastião. *Trajetórias: capitalismo neoliberal e reformas econômicas nos países da periferia*. São Paulo: Editora UNESP, 2007.

Vigevani, Tullo. "La via del pragmatismo responsabile: la politica estera del Brasile". *Politica Internazional*, vol. 11–12, 1974: 273–335.

Vigevani, Tullo. *Questão nacional e política exterior. Um estudo de caso: formulação da política internacional do Brasil e motivações da Força Expedicionária Brasileira*. São Paulo: University of São Paulo, 1989 (Ph.D. Dissertation).

Vigevani, Tullo; Oliveira, Marcelo Fernandes de and Cintra, Rodrigo. "Política externa no período FHC: a busca de autonomia pela integração". *Tempo Social*, vol. 15, 2004: 31–61.

Vigevani, Tullo *et al.* (orgs.). *A dimensão subnacional e as relações internacionais*. São Paulo: EDUC/Editora Unesp/EDUSC/FAPESP, 2004.

Vigevani, Tullo and Mariano, Marcelo Passini. *A ALCA e a política externa brasileira*. São Paulo: Cedec, 2005 (Cadernos Cedec, 74).

Villa, Rafael Duarte. "Política externa brasileira: capital social e discurso democrático na América do Sul". *Revista Brasileira de Ciências Sociais*, vol. 21, n. 61, 2006: 63–89.

Villa, Rafael Duarte. "Limites do ativismo venezuelano para América do Sul". *Política Externa*, vol. 16, n. 2, 2007: 37–49.

Zúquete, José Pedro. "The missionary politics of Hugo Chávez". *Latin American Politics and Society*, vol. 50, n. 1, 2008: 91–121.

Waltz, Kenneth N. *Theory of international politics*. Massachusetts: Addison-Wesley Publishing Company, 1979.

Waltz, Kenneth N. "Structural realism after the Cold War". *International Security*, vol. 25, n. 1, 2000: 5–41.

Wanderley, Luiz Eduardo and Vigevani, Tullo (orgs.). *Governos subnacionais e sociedade civil: integração regional e Mercosul*. São Paulo: EDUC/Editora Unesp/ FAPESP, 2005.

Weber, Max. *Economia e sociedade: Fundamentos da sociologia compreensiva*. Brasília: Editora UnB, 1991.

Wendt, Alexander. "Collective identity formation and the international state". *American Political Science Review*, vol. 88, n. 2, 1994: 181–219.

Wendt, Alexander. *Social theory of international politics*. Cambridge: Cambridge University Press, 1999.

Weyland, Kurt. "The rise and fall of president Collor and its impact on Brazilian democracy". *Journal of Interamerican Studies and World Affairs*, vol. 35, n. 1, 1993: 1–37.

Weyland, Kurt. "The fragmentation of the business in Brazil". In: Francisco Durand and Eduardo Silva (eds.). *Organized business, economic change, and democracy in Latin America*. Miami: North-South Center Press, 1999.

Appendixes

Basic Data on Brazilian Foreign Policy

Appendix 1 Foreign Relations Ministers by Administration

PRESIDENT	*FOREIGN RELATIONS MINISTERS*
José Sarney (1985–1990)	Olavo Setúbal (From March, 1985 to March 1986) Roberto de Abreu Sodré (From March 1986 to January 1990)
Fernando Collor de Mello (1990–1992)	José Francisco Rezek (From January 1990 to April 1992) Celso Lafer (From April to October 1992)
Itamar Franco (1992–1994)	Fernando Henrique Cardoso (From October 1992 to May 1993) Celso Amorim (From May 1993 to December 1994)
Fernando Henrique Cardoso (1995–1998) Fernando Henrique Cardoso (1999–2002)	Luiz Felipe Lampréia (From January 1995 to January 2001) Celso Loafer (From January 2001 to December 2002)
Luiz Inácio Lula da Silva (2003–2006) Luiz Inácio Lula da Silva (2007– . . .)	Celso Amorim (From January 2003 to the time this book went to press)

Appendix 2 Brazilian Ministry of Foreign Affairs—Short Version Organization Chart, Based on Decree 5.979, December 6, 2006

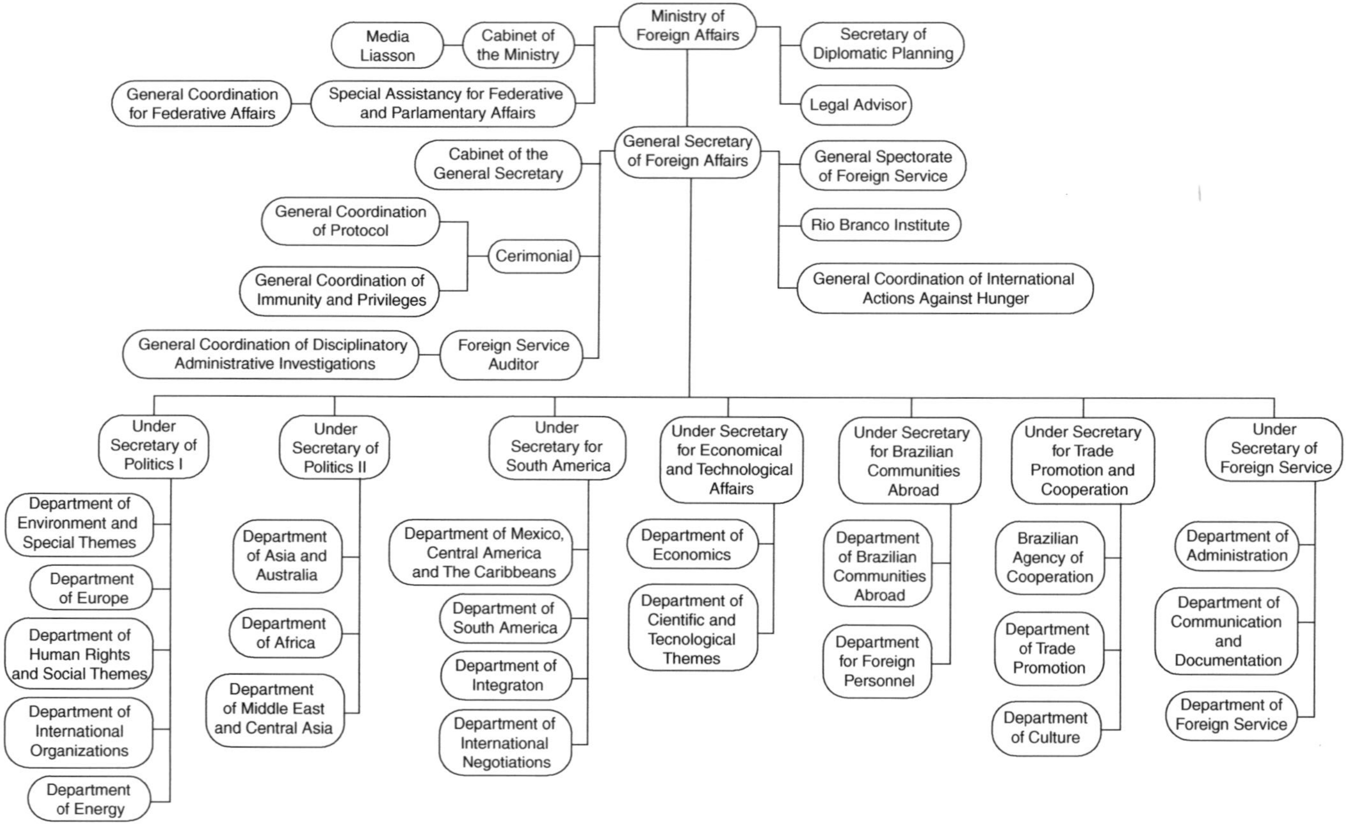

Source: MRE

Appendix 3 Mercosur's Economic Asymmetry

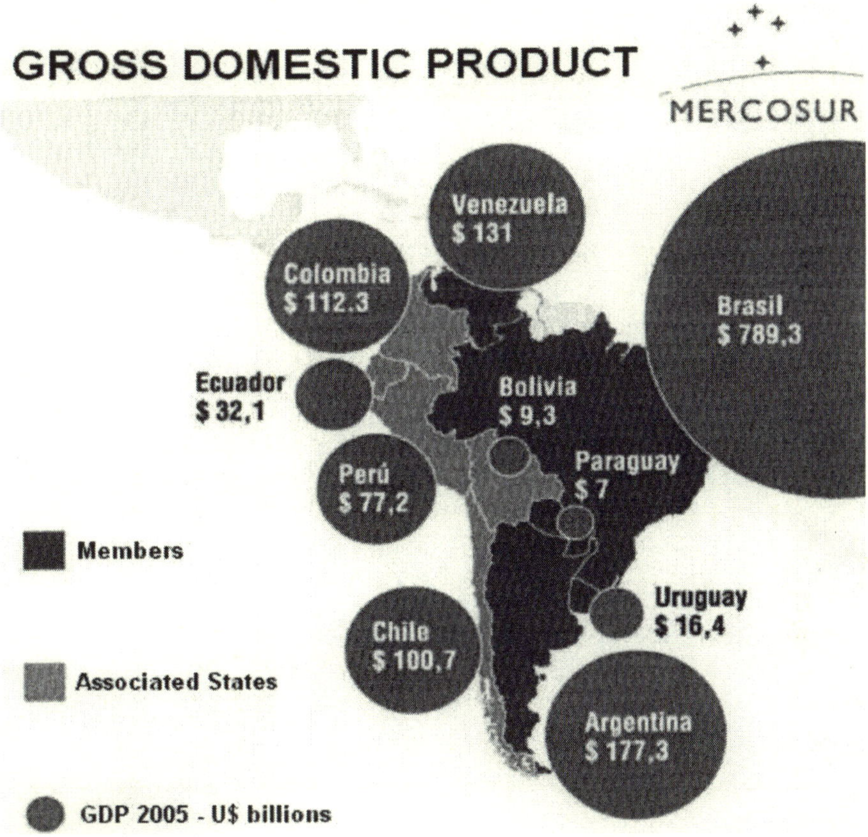

Source: Mercosul

Appendix 4 Chronology

1985

15 March	José Sarney assumes the presidency of the Nova República, with Olavo Egydio Setubal as his Minister of Foreign Relations
21 April	President Tancredo Neves dies
21 August	Creation of the Contadora Group for the pacification of Central America
7 September	US government announces investigations of the Brazilian IT sector, and retaliations in cases of non-compliance with intellectual property rights, pharmaceutical patents and software piracy
23 September	New York—Speech by the President of the Republic at the 40th UN General Assembly centered on the theme of the foreign debt of Latin American countries
9 October	Announcement of the Baker Plan for dealing with the foreign debt issue
30 November	Signing of the Iguaçu Declaration on peaceful cooperation on nuclear energy matters by the presidents of Argentina and Brazil

1986

14 February	Roberto Costa de Abreu Sodré takes office as Minister of Foreign Relations
1 March	Launch of the Cruzado Plan
14 July	Brazil reestablishes diplomatic relations with Cuba
10 and 11 September	Visit by President José Sarney to the United States to discuss US trade retaliations with President Ronald Reagan
20 September	Start of the GATT Uruguay Round
27 October	Declaration of the South Atlantic Peace and Cooperation Zone proposed by Brazil approved by the UN
11 December	Brasília—Signing of the Act of Friendship between Brazil, Argentina and Uruguay

1987

20 February	Announcement of the interruption of foreign debt interest payments by Minister of Finance Dilson Funaro
15 October	Brazil is elected non-permanent member of the UN Security Council

1988

13 April	Global System of Trade Preferences Among Developing Countries (GSTP) adopted by the G-77
22 July	Announcement by the USTR of sanctions against Brazil, as per Section 301 of the Trade Act, as a result of the trade disputes between the two countries
5 October	New Brazilian Constitution promulgated
17–21 October	Visit to the Soviet Union by President José Sarney and a business delegation; signing of agreements in the fields of scientific-technological cooperation, integration for peace and international cooperation
22 December	Assassination of Chico Mendes

1989

2 February	Caracas—Meeting between presidents Sarney and Fidel Castro
10 March	Announcement of the Brady Plan proposal
8 May	Establishment of diplomatic relations with the Socialist Republic of Vietnam
4 June	Statement in repudiation of the repression by the Chinese government of pro-democracy protesters in Tiananmen Square in Beijing
7 September	Belgrade—Creation of the Non-Aligned Countries Summit, the Group of 15
25 September	President José Sarney speaks at the 44th UN General Assembly on the questions of democracy and the economic exploitation of poor countries
1 November	São Luís do Maranhão—1st Summit Meeting of Heads of State of countries whose official language is Portuguese and creation of the International Portuguese Language Institute in Cabo Verde

17 December	Fernando Collor de Mello wins Brazil's direct presidential elections

1990

15 March	Jurist José Francisco Rezek becomes Minister of Foreign Relations; new anti-inflation plan announced by Economy Minister Zélia Cardoso de Mello
6 July	Signing of the Buenos Aires Act by Brazil and Argentina, in order to form a bilateral common market
22 to 30 September	Participation in the 45th UN General Assembly with a speech promoting liberal policies and privatization
28 November	Signing of the Argentine-Brazilian Declaration on Common Nuclear Policy
3 December	Visit to Brazil by President George Bush of the United States
20 December	Signing of the Economic Complementation Agreement between Brazil and Argentina

1991

26 March	Signing of the Treaty of Asunción Establishing the Common Market of the South (Mercosur)
19 June	Conclusion of the 4+1 Agreement
18 and 19 July	Guadalajara—1st Ibero-American Summit

1992

29 January	Agreement signed between Brazil and the IMF on foreign debt re-scheduling
10 and 11 February	Manaus—2nd Meeting of Presidents of Amazonian Countries
7 April	Suspension of ongoing bilateral projects in Peru due to the "self-coup" staged by President Alberto Fujimori
13 April	Jurist and political scientist Celso Lafer becomes Minister of Foreign Relations
29 May	Conclusion of the inter-institutional cooperation agreement between Mercosur and the Commission of the European Communities
3 to 14 June	Rio de Janeiro—Holding of the UN Conference on Environment and Development, Rio 92

23 and 24 July	Madrid—2nd Ibero-American Summit
25 September	Washington—Brazil's joining of the American Convention on Human Rights formally announced
29 September	Impeachment of President Fernando Collor de Mello
5 October	Vice-President Itamar Franco takes office as President of the Republic, with Fernando Henrique Cardoso as his Minister of Foreign Relations
23 October	Visit by President Itamar Franco to Senegal for the 2nd Summit Meeting of the G-15
2 December	Buenos Aires—Launch of the Amazonian Initiative at the 6th Summit Meeting of the Rio Group

1993

1 January	Brazil takes up a non-permanent seat on the UN Security Council
17 February	Signing of the commercial contract for the purchase of Bolivian natural gas in the presence of the presidents of the two countries; start of construction of the Brazil–Bolivia gas pipeline
21 May	Ambassador Celso Luiz Nunes Amorim takes charge at the Ministry of Foreign Relations, while Fernando Henrique Cardoso becomes Minister of Finance
15 and 16 July	Salvador—3rd Ibero-American Summit
24 September	Creation of the Association of Coffee Producing Countries
27 September	In a speech to the 48th UN General Assembly, Minister Celso Amorim criticizes the concepts of duty of intervention and good governance

1994

15 April	Conclusion of the Uruguay Round; Marrakesh Agreement establishes the World Trade Organization to substitute the GATT-1947
30 May	Mexico City—Brazil signs up to the Treaty of Tlateloco
9 June	Belém—24th General Assembly of the Organization of American States (OAS) and approval of the Belém do Pará Convention

1 July	Implementation of the Real Plan
22 September	Brasília—3rd Meeting of the South Atlantic Peace and Cooperation Zone
9–11 December	Miami—1st Summit of the Americas; the aim is to create the Free Trade Area of the Americas and sign the Miami Declaration of Principles
17 December	Approval of the Ouro Preto Protocol instituting Mercosur

1995

1 January	Fernando Henrique Cardoso takes office as President of the Republic, with Ambassador Luiz Felipe Lampreia heading the Ministry of Foreign Relations; the Mercosur Customs Union comes into force, with the adoption of a common external tariff
15 September	Ambassador Rubens Ricupero becomes UNCTAD secretary-general
24 October	Special meeting of heads of State and government to celebrate the 50th anniversary of the UN

1996

10 April	New Intellectual Property Law approved by Congress
17 July	Official constitution of the Community of Portuguese Language Countries
24 September	51st UN General Assembly and signing of the Comprehensive Nuclear-Test-Ban Treaty
6 November	Francisco Rezek is elected judge of the International Court of Justice
17 December	Fortaleza—Talks on the Free Trade Area between Mercosur and Bolivia, Mercosur's new associate member

1997

6 August	Petroleum Law ends Petrobras' monopoly of oil exploration
13 October	Visit to Brazil by President Bill Clinton of the United States
10 December	Approval of the Kyoto Protocol with the adoption of the Clean Development Mechanism proposed by Brazil

1998

16 April	Buenos Aires—Creation of the Free Trade Area between Mercosur and the Andean Community
1 May	Brazil is removed from Section 301 of the US Trade Law
18 May	Repudiation of the Memorandum of Understanding with India on cooperation for peaceful uses of nuclear energy, after that country's nuclear tests (and Pakistan's)
8 June	President Fernando Henrique Cardoso visits US President Bill Clinton at Camp David; announcement of the creation of the National Anti-Drugs Department during a Special Assembly at the UN
12 and 13 July	Visit to Brazil by UN Secretary-General Kofi Annan
17 July	Approval of the Rome Statute creating the International Criminal Court
20–23 July	Visit to Brazil by President Nelson Mandela of South Africa
4 October	Fernando Henrique Cardoso is reelected president
13 November	Brazil signs a new agreement with the IMF to obtain financial aid worth US$41.5 billion

1999

4 January	Brazil assumes the UN Security Council presidency for the month
13 January	Devaluation of the national currency, frozen since 1994; return to a floating exchange rate
9 February	First stretch of the Brazil–Bolivia gas pipeline opened
30 April	Inclusion of Brazil in the observation list of Section 301 of the US Trade Law
28 and 29 June	Rio de Janeiro—1st Latin America and Caribbean–European Union Summit
25 September	Creation of the financial Group of 20 between the G-7 and developing countries
14 October	Taiyuan—Launch of the first Sino-Brazilian satellite
13 to 16 November	Visit to Cuba by President Fernando Henrique Cardoso; 9th Ibero-American Summit
20 and 21 November	Florence—President of the Republic participates in meeting on "Progressive Governance for the 21st Century"

24 November	Mercosur–European Union Bi-regional Negotiations Committee meeting

2000

7 to 9 March	Visit by President Fernando Henrique Cardoso to Portugal for the celebrations of the 500th anniversary of Pedro Álvares Cabral's voyage; signing of the new Treaty of Friendship, Cooperation and Consultation between Brazil and Portugal
31 August	Brasília—1st Meeting of South American Presidents
7 December	Opening of the Itamaraty Representation Office in São Paulo
15 December	Florianópolis—Visit to Brazil by President Thabo Mbeki of South Africa and signing of the Mercosur–South Africa Framework Agreement

2001

25 to 30 January	Porto Alegre—First gathering of the World Social Forum
29 January	Celso Lafer becomes Minister of Foreign Relations
29 and 30 March	Santiago—1st Meeting of Foreign Ministers of the Forum for East Asia–Latin America Cooperation
3 April	Visit to Brazil by President Hugo Chávez of Venezuela; proposal to join the Mercosur
20 to 22 April	Quebec—3rd Summit of the Americas; government states that the FTAA is "an option and not destiny"
25 June	Removal of US complaint at the WTO about Brazilian legislation in the field of pharmaceutical patents
8 to 11 July	Visit to Brazil by European Union Trade Commissioner Pascal Lamy
25 July	Presentation at the International Whaling Commission of a proposal to create a sanctuary in the South Atlantic
30 July to 1 August	Visit to Brazil by Prime Minister Tony Blair of Great Britain
14 August	Creation of the Brazil–Argentine Agency on Nuclear Energy Applications

30 October	Paris—Speech by President Fernando Henrique Cardoso at the French National Assembly advocates a “new” international contract
9 to 13 November	Doha—4th WTO Ministerial Conference; Brazilian threat to break the patents of HIV/AIDS drugs; launch of the Doha Development Agenda
10 November	56th UN General Assembly; President of the Republic calls for globalization with solidarity

2002

14 February	Russia declares its support for Brazil becoming a permanent member of the UN Security Council; visit to Brazil by Chancellor Gerhard Schöder of Germany, who also manifests his support for Brazil becoming a permanent member of the UN Security Council; signing of a financial cooperation agreement for the execution of tropical forest conservation projects
1 March	Visit to Brazil by President José Eduardo dos Santos of Angola, to discuss matters pertaining to the pacification of his country
22 April	Ambassador José Bustani removed from the post of Director-General of the Organisation for the Prohibition of Chemical Weapons due to US pressure
3 July	Visit to Brazil by President Vicente Fox of Mexico; signing of agreement on fixed tariff preferences between the two countries
4 and 5 July	Buenos Aires—22nd Mercosur Summit
5 to 7 August	Brasília—1st Meeting of the Brazil–South Africa Joint Committee
25 October	Paris—Brazil–France Agreement on Cooperation in the Peaceful Uses of Nuclear Energy is signed
1 November	Brazil and the USA assume the co-presidency of the FTAA negotiation process
28 November	Berlin—Opening of the Mercosur Joint Foreign Trade Promotion Center

2003

1 January	Inauguration of President Luiz Inácio Lula da Silva; Celso Amorim is the new Minister of Foreign Relations

26 January	Davos—Participation of President Luiz Inácio Lula da Silva in the World Economic Forum
6 June	Creation of the India, Brazil and South Africa (IBSA) Dialogue Forum
18 June	Asunción—Presentation of the proposal for consolidation of the Mercosur Customs Union, the Objetivo 2006
14 July	The United Kingdom declares its support for Brazil becoming a permanent member of the UN Security Council
23 September	58th UN General Assembly; President of the Republic suggests the creation of a World Committee for Fighting Hunger
16 October	Visit by President Luiz Inácio Lula da Silva to Argentina; signing of the Buenos Aires Consensus, in counter-position to the Washington Consensus
23 October	Brazil elected non-permanent member of the UN Security Council for the ninth time
6 November	China declares its support for Brazil becoming a permanent member of the UN Security Council
11 and 12 December	Brasília—Ministerial Meeting of the G-20 for the WTO Doha Round

2004

1 January	Reciprocal procedures adopted for controlling the entry of US citizens in Brazil
20 January	Geneva—Meeting between presidents Luiz Inácio Lula da Silva, Jacques Chirac of France and Ricardo Lagos of Chile, and UN Secretary-General Kofi Annan for the creation of a global fund for fighting hunger and poverty
22 to 26 May	Visit by President Luiz Inácio Lula da Silva to China with a business delegation
28 May	Guadalajara—3rd European Union–Latin America Summit; departure of the first Brazilian contingent to the UN Stabilization Mission in Haiti
13 to 18 June	São Paulo—11th UNCTAD General Conference, with the adoption of the São Paulo Consensus
11 to 16 November	Visit by President Hu Jintao of China due to Brazil's recognition of China as a market economy

16 December	Belo Horizonte—Preferential trade agreement signed between Mercosur and the Southern African Customs Union
17 December	Ouro Preto—27th Mercosur Summit; formalization of the entry of Colombia, Ecuador and Venezuela as associate States

2005

19 January	Letícia—Meeting between presidents Luiz Inácio Lula da Silva and Alvaro Uribe Vélez of Colombia
14 February	Caracas—Working visit to Venezuela; meeting with President Hugo Chávez
23 March	Brasília—Courtesy visit by Secretary of Defense Donald Rumsfeld of the United States
26 April	Brasília—Working visit by Secretary of State Condoleezza Rice of the United States
13 to 15 July	Official visit to France for the festivities of the Year of Brazil in France
1 August	Brasília—Courtesy visit by Secretary of the Treasury John Snow of the United States
11 August	Working visit by President Hugo Chávez of Venezuela
8 September	Puerto Maldonado—Visit to Peru for the start of work on the Inter-Ocean Highway
6 November	Working visit by President George W. Bush of the United States
30 November	Puerto Iguazú—Commemorative gathering for the 20th anniversary of the Brazil–Argentina integration process; signing of acts by presidents Lula and Kirchner
8 and 9 December	Mercosur Summit Meeting, with political decision in favor of the acceptance of Venezuela as a full member of the bloc
14 December	Working visit to Colombia; meeting with President Álvaro Uribe
15 December	Visit by World Bank President Paul Wolfowitz
16 December	Porto de Suape—Working visit by President Hugo Chávez of Venezuela for the formal launch of the future Abreu e Lima bi-national refinery

2006

10 January	Visit to Brazil by IMF Managing-Director Rodrigo Rato for the payment, brought forward by Brazil, of the US$15.57 billion balance owed as part of the aid package contracted in 2003
12 February	Visit to the Republic of South Africa; participation in the Progressive Governance Summit meeting, with heads of government from 13 other countries
6 March	State visit to the United Kingdom; meetings with Queen Elizabeth II and Prime Minister Tony Blair
26 April	Tripartite meeting between the presidents of Brazil, Argentina and Venezuela
15 to 17 July	St. Petersburg—Participation in enlarged G-8 meeting
21 July	Córdoba—30th Mercosur Summit and enlarged meeting with heads of State of associate countries, with the presence of President Fidel Castro for the signing of the Mercosur trade agreement with Cuba
13 September	1st Summit of the India, Brazil and South Africa—IBSA Dialogue Forum (G-3), with the presence of Prime Minister Manmohan Singh of India and President Thabo Mbeki of South Africa
19 September	New York—President Lula speech at the opening of the 61st UN General Assembly; launch of the International Drug Purchase Facility (UNITAID); President Lula named "Statesman of the Year" by the Appeal of Conscience Foundation and attends award ceremony

2007

17 and 18 January	Geneva—1st Special Session of the of the World Intellectual Property Organization (WIPO)
2 and 3 March	Georgetown—19th Rio Group Summit Meeting
8 and 9 March	Visit to Brazil by President George W. Bush of the United States
21 March	Brasília—10th Meeting of the Brazil–European Union Joint Committee
30 and 31 March	Washington—Visit by President Lula to the United States

11 to 13 April	New Delhi—Visit by Minister Celso Amorim to India; takes part in meetings on the WTO Doha Round and in the 3rd Meeting of the Brazil–India Joint Committee
17 and 18 May	Brussels—Trip by Minister Celso Amorim to take part in a meeting of the G-4 on the WTO Doha Round
3 to 5 June	New Delhi—State visit by President Lula to India Panama City—37th OAS General Assembly
4 July	Lisbon—Visit by President Lula to Portugal on the occasion of the 1st Brazil–European Union Summit
30 August	Brasília—1st meeting of the Brazil–China Joint Working Group
25 September to 7 October	New York—General debate of the 62nd UN General Assembly
17 October	2nd Summit of the India, Brazil and South Africa—IBSA Dialogue Forum (G-3)
11 to 13 November	Brasília—Visit to Brazil by UN Secretary-General Ban Ki-Moon

2008

6 March	Spain deports large numbers of Brazilians; Ministry of Foreign Relations considers applying reciprocity rule
13 to 15 March	Brasília and Salvador—Visit by Secretary of State Condoleezza Rice of the United States
20 to 25 April	Accra—12th UN Conference on Trade and Development—UNCTAD XII
14 April	UN Special Rapporteur on the Right to Food Jean Ziegler begins controversy over Brazil's large-scale production of ethanol, a bio-fuel produced from sugarcane
16 May	Ekaterinburg—Ministerial meeting of BRIC countries
2 June	Definitive Brazilian victory in WTO panel against the USA regarding cotton subsidies

Index

About the Authors

Tullo Vigevani is full professor of political science at São Paulo State University (UNESP), researcher at both the Center for Studies on Contemporary Culture (CEDEC) and the National Institute of Science and Technology for Studies on the United States, and coordinator of the Graduate Program on International Relations of São Paulo State University, University of Campinas, and Pontifical Catholic University of São Paolo.

Gabriel Cepaluni is assistant professor of international relations at São Paulo State University (UNESP). He received his PhD from the Department of Political Science at the University of São Paulo in 2010 and was a visiting researcher in the Department of Government at Georgetown University (2008–2009).